Fodor's

THIRD New EDITION

Norway

D1510146

Reprinted from *Fodor's Scandinavia*

Fodor's Travel Publications, Inc.
New York • Toronto • London • Sydney • Auckland
http://www.fodors.com/

Fodor's Norway

Editor: Rebecca Miller

Contributors: Glen Berger, Melody Favish, Anto Howard, Karina Porcelli, Linda K. Schmidt, Mary Ellen Schultz, Fiona Smith

Creative Director: Fabrizio La Rocca

Cartographer: David Lindroth

Cover Photograph: E. Nagele/FPG International

Text Design: Between the Covers

Copyright

Special Sales

Fodor's Travel Publications are available at special discounts for bulk purchases for sales promotions or premiums. Special editions, including personalized covers, excerpts of existing guides, and corporate imprints, can be created in large quantities for special needs. For more information, contact your local bookseller or write to Special Markets, Fodor's Travel Publications, 201 East 50th Street, New York, NY 10022. Inquiries from Canada should be directed to your local Canadian bookseller or sent to Random House of Canada, Ltd., Marketing Department, 1265 Aerowood Drive, Mississauga, Ontario L4W 1B9. Inquiries from the United Kingdom should be sent to Fodor's Travel Publications, 20 Vauxhall Bridge Road, London, England SW1V 2SA.

PRINTED IN THE UNITED STATES OF AMERICA

10 9 8 7 6 5 4 3 2 1

CONTENTS

ON THE ROAD WITH FODOR'S

A GOOD TRAVEL GUIDE is like a wonderful traveling companion. It's charming, it's brimming with sound recommendations and solid ideas, it pulls no punches in describing lodging and dining establishments, and it's consistently full of fascinating facts that make you view what you've traveled to see in a rich new light. In the creation of *Norway*, we at Fodor's have gone to great lengths to provide you with the very best of all possible traveling companions—and to make your trip the best of all possible vacations.

About Our Writer

Fiona Smith, educated at Trinity College Dublin and University College Galway, has lived in Stavanger, Norway, since 1993.

What's New

According to polls taken in fall 1995, Gro Harlem Brundtland is still Norway's most popular person, an honor she shares with explorer Thor Heyerdahl. The prime minister's political failure to lead Norwegians into the EU has done nothing to diminish her stature or weaken the country's economy. Despite gloomy predictions, Norway has not suffered any aftershocks from its rejection of the EU. Unemployment is low and morale is high. However, Norway is still struggling to define its relationship with the outside world, despite its high profile as an international peacemaker. Considerable gains for the right wing, anti-immigration Progress Party in September 1995's local elections have given liberal Norway a jolt and reopened the debate on Norwegian values.

The tourist's money will go a bit farther in 1996, due to a slight decline in visitors to Norway and a resulting increase in competition. Tourists can expect to reap the benefits of lower prices when it comes to accommodation and food. Prices for Norwegian arts and crafts remain steep, however.

Oslo is playing host to the Eurovision Song Contest in spring 1996. The staging of this much-hyped event will give Norway the opportunity to present its natural beauty and traditions to millions of viewers all over Europe .

How to Use this Book

Organization

Up front is the **Gold Guide,** comprising two sections on gold paper that are chockfull of information about traveling within your destination and traveling in general. Both are in alphabetical order by topic. **Important Contacts A to Z** gives addresses and telephone numbers of organizations and companies that offer destination-related services and detailed information or publications. Here's where you'll find information about how to get to Norway from wherever you are. **Smart Travel Tips A to Z,** the Gold Guide's second section, gives specific tips on how to get the most out of your travels, as well as information on how to accomplish what you need to in Norway.

Stars

Stars in the margin are used to denote highly recommended sights, attractions, hotels, and restaurants.

Restaurant and Hotel Criteria and Price Categories

Restaurants and lodging places are chosen with a view to giving you the cream of the crop in each location and in each price range. In all restaurant price charts, costs are per person, excluding drinks, tip, and tax. In hotel price charts, rates are for standard double rooms, excluding taxes.

Restaurant Prices

CATEGORY	COST*
$$$$	over NKr450
$$$	NKr300–NKr450
$$	NKr150–NKr300
$	under NKr150

*per person for a three-course meal, including tax and 12½% service charge

Hotel Prices

CATEGORY	MAJOR CITIES*	OTHER AREAS*
$$$$	over NKr1,300	over NKr1,000
$$$	NKr1,000–NKr1,300	NKr850–NKr1,000
$$	NKr800–NKr1,000	NKr650–NKr850
$	under NKr800	under NKr650

All prices are for a standard double room, including service and 23% VAT

Hotel Facilities

Note that in general you incur charges when you use many hotel facilities. We wanted to let you know what facilities a hotel has to offer, but we don't always specify whether or not there's a charge, so when planning a vacation that entails a stay of several days, it's wise to ask what's included in the rate.

Hotel Meal Plans

Assume that hotels operate on the **European Plan** (EP, with no meals) unless we note that they use the **American Plan** (AP, with all meals), the **Modified American Plan** (MAP, with breakfast and dinner daily), or the **Continental Plan** (CP, with a Continental breakfast daily).

Dress Code in Restaurants

What to Wear section at the beginning of the individual chapters' dining sections tells you what's most common in that area. In general, we note a dress code only when men are required to wear a jacket or a jacket and tie.

Credit Cards

The following abbreviations are used: **AE,** American Express; **DC,** Diners Club; **MC,** MasterCard; and **V,** Visa. Discover is not accepted outside the United States.

Please Write to Us

Everyone who has contributed to *Fodor's Norway* has worked hard to make the text accurate. All prices and opening times are based on information supplied to us at press time, and the publisher cannot accept responsibility for any errors that may have occurred. The passage of time will bring changes, so it's always a good idea to call ahead and confirm information when it matters—particularly if you're making a detour to visit specific sights or attractions. When making reservations at a hotel or inn, be sure to speak up if you have a disability or are traveling with children, if you prefer a private bath or a certain type of bed, or if you have specific dietary needs or any other concerns.

Were the restaurants we recommended as described? Did our hotel picks exceed your expectations? Did you find a museum we recommended a waste of time? We would love your feedback, positive and negative. If you have complaints, we'll look into them and revise our entries when the facts warrant it. If you've happened upon a special place that we haven't included, we'll pass the information along to the writers so they can check it out. So please send us a letter or postcard (we're at 201 East 50th Street, New York, New York 10022). We look forward to hearing from you. And in the meantime, have a wonderful trip!

Karen Cure

Karen Cure
Editorial Director

Scandinavia

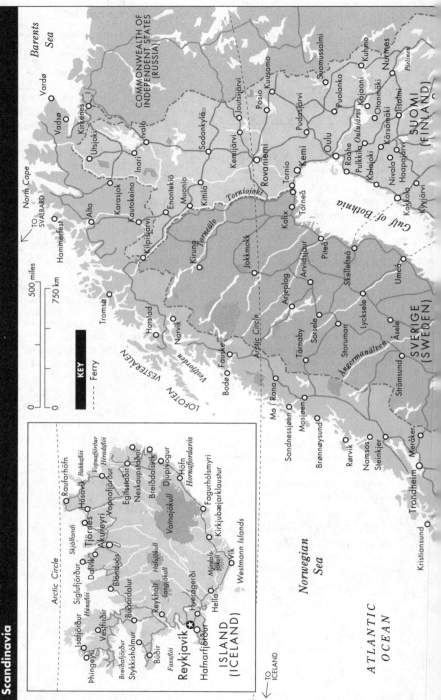

Barents
Sea

Vardø
Vadsø
Kirkenes
Ulsjoki

North Cape
TO
SVALBARD

COMMONWEALTH OF
INDEPENDENT STATES
(RUSSIA)

Hammerfest
Alta
Karasjok
Inari
Ivalo
Sodankylä
Posio
Kuusamo
Suomussalmi
Kuhmo
Nurmes

Kautokeino
Enontekiö
Muonio
Kittilä
Kemijärvi
Joutsijärvi
Pudasjärvi
Puolanka
Kajaani
Otanmäki

Kilpisjärvi
Torniojoki
Rovaniemi
Oulu
Ontojoki
Kärsämäki
Nivala
Iisalmi

Tromsø
Kiruna
Torneälv
Tornio
Kemi
Rahe
Pulkkila
Oulujärvi
Kälviäjoki
Haapajärvi
Pielinen

Harstad
Narvik
Jokkmokk
Kalix
Torneå
SUOMI
(FINLAND)

Vesfjorden
Fauske
Bodø
Arjeplog
Arvidsjaur
Piteå
Skellefteå
Umeå
Kokkola
Kyröjärvi

Arctic Circle
Tärnaby
Sorsele
Storuman
Lycksele
Äsele

LOFOTEN VESTERÅLEN
Mo i Rana
Sandnessjøen
Mosjøen
Strömsund
Ångermanälven

Brønnøysund
Rørvik
Namsos
Steinkjer
Meråker

SVERIGE
(SWEDEN)

Trondheim
Kristiansund

Gulf of Bothnia

KEY
— — — Ferry

0   500 miles
0   750 km

ISLAND (ICELAND)

Arctic Circle

Þingeyri
Ísafjörður
Vestfirðir
Siglufjörður
Hvanndalur
Skjalfandi
Raufarhöfn
Bakkaflói

Breiðafjörður
Stykkishólmur
Búðir
Búðardalur
Blönduós
Dalvík
Akureyri
Tjörnes
Húsavík
Vopnafjörður
Vopnafjörður
Héraðsflói

Faxaflói
Reykholt
Langjökull
Hofsjökull
Egilsstaðir
Neskaupstaður
Breiðdalsvík
Djúpivogur

Reykjavík
Hafnarfjörður
Hveragerði
Hella
Myrdals Jökull
Vatnajökull
Höfn
Hornafjarðarós
Fagurhólsmyri
Kirkjubæjarklaustur

TO
ICELAND
Vík
Westmann Islands

ATLANTIC
OCEAN

Norwegian
Sea

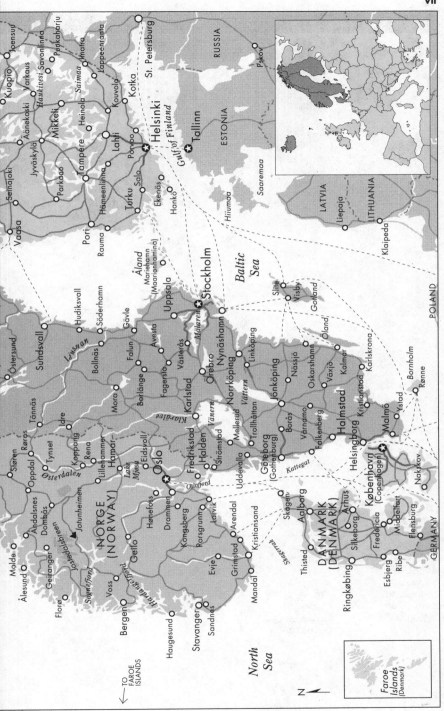

World Time Zones

Numbers below vertical bands relate each zone to Greenwich Mean Time (0 hrs.).
Local times frequently differ from these general indications,
as indicated by light-face numbers on map.

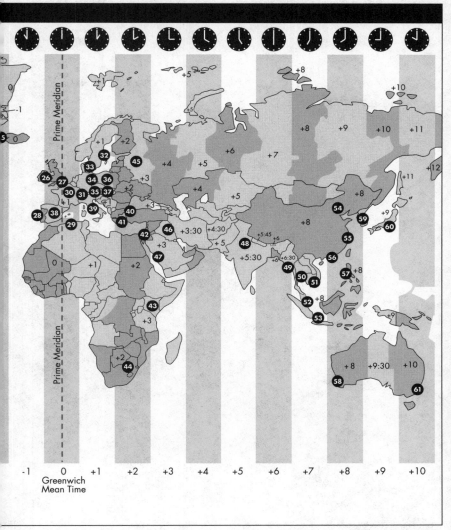

-1   0   +1   +2   +3   +4   +5   +6   +7   +8   +9   +10

Greenwich
Mean Time

Norway

TO
SVALBARD

North Cape

Vardø

Vadsø

Hammerfest

Kirkenes

Alta

ATLANTIC
OCEAN

Karasjok

Tromsø

Kautokeino

VESTERÅLEN

Harstad

FINLAND

Norwegian
Sea

LOFOTEN

Narvik

Vestfjorden

Bodø

Fauske

Arctic   Circle

Mo i Rana

Sandnessjøen

Mosjøen

Eb

Brønnøysund

SWEDEN

Gulf of Bothnia

Rørvik

Namsos

Steinkjer

Trondheim

Meråker

Støren

Kristiansund

Røros

Molde

70

Oppdal

Ålesund

Andalsnes

Tynset

Osterdalen

Geiranger

Dombås

Nord fjord

Otta

Gudbrandsdalen

Florø

Jostedalsbreen

Koppang

Sogne fjord

Rena

Lillehammer

Voss

Lake
Mjøsa

Hamar

Geilo

Baltic Sea

Bergen

Hønefoss

Eidsvoll

Hardangerfjord

Drammen

Oslo

Kongsberg

Fredrikstad

Haugesund

Larvik

Porsgrunn

Halden

Stavanger

Arendal

Oslofjord

N

Sandnes

Evje

Skagerrak

200 miles

Grimstad

0

Mandal

Kristiansand

Kattegat

300 km

IMPORTANT CONTACTS A TO Z

An Alphabetical Listing of Publications, Organizations, and Companies That Will Help You Before, During, and After Your Trip

No single travel resource can give you every detail about every topic that might interest or concern you at the various stages of your journey—when you're planning your trip, while you're on the road, and after you get back home. The following organizations, books, and brochures will supplement the information in *Fodor's Norway*. For related information, including both basic tips on visiting Norway and background information on many of the topics below, study Smart Travel Tips A to Z, the section that follows Important Contacts A to Z.

A

AIR TRAVEL

The major gateway to Norway is **Oslo Fornebu Airport.** Other international airports include **Bergen, Kristiansand, Sandefjord, Stavanger,** and **Trondheim.**

Flying time from New York to Oslo is 7½ hours; from Chicago, 11 hours; from Los Angeles, 14 hours; and from the U.K., 2 hours.

CARRIERS

Scandinavian Airlines (SAS) (☎ 800/221–2350) offers nonstop flights to Oslo from Newark, as well as service from many other major U.S. cities. **Finnair** (☎ 800/950–5000) offers flights to Norway via Helsinki, and **Icelandair** (☎ 800/223–5500) has service to Norway via Reykjavík. During winter months, stopovers for business class passengers are often free and include hotel.

Carriers serving Norway from the U.K. include **SAS** (☎ 0171/734–4020; FAX 0171/465–0537) and **British Airways** (☎ 0181/897–4000), both serving Oslo and Stavanger

WITHIN NORWAY➤ **SAS** (☎ 810/03–300) serves most major cities, including Svalbard. **Braathens SAFE** (SAFE stands for the "South Asian and Far Eastern" routes of the parent shipping company; ☎ 67/59–70–00) is the major domestic airline, serving cities throughout the country and along the coast as far north as Tromsø and Svalbard. **Widerøe** (☎ 22/73–66–00) serves smaller airports (with smaller planes), mostly along the coast, and in northern Norway. **Norsk Air** (☎ 33/46–90–00), a subsidiary of Widerøe, provides similar services in the southern part of the country. **Coast Air** (☎ 52/83–41–10) and **Norlink** (☎ 77/67–57–80), an SAS subsidiary, are commuter systems linking both smaller and larger airports.

COMPLAINTS

To register complaints about charter and scheduled airlines, contact the U.S. Department of Transportation's **Office of Consumer Affairs** (400 7th St. NW, Washington, DC 20590, ☎ 202/366–2220 or 800/322–7873).

CONSOLIDATORS

Established consolidators selling to the public include **BET World Travel** (841 Blossom Hill Rd., Suite 212-C, San Jose, CA 95123, ☎ 408/229–7880 or 800/747–1476), **Euram Tours** (1522 K St. NW, Suite 430, Washington DC, 20005, ☎ 800/848–6789), **TFI Tours International** (34 W. 32nd St., New York, NY 10001, ☎ 212/736–1140 or 800/745–8000), **UniTravel** (Box 12485, St. Louis, MO 63132, ☎ 314/569–0900 or 800/325–2222), and **Travac Tours and Charter** (989 6th Ave., 16th Floor, New York, NY 10018, ☎ 212/563–3303 or 800/872–8800; 2601 E. Jefferson, Orlando, FL 32803, ☎ 407/896–0014 or 800/872–8800). **FLY-ASAP** (3824 E. Indian School Road, Phoenix, AZ 85018, ☎ 800/359–2727) isn't a discounter, but gets good deals from among published fares, and

THE GOLD GUIDE / IMPORTANT CONTACTS

gets discount tickets from consolidators.

PUBLICATIONS

For general information about charter carriers, ask for the Office of Consumer Affairs' brochure **"Plane Talk: Public Charter Flights."** The Department of Transportation also publishes a 58-page booklet, **"Fly Rights"** ($1.75; Consumer Information Center, Dept. 133-B, Pueblo, CO 81009).

For other tips and hints, consult the Consumers Union's monthly **"Consumer Reports Travel Letter"** ($39 a year; Box 53629, Boulder CO 80322, ☎ 800/234–1970) and the newsletter **"Travel Smart"** ($37 a year; 40 Beechdale Rd., Dobbs Ferry, NY 10522, ☎ 800/327–3633); *The Official Frequent Flyer Guidebook,* by Randy Petersen ($14.99 plus $3 shipping; 4715-C Town Center Dr., Colorado Springs, CO 80916, ☎ 719/597–8899 or 800/487–8893); *Airfare Secrets Exposed,* by Sharon Tyler and Matthew Wonder (Universal Information Publishing; $16.95 plus $3.75 shipping from Sandcastle Publishing, Box 3070-A, South Pasadena, CA 91031, ☎ 213/255–3616 or 800/655–0053); and *202 Tips Even the Best Business Travelers May Not Know,* by Christopher McGinnis ($10 plus $3.00 shipping; Irwin Professional Publishing, 1333 Burr Ridge Parkway, Burr Ridge, IL 60521, ☎ 800/634–3966).

B

BETTER BUSINESS BUREAU

For local contacts in the home town of a tour operator you may be considering, consult the **Council of Better Business Bureaus** (4200 Wilson Blvd., Arlington, VA 22203, ☎ 703/276–0100).

BUS TRAVEL

WITHIN NORWAY➤ Most long-distance buses leave from **Bussterminalen** (Galleri Oslo, Schweigaardsgt., 10, ☎ 22/17-01-66), close to Oslo Central Station. **Nor-Way Bussekspress** (Bussterminalen, ☎ 22/17–52–90, FAX 22/17–59–22) has more than 40 different bus services, covering 10,000 kilometers (6,200 miles) and 500 destinations, and can arrange any journey. One of its participating services, **Feriebussen** (Østerdal Billag A/S, 2560 Alvdal, ☎ 62/48–74–00) offers five package tours with English-speaking guides.

C

CAR RENTAL

Major car-rental companies represented in Norway include **Avis** (☎ 800/331–1084, 800/879–2847 in Canada), **Budget** (☎ 800/527–0700, 0800/181–181 in the U.K.), **Dollar** (known as Eurodollar outside North America, ☎ 800/800–4000, 0171/262–0161 in the U.K.), **Hertz** (☎ 800/654–3001, 800/263–0600 in Canada, 0181/679–

1799 in the U.K.), and **National** (sometimes known as Europcar InterRent outside North America; ☎ 800/227–3876, 0181/897–0811 in the U.K.).

RENTAL WHOLESALERS

Contact **Auto Europe** (Box 7006, Portland, ME 04112, ☎ 207/828–2525 or 800/223–5555), or the **Kemwel Group** (106 Calvert St., Harrison, NY 10528, ☎ 914/835–5555 or 800/678–0678).

CHILDREN AND TRAVEL

FLYING

Look into **"Flying With Baby"** ($5.95 plus $1 shipping; Third Street Press, Box 261250, Littleton, CO 80126, ☎ 303/595–5959), cowritten by a flight attendant. **"Kids and Teens in Flight,"** free from the U.S. Department of Transportation's Office of Consumer Affairs, offers tips for children flying alone. Every two years the February issue of *Family Travel Times* (*see* Know-How, *below*) details children's services on three dozen airlines.

GAMES

The gamemeister, Milton Bradley, has games to help keep little (and not so little) children from getting fidgety while riding in planes, trains, and automobiles. Try packing the *Travel Battleship* sea battle game ($7), *Travel Connect Four,* a vertical strategy game ($8), the *Travel Yahtzee* dice game ($6), the *Travel*

Trouble dice and board game ($7), and the *Travel Guess Who* mystery game ($8).

KNOW-HOW

Family Travel Times, published four times a year by Travel with Your Children (TWYCH, 45 W. 18th St., New York, NY 10011, ☎ 212/206–0688; annual subscription $40), covers destinations, types of vacations, and modes of travel.

The *Family Travel Guides* catalogue ($1 postage; ☎ 510/527–5849) lists about 200 books and articles on family travel. *Traveling with Children—And Enjoying It,* by Arlene K. Butler ($11.95 plus $3 shipping; Globe Pequot Press, Box 833, 6 Business Park Rd., Old Saybrook, CT 06475, ☎ 203/395–0440 or 800/243–0495, 800/962–0973 in CT) helps plan your trip with children, from toddlers to teens. Also check *Take Your Baby and Go! A Guide for Traveling with Babies, Toddlers and Young Children,* by Sheri Andrews, Judy Bordeaux, and Vivian Vasquez ($5.95 plus $1.50 shipping; Bear Creek Publications, 2507 Minor Ave., Seattle, WA 98102, ☎ 206/322–7604 or 800/326–6566). *Innocents Abroad: Traveling with Kids in Europe,* by Valerie Wolf Deutsch and Laura Sutherland ($15.95 plus $2 shipping; Penguin USA, 120 Woodbine St., Bergenfield, NJ 07621, ☎ 201/387–0600 or 800/253–6476), covers

child- and teen-friendly activities, food, and transportation.

CUSTOMS

U.S. CITIZENS

The **U.S. Customs Service** (Box 7407, Washington, DC 20044, ☎ 202/927–6724) can answer questions on duty-free limits and publishes a helpful brochure, **"Know Before You Go."** For information on registering foreign-made articles, call 202/927–0540.

CANADIANS

Contact **Revenue Canada** (2265 St. Laurent Blvd. S, Ottawa, Ontario, K1G 4K3, ☎ 613/993–0534) for a copy of the free brochure **"I Declare/ Je Déclare"** and for details on duties that exceed the standard duty-free limit.

U.K. CITIZENS

HM Customs and Excise (Dorset House, Stamford St., London SE1 9NG, ☎ 0171/202–4227) can answer questions about U.K. customs regulations and publishes **"A Guide for Travellers,"** detailing standard procedures and import rules.

D
FOR TRAVELERS WITH DISABILITIES

COMPLAINTS

To register complaints under the provisions of the Americans with Disabilities Act, contact the U.S. Department of Justice's **Disability Rights Section** (Box 66738, Washington, D.C. 20035, ☎ 202/

514–0301, TTY 202/514–0383, FAX 202/307–1198).

LODGING

The **Best Western** chain (☎ 800/528–1234) offers properties with wheelchair-accessible rooms in Oslo. If wheelchair-accessible rooms are not available, ground-floor rooms are provided.

ORGANIZATIONS

FOR TRAVELERS WITH HEARING IMPAIRMENTS➤ Contact the **American Academy of Otolaryngology** (1 Prince St., Alexandria, VA 22314, ☎ 703/836–4444, FAX 703/683–5100, TTY 703/519–1585).

FOR TRAVELERS WITH MOBILITY PROBLEMS➤ Contact the **Information Center for Individuals with Disabilities** (Fort Point Pl., 27–43 Wormwood St., Boston, MA 02210, ☎ 617/727–5540, 800/462–5015 in MA, TTY 617/345–9743); **Mobility International USA** (Box 10767, Eugene, OR 97440, ☎ and TTY 503/343–1284; FAX 503/343–6812), the U.S. branch of an international organization based in Belgium (*see below*) that has affiliates in 30 countries; **MossRehab Hospital Travel Information Service** (1200 W. Tabor Rd., Philadelphia, PA 19141, ☎ 215/456–9603, TTY 215/456–9602); the **Society for the Advancement of Travel for the Handicapped** (347 5th Ave., Suite 610, New York, NY 10016, ☎ 212/447–7284, FAX 212/725–8253); the **Travel Industry and**

THE GOLD GUIDE / IMPORTANT CONTACTS

Disabled Exchange (TIDE, 5435 Donna Ave., Tarzana, CA 91356, ☎ 818/344–3640, FAX 818/344–0078); and **Travelin' Talk** (Box 3534, Clarksville, TN 37043, ☎ 615/552–6670, FAX 615/552–1182).

FOR TRAVELERS WITH VISION IMPAIRMENTS➤ Contact the **American Council of the Blind** (1155 15th St. NW, Suite 720, Washington, DC 20005, ☎ 202/467–5081, FAX 202/467–5085) or the **American Foundation for the Blind** (15 W. 16th St., New York, NY 10011, ☎ 212/620–2000, TTY 212/620–2158).

IN THE U.K.

Contact the **Royal Association for Disability and Rehabilitation** (RADAR, 12 City Forum, 250 City Rd., London EC1V 8AF, ☎ 0171/250–3222) or **Mobility International** (Rue de Manchester 25, B–1070 Brussels, Belgium, ☎ 00–322–410–6297), an international clearinghouse of travel information for people with disabilities.

PUBLICATIONS

Several free publications are available from the U.S. Information Center (Box 100, Pueblo, CO 81009, ☎ 719/948–3334): **"New Horizons for the Air Traveler with a Disability"** (address to Dept. 355A), describing legally mandated changes; the pocket-size **"Fly Smart"** (Dept. 575B), good on flight safety; and the Airport Operators Council's worldwide **"Access Travel: Airports"** (Dept. 575A).

The 500-page **Travelin' Talk Directory** ($35; Box 3534, Clarksville, TN 37043, ☎ 615/552–6670) lists people and organizations who help travelers with disabilities. For specialist travel agents worldwide, consult the **Directory of Travel Agencies for the Disabled** ($19.95 plus $2 shipping; Twin Peaks Press, Box 129, Vancouver, WA 98666, ☎ 206/694–2462 or 800/637–2256) and the **Directory of Travel Agencies for the Disabled,** by Helen Hecker ($19.95 plus $3.50 handling; Disability Bookshop, Box 129, Vancouver, WA, 98666; ☎ 206/694-2462).

SPORTS AND OUTDOOR ACTIVITIES

Norway encouraged active participation sports for people with disabilities long before it became popular elsewhere and has many Special Olympics medal winners. **Beitostølen Helsesportsenter** (2953 Beitostølen, ☎ 61/34–12–00) has sports facilities for the blind and other physically challenged people as well as training programs for instructors.

TRAVEL AGENCIES AND TOUR OPERATORS

The Americans with Disabilities Act requires that travel firms serve the needs of all travelers. However, some agencies and operators specialize in making group and individual arrangements for travelers with disabilities, among them **Access Adventures** (206 Chestnut Ridge Rd., Rochester, NY 14624, ☎ 716/889–9096), run by a former physical-rehab counselor. In addition, many general-interest operators and agencies (*see* Tour Operators, *below*) can also arrange vacations for travelers with disabilities.

FOR TRAVELERS WITH HEARING IMPAIRMENTS➤ One agency is **International Express** (7319-B Baltimore Ave., College Park, MD 20740, ☎ TTY 301/699–8836, FAX 301/699–8836), which arranges group and independent trips.

FOR TRAVELERS WITH MOBILITY IMPAIRMENTS➤ A number of operators specialize in working with travelers with mobility impairments: **Accessible Journeys** (35 W. Sellers Ave., Ridley Park, PA 19078, ☎ 610/521–0339 or 800/846–4537, FAX 610/521–6959), a registered nursing service that arranges vacations; **Flying Wheels Travel** (143 W. Bridge St., Box 382, Owatonna, MN 55060, ☎ 507/451–5005 or 800/535–6790), a travel agency that specializes in European cruises and tours; **Hinsdale Travel Service** (201 E. Ogden Ave., Suite 100, Hinsdale, IL 60521, ☎ 708/325–1335 or 800/303–5521), a travel agency that will give you access to the services of wheelchair traveler Janice Perkins; and **Wheelchair Journeys** (16979 Redmond Way, Redmond, WA 98052, ☎ 206/

885–2210), which can handle arrangements worldwide.

FOR TRAVELERS WITH DEVELOPMENTAL DISABILITIES➤ Contact the nonprofit **New Directions** (5276 Hollister Ave., Suite 207, Santa Barbara, CA 93111, ☎ 805/967–2841), for travelers with developmental disabilities and their families as well as the general-interest operations above.

DISCOUNT CLUBS

Options include **Great American Traveler** ($49.95 annually; Box 27965, Salt Lake City, UT 84127, ☎ 800/548–2812), **Moment's Notice Discount Travel Club** ($25 annually, single or family; 7301 New Utrecht, New York, NY 11204, ☎ 718/234–6295), **Travelers Advantage** ($49 annually, single or family; CUC Travel Service, 49 Music Sq. W, Nashville, TN 37203, ☎ 800/548–1116 or 800/648–4037), and **Worldwide Discount Travel Club** ($50 annually for family, $40 single; 1674 Meridian Ave., Miami Beach, FL 33139, ☎ 305/534–2082).

E
ELECTRICITY

Send a self-addressed, stamped envelope to the **Franzus Company** (Customer Service, Dept. B50, Murtha Industrial Park, Box 142, Beacon Falls, CT 06403, ☎ 203/723–6664) for a copy of the free brochure "Foreign Electricity Is No Deep Dark Secret."

F
FERRY TRAVEL

FROM THE UNITED KINGDOM

Color Line (Tyne Commission Quay, North Shields [near Newcastle] LEN29 6EA, ☎ 091/296-1313, Skoltegrunnskaien, 5000 Bergen, ☎ 55/32-27-80; or 405 Park Ave., New York, NY 10022, ☎ 800/323-7436), has three departures a week between Bergen, Stavanger, and Newcastle during the summer season (May 22–Sept. 10), two during the rest of the year. Crossings take about 22 hours. Monday sailings stop first in Stavanger and arrive in Bergen six hours later; the other trips stop first in Bergen. **DFDS/ Scandinavian Seaways** (DFDS Travel Centre, 15 Hanover St., London WIR 9HG, ☎ 0171/493–6696, FAX 0171–493–4668; DFDS Seaways USA Inc., 6555 NW 9th Ave., Suite 207, Fort Lauderdale, FL 33309, ☎ 800/533–3755, FAX 945/491–7958) has a crossing between Harwich and Göteborg, Sweden, a 4½-hour drive from Oslo.

WITHIN NORWAY

Ferries and passenger ships remain important means of transportation in Norway. Along west-coast fjords, car ferries are a way of life. More specialized boat service includes hydrofoil/catamaran trips between Stavanger, Haugesund, and Bergen. There are also fjord cruises out of these cities and others in the north. **Color Line** (Box 1422, Vika 0115, Oslo, ☎ 22/83–60–10, FAX 22/83–07–76) is a major carrier in Norwegian waters. You can also sail along the magnificent west coast of Norway with the **Fjord Line** (Slottsgatan 1, N–5023 Bergen, Norway, ☎ 47/55–32–37–70, FAX 47/55–32–38–15).

Norway's most renowned boat trip is the *Hurtigruten,* or the Coastal Express, which departs from Bergen and stops at 36 ports in six days, ending with Kirkenes, near the Russian border, before turning back. Tickets can be purchased for the entire journey or for individual legs. Shore excursions are arranged at all ports. Tickets are available through **Bergen Line** travel agents (405 Park Ave., New York, NY 10022, ☎ 800/323-7436), or directly from the companies that run the service: **FFR** (9600 Hammerfest, ☎ 78/41-10–00), **OVDS** (8501 Narvik, ☎ 76/92–37-00), **Hurtigruten Booking** (Kjøpmannsgt. 52, 7011 Trondheim, ☎ 73/51–51–20, FAX 73/51-51–46), and **TFDS** (9000 Tromsø, ☎ 77/68–60–88).

G
GAY AND LESBIAN TRAVEL

ORGANIZATIONS

The **International Gay Travel Association** (Box 4974, Key West, FL 33041, ☎ 800/448-8550), a consortium of 800 businesses,

THE GOLD GUIDE / IMPORTANT CONTACTS

can supply names of travel agents and tour operators.

PUBLICATIONS

The premier international travel magazine for gays and lesbians is **Our World** ($35 for 10 issues; 1104 N. Nova Rd., Suite 251, Daytona Beach, FL 32117, ☎ 904/441–5367). The 16-page monthly **"Out & About"** ($49 for 10 issues; ☎ 212/645–6922 or 800/929–2268), covers gay-friendly resorts, hotels, cruise lines, and airlines.

TOUR OPERATORS

Cruises and resort vacations are handled by **R.S.V.P. Travel Productions** (2800 University Ave. SE, Minneapolis, MN 55414, ☎ 800/328–7787) for gays, **Olivia** (4400 Market St., Oakland, CA 94608, ☎ 800/631–6277) for lesbian travelers, and **Toto Tours** (1326 W. Albion Suite 3W, Chicago, IL 60626, ☎ 312/274–8686 or 800/565–1241), which has group tours worldwide.

TRAVEL AGENCIES

The largest agencies serving gay travelers are **Advance Travel** (10700 Northwest Freeway, Suite #160, Houston, TX 77092, ☎ 713/682–2002 or 800/695–0880), **Islanders/Kennedy Travel** (183 10th St., New York, NY 10014, ☎ 212/242–3222 or 800/988–1181), **Now Voyager** (4406 18th St., San Francisco, CA 94114, ☎ 415/626–1169 or 800/255–6951), and **Yellowbrick Road** (1500 W. Balmoral Ave.,

Chicago, IL 60640, ☎ 312/561–1800 or 800/642–2488). **Skylink Women's Travel** (746 Ashland Ave., Santa Monica, CA 90405, ☎ 310/452–0506 or 800/225-5759) works with lesbians.

H
HEALTH ISSUES

FINDING A DOCTOR

For members, the **International Association for Medical Assistance to Travellers** (IAMAT, 417 Center St., Lewiston, NY 14092, ☎ 716/754–4883; 40 Regal Rd., Guelph, Ontario N1K 1B5, ☎ 519/836–0102; 1287 St. Clair Ave., Toronto, Ontario M6E 1B8, ☎ 416/652–0137; 57 Voirets, 1212 Grand-Lancy, Geneva, Switzerland; membership free) publishes a worldwide directory of English-speaking physicians meeting IAMAT standards.

MEDICAL-ASSISTANCE COMPANIES

Contact **International SOS Assistance** (Box 11568, Philadelphia, PA 19116, ☎ 215/244–1500 or 800/523–8930; Box 466, Pl. Bonaventure, Montréal, Québec, H5A 1C1, ☎ 514/874–7674 or 800/363–0263), **Medex Assistance Corporation** (Box 10623, Baltimore, MD 21285, ☎ 410/296–2530 or 800/573-2029), **Near Services** (Box 1339, Calumet City, IL 60409, ☎ 708/868–6700 and 800/654–6700), and **Travel Assistance International** (1133 15th St. NW, Suite 400, Washington, DC 20005,

☎ 202/331–1609 or 800/821–2828). Because these companies also sell death-and-dismemberment, trip-cancellation, and other insurance coverage, there is some overlap with the travel-insurance policies sold by the companies listed under Insurance, *below.*

I
INSURANCE

Travel insurance covering baggage, health, and trip cancellation or interruptions available from **Access America** (Box 90315, Richmond, VA 23286, ☎ 804/285–3300 or 800/284–8300), **Carefree Travel Insurance** (Box 9366, 100 Garden City Plaza, Garden City, NY 11530, ☎ 516/294–0220 or 800/323–3149), **Near Services** (Box 1339, Calumet City, IL 60409, ☎ 708/868–6700 or 800/654–6700), **Tele-Trip** (Mutual of Omaha Plaza, Box 31716, Omaha, NE 68131, ☎ 800/228–9792), **Travel Insured International (Box 280568, East Hartford, CT 06128-0568,** ☎ 203/528–7663 or 800/243–3174), Travel Guard International (1145 Clark St., Stevens Point, WI 54481, ☎ 715/345–0505 or 800/826–1300), and Wallach & Company (107 W. Federal St., Box 480, Middleburg, VA 22117, ☎ 703/687–3166 or 800/237–6615).

IN THE U.K.

The **Association of British Insurers** (51 Gresham St., London

EC2V 7HQ, ☎ 0171/600–3333; 30 Gordon St., Glasgow G1 3PU, ☎ 0141/226–3905; Scottish Provident Bldg., Donegall Sq. W, Belfast BT1 6JE, ☎ 01232/249176; and other locations) gives advice by phone and publishes the free **"Holiday Insurance,"** which sets out typical policy provisions and costs.

L
LODGING

APARTMENT AND VILLA RENTAL

Contact **Europa-Let** (92 N. Main St., Ashland, OR 97520, ☎ 503/482–5806 or 800/462–4486).

HOME EXCHANGE

Principal clearinghouses include **HomeLink International/Vacation Exchange Club** ($70 annually; Box 650, Key West, FL 33041, ☎ 305/294–1448 or 800/638–3841), which gives members four annual directories, with a listing in one, plus updates, and **Intervac International** ($65 annually; Box 590504, San Francisco, CA 94159, ☎ 415/435–3497), which has three annual directories.

M
MONEY MATTERS

ATMS

For specific foreign **Cirrus** locations, call 800/424–7787; for foreign **Plus** locations, consult the Plus directory at your local bank.

CURRENCY EXCHANGE

If your bank doesn't exchange currency,

contact **Thomas Cook Currency Services** (41 E. 42nd St., New York, NY 10017, or 511 Madison Ave., New York, NY 10022, ☎ 212/757–6915 or 800/223–7373 for locations) or **Ruesch International** (☎ 800/424–2923 for locations).

WIRING FUNDS

Funds can be wired via **American Express MoneyGram**ˢᴹ (☎ 800/926–9400 from the U.S. and Canada for locations and information).

P
PASSPORTS
AND VISAS

U.S. CITIZENS

For fees, documentation requirements, and other information, call the **Office of Passport Services** information line (☎ 202/647–0518).

CANADIANS

For fees, documentation requirements, and other information, call the Ministry of Foreign Affairs and International Trade's **Passport Office** (☎ 819/994–3500 or 800/567–6868).

U.K. CITIZENS

For fees, documentation requirements, and to get an emergency passport, call the **London Passport Office** (☎ 0171/271–3000).

PHONE MATTERS

The country code for Norway is 47. For local access numbers abroad, contact **AT&T** USADirect (☎ 800/874–4000), **MCI** Call USA (☎ 800/444–4444), or **Sprint** Express (☎ 800/793–1153).

PHOTO HELP

The **Kodak Information Center** (☎ 800/242–2424) answers consumer questions about film and photography.

R
RAIL TRAVEL

DISCOUNT PASSES

The **EurailPass,** valid for unlimited first-class train travel through 17 countries, including Norway, is an excellent value if you plan to travel around the Continent. To buy a pass, apply through your travel agent or **Rail Europe** (226–230 Westchester Ave., White Plains, NY 10604, ☎ 800/848–7245; or 2087 Dundas E., Suite 105, Mississauga, Ontario L4X 1M2, ☎ 800/361–7245); **DER Tours** (9501 W. Devon Ave., Rosemont, IL 60018, ☎ 800/782–2424, FAX 800/282–7474); or **CIT Tours Corp.** (342 Madison Ave., Suite 207, New York, NY 10173, ☎ 212/697–2100 or 800/248–8687; 310/670–4269 or 800/248–7245 in western U.S.).

Within Norway, the **ScanRail Pass** is valid for unlimited rail travel and offers free and discounted crossings on several ferry lines. A second-class adult pass costs $159 for five travel days within a period of 15 days and $275 for 10 days of rail travel. The first-class rates are about $199 and $339 respectively. A **Youth ScanRail Pass** is available to travelers from 12 to 26 and costs 75% of the adult fare

THE GOLD GUIDE / IMPORTANT CONTACTS

($119 for five days and $206 for 10 days in second class). Children from 4 to 11 travel for half-fare, and children under 4 on laps travel free. If you want the flexibility of a car combined with the speed and comfort of the train, try **ScanRail 'n Drive** (from **$229** per person, based on two adults sharing an economy car, or $299 for an adult traveling solo). This pass gives you a four-or nine-day ScanRail pass, plus three days of car rental to use within a 14- or 21-day period. These passes can be purchased from Rail Europe (see above), DER (see above), and the **NSB** (Norwegian State Railways) travel agency in London (☎ 0171/930–6666).

S
SENIOR CITIZENS

EDUCATIONAL TRAVEL

The nonprofit **Elderhostel** (75 Federal St., 3rd Floor, Boston, MA 02110, ☎ 617/426–7788), for people 60 and older, has offered inexpensive study programs since 1975. Dozens of courses in Norway are available. Fees for two- to three-week trips—including room, board, and transportation from the United States—range from $2,000 to $5,000.

For people 50 and over and their children and grandchildren, **Interhostel** (University of New Hampshire, 6 Garrison Ave., Durham, NH 03824, ☎ 603/862–1147 or 800/733–9753) runs 10-day

summer programs involving lectures, field trips, and sightseeing. Most last two weeks and cost $2,125–$3,100, including airfare.

ORGANIZATIONS

Contact the **American Association of Retired Persons** (AARP, 601 E St. NW, Washington, DC 20049, ☎ 202/434–2277; $8 per person or couple annually). Its Purchase Privilege Program gets members discounts on lodging, car rentals, and sightseeing.

For other discounts on lodgings, car rentals, and other travel products, along with magazines and newsletters, contact **Mature Outlook** (subscription $9.95 annually; 6001 N. Clark St., Chicago, IL 60660, ☎ 312/465–6466 or 800/336–6330).

PUBLICATIONS

"The Mature Traveler" ($29.95; Box 50400, Reno, NV 89513, ☎ 702/786–7419), a monthly newsletter, covers travel deals.

SPORTS AND THE OUTDOORS

BICYCLING

Den Norske Turistforening (DNT, Box 1963 Vika, 0125 Oslo 1, ☎ 22/83–25–50, FAX 22/83–24–78) provides inexpensive lodging for cyclists planning overnight trips. You can also contact **Syklistenes Landsforening** (Maridalsvn. 60, 0458 Oslo 4, ☎ 22/71–92–93) for general information and maps, as well as

the latest weather conditions.

CAMPING

Norway has more than 900 inspected and classified campsites, many with showers, bathrooms, and hookups for electricity. Most also have cabins or chalets to rent by the night or longer. For more information and a list of sites, contact local tourist offices, the **Norwegian Automobile Federation** (Storgt. 2, 0155 Oslo 1, ☎ 22/34–14–00), or the **Scandinavian Tourist Board** (see Visitor Information below).

CANOEING

There are plenty of lakes and streams for canoeing in Norway, as well as rental facilities. Contact **Norges Padleforbund** (Hauger Skolevei 1, 1351 Bærum, ☎ 67/15–46–00) for a list of rental companies and regional canoeing centers.

DIVING

Diving is very well-organized and popular in Norway, especially on the west coast. Contact **Norges Dykkforbund** (Hauger Skolevei 1, 1351 Bærum, ☎ 67/15–46–00) for a list of diving centers.

GOLF

Golf came to Norway only recently, but the country has gone golf-crazy–there is even a course on Arctic Spitsbergen. For information about guest privileges and greens fees, contact **Oslo Golfklubb** (Bogstad, 0740 Oslo 7, ☎ 22/50–44–02, FAX

22/73–09–12); **Bergen Golfklubb** (Boks 470, 5001 Bergen, ☎ 55/18–20–77); **Stavanger Golfklubb** (Longebakken 45, 4042 Hafrsfjord, ☎ 51/55-54-31); or **Trondheim Golfklubb** (Boks 169, 7001 Trondheim, ☎ 73/53–18–85).

HIKING

Den Norske Turistforening (*see* Bicycling, *above*) and affiliated organizations administer cabins and tourist facilities in the central and northern mountainous areas of the country and will arrange group hikes. They have English brochures that can be ordered by mail or bought at their offices in many towns throughout Norway.

HORSEBACK RIDING

Most cities and resort areas have stables, which rent chunky Norwegian fjord ponies and horses. **Steinseth Ridesenter** (Sollivn. 74, 1370 Asker, ☎ 66/78–75–46) is a 30-minute drive from Oslo. Many resorts specialize in mountain pack trips; riding camps are in operation every summer.

MOUNTAIN CLIMBING

The mountains of the Lofoten Islands and the Lyngen area of Troms County offer alpine-class mountaineering. **Den Norske Turistforening** (*see* Bicycling, *above*) has information.

PARAGLIDING/ HANGGLIDING

The mountains and hills of Norway provide excellent take-off spots. However, winds and weather conspire to

make conditions unpredictable. For details on local clubs, regulations, and equipment rental, contact **Norsk Aeroklubb** (Moellesvingen 2, 0854 Oslo, ☎ 22/93–03–00).

RAFTING

Rafting excursions are offered throughout Norway. For more information, contact: **Flåteopplevelser** (Postboks 227, 2051 Jessheim, ☎ 63/97–29–04); **Norwegian Wildlife and Rafting** (2254 Lundersæter, ☎ 62/82–97–24); or **Dagali-Voss Rafting** (Dagali, 3580 Geilo, ☎ 32/09–38–20).

RUNNING

Grete Waitz and Ingrid Kristiansen have put Norway on the marathon runners' map in recent years. The first national marathon championships were held in Norway in 1897 and the Oslo Marathon always attracts a large following. **Norges Friidretts Forbund** (Karl Johans Gt. 2, 0104 Oslo, ☎ 22/42–03–03) has information about local clubs and competitions.

SAILING

Both the late King Olav V and the present King Harald V won Olympic gold medals in sailing. Sailing in Oslofjorden and among the islands of the southern coast is a favorite summer pastime. Contact **Norges Seilforbund** (Hauger Skolevei 1, 1351 Bærum, ☎ 67/56–85–75) about facilities around the country; for the Oslo region, contact **KNS**

(The Royal Norwegian Sailing Association; Huk Aveny 1, 0287 Oslo 2, ☎ 22/43–74–10).

SKIING

Skiforeningen (Kongevn. 5, 0390 Oslo 3, ☎ 22/92–32–00) provides national snow-condition reports. But winter's not the only time for skiing in Norway–summer skiing on a glacier can be quite a novelty. Ski centers in operation over the summer include: **Finse Skisenter** (3590 Finse, ☎ 55/52–67-44); **Galdhøpiggen Sommerskisenter** (2686 Bøverdalen, ☎ 61/21-21-42); and **Stryn Sommerskisenter** (6880 Stryn, ☎ 57/87–19–95).

WINDSURFING

The best windsurfing (a new sport here) is in western Norway. Centers include: **Selje Sjøsportsenter** (6740 Selje, ☎ 57/85–61–07) and **Stavanger Surfsentrum** (4012 Stavanger, ☎ 51/53–11–22).

STUDENTS

GROUPS

Major tour operators include **Contiki Holidays** (300 Plaza Alicante, Suite 900, Garden Grove, CA 92640, ☎ 714/740–0808 or 800/466–0610).

HOSTELING

Contact **Hostelling International–American Youth Hostels** (733 15th St. NW, Suite 840, Washington, DC 20005, ☎ 202/783–6161) in the United States, **Hostelling International–Canada** (205 Catherine St., Suite 400,

Ottawa, Ontario K2P 1C3, ☎ 613/237–7884) in Canada, and the **Youth Hostel Association of England and Wales** (Trevelyan House, 8 St. Stephen's Hill, St. Albans, Hertfordshire AL1 2DY, ☎ 01727/855215 and 01727/845047) in the United Kingdom. Membership ($25 in the U.S., C$25 in Canada, and £9 in the U.K.) gets you access to 5,000 hostels worldwide that charge $7–$20 nightly per person.

I.D. CARDS

To be eligible for discounts on transportation and admissions, get the **International Student Identity Card** (ISIC) if you're a bona fide student or the **International Youth Card** (IYC) if you're under 26. In the United States, the ISIC and IYC cards cost $16 each and include basic travel accident and illness coverage, plus a toll-free travel hot line. Apply through the Council on International Educational Exchange (*see* Organizations, *below*). Cards are available for $15 each in Canada from Travel Cuts (187 College St., Toronto, Ontario M5T 1P7, ☎ 416/979–2406 or 800/667–2887) and in the United Kingdom for £5 each at student unions and student travel companies.

ORGANIZATIONS

A major contact is the **Council on International Educational Exchange** (CIEE, 205 E. 42nd St., 16th Floor, New York, NY 10017, ☎ 212/661–1450) with locations in Boston (729

Boylston St., 02116, ☎ 617/266–1926), Miami (9100 S. Dadeland Blvd., 33156, ☎ 305/670–9261), Los Angeles (1093 Broxton Ave., 90024, ☎ 310/208–3551), 43 other college towns nationwide, and the United Kingdom (28A Poland St., London W1V 3DB, ☎ 0171/437–7767). Twice a year, it publishes *Student Travels* magazine. The CIEE's Council Travel Service is the exclusive U.S. agent for several student-discount cards.

Campus Connections (325 Chestnut St., Suite 1101, Philadelphia, PA 19106, ☎ 215/625–8585 or 800/428–3235) specializes in discounted accommodations and airfares for students. The **Educational Travel Centre** (438 N. Frances St., Madison, WI 53703, ☎ 608/256–5551) offers rail passes and low-cost airline tickets, mostly for flights departing from Chicago. For air travel only, contact **TMI Student Travel** (100 W. 33rd St., Suite 813, New York, NY 10001, ☎ 800/245–3672).

In Canada, also contact **Travel Cuts** (*see* above).

PUBLICATIONS

See the *Berkeley Guide to Europe* ($18.95; Fodor's Travel Publications, 800/533–6478 or from bookstores).

T

TOUR OPERATORS

Among the companies selling tours and pack-

ages to Norway, the following have a proven reputation, are nationally known, and offer plenty of options.

GROUP TOURS

Super-deluxe tours of Norway are available from two very reputable operators, **Abercrombie & Kent** (1520 Kensington Rd., Oak Brook, IL 60521, ☎ 708/954–2944 or 800/323–7308) and **Travcoa** (Box 2630, Newport Beach, CA, 92658, ☎ 714/476–2800 or 800/992–2003). For deluxe programs, try well-known **Tauck Tours** (11 Wilton Rd., Westport CT 06881, ☎ 203/226–6911 or 800/468–2825) or **Maupintour** (Box 807, Lawrence KS 66044, ☎ 913/843–1211 or 800/255–4266). Another operator falling between deluxe and first-class is **Globus** (5301 South Federal Circle, Littleton, CO 80123, ☎ 303/797–2800 or 800/221–0090). First-class and first-class superior programs are sold by **Bennett Tours** (270 Madison Ave., New York, NY 10016, ☎ 212/532–5060 or 800/221–2420), **Brendan Tours** (15137 Califa St., Van Nuys, CA 91411, ☎ 818/785–9696 or 800/421–8446), **Caravan Tours** (401 N. Michigan Ave., Chicago, IL 60611, ☎ 312/321–9800 or 800/CARAVAN), **Delta Dream Vacations** (800/872–7786), **Finway** (☎ 800/526–4927), **Insight International** (745 Atlantic Ave., Boston MA 0211, ☎ 617/482–2000 or

800/582–8380), **Scantours** (1535 Sixth St., Suite 205, Santa Monica, CA 90401, ☎ 310/451–0911 or 800/223–7226), and **Trafalgar Tours** (21 E. 26th St., New York, NY 10010, ☎ 212/689–8977 or 800/854–0103). For budget and tourist class programs, try **Cosmos** (*see* Globus, *above*).

PACKAGES

Independent vacation packages are available from all the group-tour operators above. You may also want to contact Holiday Tours of America (☎ 800/677–6454).

THEME TRIPS

ADVENTURE➤ For Norwegian adventures, from whalewatching to dogsledding, contact **Borton Overseas** (1621 E. 79th St., Bloomington, MN 55425, ☎ 612/883–0704 or 800/843–0602). For wintertime advenutures, call **Scandinavian Special Interest Network** (38 Valley View Trail, Sparta, NJ 07871, ☎ 201/729–8961, FAX 201/729–6565). **All Adventure Travel** (5589 Arapahoe 208, Boulder, CO 80303, ☎ 800/537–4025), with more than 80 tour operators members, can satisfy virtually any special interest in Norway.

BICYCLING➤ Bike trips in Norway are available from **Backroads** (1516 5th St., Suite A550, Berkeley, CA 94710, ☎ 510/527–1555 or 800/462–2848).

BIRD-WATCHING➤ Northern Norway contains some of northern Europe's largest bird sanctuaries and teems with fantastic numbers of seabirds, including cormorants, razorbills, auks, guillemots, eider ducks, puffins, and even eagles. Contact **Borton Overseas** (*see* Adventure, *above*) or the **Scandinavian Tourist Board** (*see* Visitor Information *below*).

CRUISING➤ For a cruise of Norway's fjords, contact **EuroCruises** (303 W. 13th St., New York, NY 10014, ☎ 212/691–2099 or 800/688–3876). Also try **KD River Cruises of Europe** (2500 Westchester Ave., Purchase, NY 10577, ☎ 914/696–3600 or 800/346–6535) and **Swan Hellenic/Esplanade Tours** (581 Boylston St., Boston, MA 02116, ☎ 617/266–7465 or 800/426–5492).

FOLK ART AND CRAFTS➤ For a journey covering the wonderful arts and crafts of Norway, contact **Scandinavian Special Interest Network** (*see* Adventure, *above*).

GENEALOGY➤ Travelers of Norwegian descent interested in intensive heritage tours of their ancestral region should contact **Brekke Tours** (802 N. 43rd St., Suite D, Grand Forks, ND 58203, ☎ 701/772–8999 or 800/437–5302).

MUSIC➤ **Dailey-Thorp Travel** (330 W. 58th St., New York, NY 10019, ☎ 212/307–1555; book through travel agents) specializes in classical music and opera programs throughout Norway; its packages include tickets that are otherwise very hard to get.

FROM THE U.K.

Contact **Scandinavian Travel Service** (29a Nork Way, Banstead, Surrey SM7 1PB, ☎ 01737/212500) and **Scantours** (21–24 Cockspur St., London SW1Y 5BN, ☎ 0171/839–2927).

ORGANIZATIONS

The **National Tour Association** (546 E. Main St., Lexington, KY 40508, ☎ 606/226–4444 or 800/755–8687) and **United States Tour Operators Association** (USTOA, 211 E. 51st St., Suite 12B, New York, NY 10022, ☎ 212/750–7371) can provide lists of member operators and information on booking tours.

PUBLICATIONS

Consult the brochure *"On Tour"* and ask for a current list of member operators from the National Tour Association (*see* Organizations, *above*). Also get a copy of the *"Worldwide Tour & Vacation Package Finder"* from the USTOA (*see* Organizations, *above*) and the Better Business Bureau's *"Tips on Travel Packages"* (publication No. 24-195, $2; 4200 Wilson Blvd., Arlington, VA 22203.

TRAVEL AGENCIES

For names of reputable agencies in your area, contact the **American Society of Travel Agents** (1101 King St., Suite 200, Alexandria, VA 22314, ☎ 703/739–2782).

THE GOLD GUIDE / IMPORTANT CONTACTS

U

U.S. GOVERNMENT TRAVEL BRIEFINGS

The U.S. Department of State's Overseas Citizens Emergency Center (Room 4811, Washington, DC 20520; enclose SASE) issues **Consular Information Sheets,** which cover crime, security, political climate, and health risks as well as embassy locations, entry requirements, currency regulations, and other routine matters. For the latest information, stop in at any U.S. passport office, consulate, or embassy; call the interactive hot line (☎ 202/ 647–5225 or fax 202/ 647-3000); or, with your PC's modem, tap into the Bureau of Consular Affairs' computer bulletin board (☎ 202/ 647–9225).

V

VISITOR INFORMATION

Contact the **Scandinavian Tourist Board,** 655 3rd Ave., New York, NY 10017, ☎ 212/ 949–2333, FAX 212/ 983–5260.

In the U.K., contact the **Norwegian Tourist Board** (5 Lower Regent St., London SW1Y 4LR, ☎ 0171/839–6255, FAX 0171/839–6014).

PUBLICATIONS

The Norwegian Tourist Office's "Tourist Timetables" is particularly useful. It includes information about ships, trains, planes, buses, and ferries traveling to and around Norway.

W

WEATHER

For current conditions and forecasts, plus the local time and helpful travel tips, call the **Weather Channel Connection** (☎ 900/932– 8437; 95¢ per minute) from a touch-tone phone.

SMART TRAVEL TIPS A TO Z

Basic Information on Traveling in Norway and Savvy Tips to Make Your Trip a Breeze

The more you travel, the more you know about how to make trips run like clockwork. To help make your travels hassle-free, Fodor's editors have rounded up dozens of tips from our contributors and travel experts all over the world, as well as basic information on visiting Norway. For names of organizations to contact and publications that can give you more information, see Important Contacts A to Z, *above.*

A
AIR TRAVEL

If time is an issue, **always look for nonstop flights,** which require no change of plane. If possible, **avoid connecting flights,** which stop at least once and can involve a change of plane, although the flight number remains the same; if the first leg is late, the second waits.

CUTTING COSTS

The Sunday travel section of most newspapers is a good source of deals.

MAJOR AIRLINES➤ The least-expensive airfares from the major airlines are priced for round-trip travel and are subject to restrictions. You must usually **book in advance and buy the ticket within 24 hours** to get cheaper fares, and you may have to **stay over a Saturday night.** The lowest fare is subject to availability, and only a small percentage of the plane's total seats are sold at that price. It's good to **call a number of airlines, and when you are quoted a good price, book it on the spot**—the same fare on the same flight may not be available the next day. Airlines generally allow you to change your return date for a $25 to $50 fee, but most low-fare tickets are nonrefundable. However, if you don't use it, you can apply the cost toward the purchase price of a new ticket, again for a small charge.

CONSOLIDATORS➤ Consolidators, who buy tickets at reduced rates from scheduled airlines, sell them at prices below the lowest available from the airlines directly—usually without advance restrictions. Sometimes you can even get your money back if you need to return the ticket. Carefully read the fine print detailing penalties for changes and cancellations. If you doubt the reliability of a consolidator, **confirm your reservation with the airline.**

ALOFT

AIRLINE FOOD➤ If you hate airline food, **ask for special meals when booking.** These can be vegetarian, low-cholesterol, or kosher, for example; commonly prepared to order in smaller quantities than standard catered fare, they can be tastier.

JET LAG

To avoid this syndrome, which occurs when travel disrupts your body's natural cycles, try to maintain a normal routine. At night, **get some sleep.** By day, move about the cabin to **stretch your legs, eat light meals, and drink water—not alcohol.**

SMOKING➤ Smoking is banned on all flights within the U.S. of less than six hours' duration and on all Canadian flights; the ban also applies to domestic segments of international flights aboard U.S. and foreign carriers. Delta has banned smoking system-wide. On U.S. carriers flying to Norway and other destinations abroad, a seat in a no-smoking section must be provided for every passenger who requests one, and the section must be enlarged to accommodate such passengers if necessary as long as they have complied with the airline's deadline for check-in and seat assignment. If smoking bothers you, request a seat far from the smoking section.

Foreign airlines are exempt from these rules but do provide no-smoking sections.

British Airways has banned smoking; some nations have banned smoking on all domestic flights, and others may ban smoking on some flights. Talks continue on the feasibility of broadening no-smoking policies.

WITHIN NORWAY

If you are traveling from south to north in Norway, flying is a necessity: Stavanger in southern Norway is as close to Rome, Italy, as it is to the northern tip of Norway.

A number of special fares are available within Norway year-round, including air passes, family tickets, weekend excursions, and youth (up to the age of 26) and senior (over 67) discounts. Youth fares are cheapest when purchased from the automatic ticket machines at the airport on the day of departure. All Norwegian routes have reduced rates from July through the middle of August, and tickets can be purchased on the spot.

SAS offers special "Jackpot" fares all year within Norway, as well as reasonable "Visit Norway" fares which must be purchased in the United States in conjunction with an SAS flight to Scandinavia. SAS "Visit Norway" passes can be bought at your travel agent when you purchase your flight.

B
BUS TRAVEL

Long-distance buses usually take longer than trains and fares are only slightly lower. However, virtually every settlement on the mainland is served by bus, and for anyone with a desire to get off the beaten track, a pay-as-you-go, open-ended bus trip can be one of the best ways to see Norway.

C
CAMERAS, CAMCORDERS, AND COMPUTERS

LAPTOPS

Before you depart, **check your portable computer's battery,** because you may be asked at security to turn on the computer to prove that it is what it appears to be. At the airport, you may prefer to **request a manual inspection,** although security X-rays do not harm hard-disk or floppy-disk storage. Also, **register your foreign-made laptop with U.S. Customs.** If your laptop is U.S.-made, call the consulate of the country you'll be visiting to find out whether or not it should be registered with local customs upon arrival. You may want to **find out about repair facilities at your destination** in case you need them.

PHOTOGRAPHY

If your camera is new or if you haven't used it for a while, **shoot and develop a few rolls of film** before you leave. Always **store film in a cool, dry place**—never in the car's glove compartment or on the shelf under the rear window.

Every pass of film through an X-ray machine increases the chance of clouding. To protect it, carry it in a clear plastic bag and **ask for hand inspection at security.** Such requests are virtually always honored at U.S. airports, and usually are accommodated abroad. Don't depend on a lead-lined bag to protect film in checked luggage—the airline may increase the radiation to see what's inside.

VIDEO

Before your trip, **test your camcorder, invest in a skylight filter to protect the lens, and charge the batteries.** (Airport security personnel may ask you to turn on the camcorder to prove that it's what it appears to be.) The batteries of most newer camcorders can be recharged with a universal or worldwide AC adapter charger (or multivoltage converter), usable whether the voltage is 110 or 220. All that's needed is the appropriate plug.

Videotape is not damaged by X-rays, but it may be harmed by the magnetic field of a walk-through metal detector, so **ask that videotapes be hand-checked.** Videotape sold in Norway is based on the PAL standard, which is different than the one used in the United States. You will not be able to view your tapes through the local TV set or view movies bought there in your home VCR. Blank tapes bought in Norway can be used for camcorder taping, but they are pricey. Some U.S. audio-visual shops convert foreign tapes to U.S. standards; contact an electronics dealer to find the nearest.

CHILDREN AND TRAVEL

In Norway children are to be seen *and* heard and are genuinely welcome in most public places.

BABY-SITTING

For recommended local sitters, **check with your hotel desk.**

DISCOUNTS

Children are entitled to discount tickets (often as much as 50% off) on buses, trains, and ferries throughout Norway, as well as reductions on special City Cards. Children under 18 pay half-price and children under 2 pay 10% on SAS round-trips. The only restriction on this discount is that the family travel together and return to the originating city in Norway at least two days later. With the ScanRail Pass—good for rail journeys throughout Norway—children under four (on lap) travel free, while those from 4 to 11 pay half-fare and those from 12–25 pay 75% of the adult fare.

DRIVING

If you are renting a car, **arrange for a car seat when you reserve.** Sometimes they're free.

FLYING

Always **ask about discounted children's fares.** On international flights, the fare for infants under age 2 not occupying a seat is generally either free or 10% of the accompanying adult's fare; children ages 2 through 11 usually pay half to two-thirds of the adult fare. On domestic flights, children under 2 not occupying a seat travel free, and older children currently travel on the lowest applicable adult fare.

BAGGAGE➤ In general, the adult baggage allowance applies for children paying half or more of the adult fare. Before departure, **ask about carry-on allowances,** if you are traveling with an infant. In general, those paying 10% of the adult fare are allowed one carry-on bag, not to exceed 70 pounds or 45 inches (length + width + height) and a collapsible stroller; you may be allowed less if the flight is full.

SAFETY SEATS➤ According to the FAA, it's a good idea to **use safety seats aloft.** Airline policy varies. U.S. carriers allow FAA-approved models, but airlines usually require that you buy a ticket, even if your child would otherwise ride free, because the seats must be strapped into regular passenger seats. Foreign carriers may not allow infant seats, may charge the child's rather than the infant's fare for their use, or may require you to hold your baby during takeoff and landing, thus defeating the seat's purpose.

FACILITIES➤ When making your reservation, **ask for children's** meals or freestanding bassinets if you need them; the latter are available only to those with seats at the bulkhead, where there's enough legroom. If you don't need a bassinet, **think twice before requesting bulkhead seats**—the only storage for in-flight necessities is in the inconveniently distant overhead bins.

LODGING

Most hotels allow children under a certain age to stay in their parents' room at no extra charge, while others charge them as extra adults; be sure to **ask about the cut-off age.**

Many youth hostels offer special facilities (including multiple-bed rooms and separate kitchens) for families with children. Family hostels also provide an excellent opportunity for children to meet youngsters from other countries. Contact Hostelling International (*see* Students in Important Contacts A to Z, *above*).

CUSTOMS AND DUTIES

ON ARRIVAL

Any adult can bring in duty-free 1 liter of alcohol (not exceeding 60% by volume), 1 liter of wine, and 2 liters of beer. Anyone over 18 years old can import 400 cigarettes duty free. Importing alcohol over the above limit is not recommended.

BACK HOME IN THE U.S.

You may bring home $400 worth of foreign

goods duty-free if you've been out of the country for at least 48 hours and haven't already used the $400 exemption, or any part of it, in the past 30 days.

Travelers 21 or older may bring back one liter of alcohol duty-free, provided the beverage laws of the state through which they reenter the United States allow it. In addition, 100 non-Cuban cigars and 200 cigarettes are allowed, regardless of your age. Antiques and works of art more than 100 years old are duty-free.

Duty-free, travelers may mail packages valued at up to $200 to themselves and up to $100 to others, with a limit of one parcel per addressee per day (and no alcohol or tobacco products or perfume valued at more than $5); outside, identify the package as being for personal use or an unsolicited gift, specifying the contents and their retail value. Mailed items do not count as part of your exemption.

IN CANADA➤ Once per calendar year, when you've been out of Canada for at least seven days, you may bring in C$300 worth of goods duty-free. If you've been away less than seven days but more than 48 hours, the duty-free exemption drops to C$100 but can be claimed any number of times (as can a C$20 duty-free exemption for absences of 24 hours or more). You cannot combine the yearly and 48-hour exemptions,

use the C$300 exemption only partially (to save the balance for a later trip), or pool exemptions with family members. Goods claimed under the C$300 exemption may follow you by mail; those claimed under the lesser exemptions must accompany you.

Alcohol and tobacco products may be included in the yearly and 48-hour exemptions but not in the 24-hour exemption. If you meet the age requirements of the province through which you reenter Canada, you may bring in, duty-free, 1.14 liters (40 imperial ounces) of wine or liquor *or* 24 12-ounce cans or bottles of beer or ale. If you are 16 or older, you may bring in, duty-free, 200 cigarettes, 50 cigars or cigarillos, and 400 tobacco sticks or 400 grams of manufactured tobacco. Alcohol and tobacco must accompany you on your return.

An unlimited number of gifts valued up to C$60 each may be mailed to Canada duty-free. These do not count as part of your exemption. Label the package "Unsolicited Gift— Value under $60." Alcohol and tobacco are excluded.

IN THE U.K.➤ Because Norway is outside the EU, you may import duty-free 200 cigarettes, 100 cigarillos, 50 cigars or 250 grams of tobacco; 1 liter of spirits or 2 liters of fortified or sparkling wine; 2 liters of still table wine; 60 milliliters of perfume;

250 milliliters of toilet water; plus £136 worth of other goods, including gifts and souvenirs.

D

DINING

For information on affordable eating, see Costs under Money and Expenses, *below.*

FOR TRAVELERS WITH DISABILITIES

Facilities for travelers with disabilities in Norway are generally good, and most of the major tourist offices offer special booklets and brochures on travel and accommodations.

When discussing accessibility with an operator or reservationist, **ask hard questions.** Are there any stairs, inside *or* out? Are there grab bars next to the toilet *and* in the shower/tub? How wide is the doorway to the room? To the bathroom? For the most extensive facilities, meeting the latest legal specifications, **opt for newer accommodations,** which more often have been designed with access in mind. Older properties or ships must usually be retrofitted and may offer more limited facilities as a result. Be sure to **discuss your needs before booking.**

DISCOUNT CLUBS

Travel clubs offer members unsold space on airplanes, cruise ships, and package tours at as much as 50% below regular prices. Membership may include a regular bulletin or access to a toll-free hot line giving details of available trips departing from three or four days to several months in the future. Most also offer 50% discounts off hotel rack rates. Before booking with a club, **make sure the hotel or other supplier isn't offering a better deal.**

DRIVING

Driving is a marvelous way to explore Norway. The roads are generally excellent and well marked with directional, distance and informational signs. All vehicles registered abroad are required to carry international liability insurance and an international accident report form, which can be obtained from automobile clubs. Collision insurance is recommended.

Driving is on the right. Dimmed headlights are mandatory at all times, as is the use of seatbelts and children's seats (when appropriate) in both front and rear seats.

Four-lane highways are the exception and are found only around major cities. Outside of main routes, roads tend to be narrow and sharply twisting, with only token guardrails, and during the summer roads are always crowded. Along the west coast, waits for ferries and passage through tunnels can be significant. **Don't expect to cover more than 240 kilometers (150 miles) in a day, especially in fjord country.**

Some roads, particularly those over moun-

tains, can close for all or part of the winter. If you drive on other than major roads in winter, make sure the car is equipped with studded tires for improved traction. Roads are not salted but are left with a hard-packed layer of snow on top of the asphalt. **If you're renting, choose a small car with front-wheel drive.** Also bring an ice scraper, snow brush, small shovel, and heavy clothes for emergencies. Although the weather along the coast is sunny, a few hours inland, temperatures may be 15° colder and snowfall is the rule rather than the exception.

Gas stations are plentiful and unleaded gasoline and diesel fuel are sold virtually everywhere from self-service gas pumps. Those marked *kort* are 24-hour pumps, which take oil company credit cards or bank cards, either of which is inserted directly into the pump. Gasoline is expensive however, running about $1.00 per liter, or roughly four times the typical U.S. price.

Also be aware that there are relatively low legal blood-alcohol limits and tough penalties for driving while intoxicated in Norway. The legal limit is a blood-alcohol percentage of 0.05%, which corresponds to a glass of wine or a bottle of low-alcohol beer. Penalties include suspension of the driver's license and fines or imprisonment, and are enforced by random police

roadblocks in urban areas on weekends. No exceptions are made for foreigners. In addition, an accident involving a driver with an illegal blood-alcohol level usually voids all insurance agreements, so the driver becomes responsible for his own medical bills and damage to the cars.

Speeding is also punished severely. Most roads are monitored by radar and cameras in gray metal boxes. Signs warning of *Automatisk Trafikkontroll* (Automatic Traffic Monitoring) are posted periodically along appropriate roads. Radar controls are frequent on weekends, especially along major highways.

Make sure you double-check all directions and have an up-to-date map before you venture out, because some highway numbers have changed in the past few years, particularly routes beginning with "E." You may come across construction in and around Oslo and other major cities.

F
FERRY TRAVEL

Along west-coast fjords, car ferries are a way of life. **Once you know your route, buy tickets for those ferries that allow advance purchase**—this lets you drive to the front of the line.

Many companies arrange package trips (*see* Tour Operators in Important Contacts A to Z, *above*), some offering a rental car and hotel accommodations as part of the deal.

I
INSURANCE

Travel insurance can protect your investment, replace your luggage and its contents, or provide for medical coverage should you fall ill during your trip. Most tour operators, travel agents, and insurance agents sell specialized health-and-accident, flight, trip-cancellation, and luggage insurance as well as comprehensive policies with some or all of these features. Before you make any purchase, **review your existing health and homeowner's policies** to find out whether they cover expenses incurred while traveling.

BAGGAGE

Airline liability for your baggage is limited to $1,250 per person on domestic flights. On international flights, the airlines' liability is $9.07 per pound or $20 per kilogram for checked baggage (roughly $640 per 70-pound bag) and $400 per passenger for unchecked baggage. Insurance for losses exceeding the terms of your airline ticket can be bought directly from the airline at check-in for about $10 per $1,000 of coverage; note that it excludes a rather extensive list of items, shown on your airline ticket.

FLIGHT

You should **think twice before buying flight insurance.** Often purchased as a last-minute impulse at the airport, it pays a lump sum when a plane crashes, either to a beneficiary if the insured dies or sometimes to a surviving passenger who loses eyesight or a limb. Supplementing the airlines' coverage described in the limits-of-liability paragraphs on your ticket, it's expensive and basically unnecessary. Charging an airline ticket to a major credit card often automatically entitles you to coverage and may also embrace travel by bus, train, and ship.

HEALTH

If your own health insurance policy does not cover you outside the U.S., **consider buying supplemental medical coverage.** It can cover from $1,000 to $150,000 worth of medical and/or dental expenses incurred as a result of an accident or illness during a trip. These policies also may include a personal-accident, or death-and-dismemberment, provision, which pays a lump sum ranging from $15,000 to $500,000 to your beneficiaries if you die or to you if you lose one or more limbs or your eyesight, and a medical-assistance provision, which may either reimburse you for the cost of referrals, evacuation, or repatriation and other services, or may automatically enroll you as a member of a particular medical-assistance company. (*See* Health Issues *in* Important Contacts A to Z, *above*.)

FOR U.K. TRAVELERS

You can buy an annual travel-insurance policy valid for most vacations during the year in which it's purchased. If you go this route, make sure it covers you if you have a preexisting medical condition or are pregnant.

TRIP

Without insurance, you will lose all or most of your money if you must cancel your trip due to illness or any other reason. Especially if your airline ticket, cruise, or package tour is nonrefundable and cannot be changed, it's essential that you **buy trip-cancellation-and-interruption insurance.** When considering how much coverage you need, look for a policy that will cover the cost of your trip plus the nondiscounted price of a one-way airline ticket should you need to return home early. Read the fine print carefully, especially sections defining "family member" and "preexisting medical conditions." Also **consider default or bankruptcy insurance,** which protects you against a supplier's failure to deliver. However, such policies often do not cover default by a travel agency, tour operator, airline, or cruise line if you bought your tour and the coverage directly from the firm in question.

L
LANGUAGE

Despite the fact that Norwegian is in the Germanic family of languages, it is a myth that someone who speaks German can understand Norwegian. Fortunately, English is widely spoken, as every Norwegian receives at least seven years of English instruction, starting in the second grade. Outside major cities however, English becomes rarer, and it's a good idea to **take along a dictionary or phrase book.** Danish, Norwegian, and Swedish are similar, and fluent speakers can generally understand each other.

Norwegian has three additional vowels, æ, ø, and å. Æ is pronounced as a short "a." The ø, sometimes printed as *oe,* is the same as ö in German and Swedish, pronounced very much like a short "u." The å is a contraction of the archaic aa and sounds like a long "o." The important thing about these characters isn't that you pronounce them correctly—foreigners usually can't—but that you know to look for them in the phone book at the very end. Mr. Søren Åstrup, for example, will be found after "Z." Æ and Ø follow.

There are two officially sanctioned languages, Bokmål and Nynorsk. Bokmål is used by 84% of the population and is the main written form of Norwegian, the language of books, as the first half of its name indicates. Nynorsk, which translates as "new Norwegian," is actually a compilation of older dialect forms from rural Norway, which evolved during

the national romantic period around the turn of this century. All Norwegians are required to study both languages and 25% of all state (NRK) television and radio broadcasting is required to be in Nynorsk.

The Sami (incorrectly called Lapp) people have their own language, which is more akin to Finnish than to Norwegian.

LODGING

Norway has several hotel chains. SAS, which is a division of the airline, has a number of luxury hotels designed for the business traveler. Many are above the Arctic Circle and are the "only game in town." Rica and Reso hotels, also luxury chains, have expanded extensively in the past few years. Best Western and Rainbow hotels are both moderate chains, found in most major towns.

The most interesting and distinctive hotel chain is Home Hotels (Swedish-owned), which has successfully converted existing historic buildings into modern functional establishments in the middle price range. All Home Hotels provide an evening meal, jogging suits, free beer, and other amenities designed to appeal to the single, usually business, traveler. **As far as value for money is concerned, Home Hotels are Norway's best buy.**

The Farmer's Association operates simple hotels in most towns and cities. These reason-

ably priced accommodations usually have "-heimen" as part of the name, such as Bondeheimen in Oslo. The same organization also runs cafeterias serving traditional Norwegian food, usually called Kaffistova. All of these hotels and restaurants are alcohol-free.

In the countryside, look for independently run inns and motels, called *fjellstue* or *pensjonat.*

In general, reservations are a good idea; it is virtually impossible to get a room on a weekday in Stockholm in late spring because large conventions soak up all available space. Countryside inns usually have space, but not always: Vacationing Germans are sometimes referred to as *vand-hunde* (water-dogs) because waterside areas attract them in large numbers. With eastern Germans suddenly more mobile, some coast-side inns have recently been filling their summer vacancies by January.

Norway's tourist season runs from May to September. Some hotels lower prices during tourist season, others raise them during the same period. It's best to ask when making reservations.

Before you leave home, **ask your travel agent about discounts** (*see* Hotels, *below*), including summer hotel checks for Best Western, Scandic, and Inter Nor hotels, a summer Fjord Pass, and enormous year-round rebates at SAS hotels for travelers over 65. All EuroClass (business class) passengers can get discounts of at least 10% at SAS hotels when they book through SAS.

Two things about hotels usually surprise North Americans: the relatively limited dimensions of Scandinavian beds and the generous size of Scandinavian breakfasts. Scandinavian queen-size beds are often about 60 inches wide or slightly less, close in size to the U.S. double bed. King-size beds (72 inches wide) are difficult to find and, if available, require special reservations.

Older hotels may have some rooms described as "double," which in fact have one double bed plus one fold-out sofa big enough for two people. This arrangement is occasionally called a "combi-room" but is being phased out.

Many older hotels, particularly the country inns and independently run smaller hotels in the cities, do not have private bathrooms. Ask ahead if this is important to you.

Breakfast is often included in the price of the hotel except in deluxe establishments. Norwegian breakfasts resemble what many people would call lunch, usually including breads, cheeses, marmalade, hams, lunch meats, eggs, juice, cereal, milk, and coffee. In contrast, the typical Continental breakfast served in other parts of Europe consists of just a roll and coffee. A general rule is that the farther north you go,

the larger the breakfasts become.

APARTMENT AND VILLA RENTALS

If you want a home base that's roomy enough for a family and comes with cooking facilities, **consider a furnished rental.** It's generally cost-wise, too, although not always— some rentals are luxury properties (economical only when your party is large). Home-exchange directories do list rentals—often second homes owned by prospective house swappers—and some services search for a house or apartment for you (even a castle if that's your fancy) and handle the paperwork. Some send an illustrated catalogue and others send photographs of specific properties, sometimes at a charge; up-front registration fees may apply.

HOME EXCHANGE

If you would like to find a house, an apartment, or other vacation property to exchange for your own while on vacation, **become a member of a home-exchange organization,** which will send you its annual directories listing available exchanges and will include your own listing in at least one of them. Arrangements for the actual exchange are made by the two parties to it, not by the organization.

HOSTELS

Norway has 90 youth hostels, but in an effort to appeal to vacationers of all ages, the name

has been changed to *vandrehjem* (travelers' homes). Norwegian hostels are among the best in the world, squeaky clean and with excellent facilities. Rooms sleep from two to six, and many have private showers. You don't have to be a member, but members get reductions, so it's worth joining. Membership can be arranged at any vandrerhjem, or you can buy a coupon book good for seven nights, which includes the membership fee. It's a good idea to **bring your own linens,** since they're usually rented by the night. If you haven't brought any, you can buy a *laken-pose* (sheet sleeping bag) at specialty stores, or one at the vandrerhjem.

HOTELS

Inn Checks, or prepaid hotel vouchers, are offered for accommodations ranging from first-class hotels to country cottages. These vouchers, which must be purchased from travel agents or from the Scandinavian Tourist Board (*see* Visitor Information in Important Contacts A to Z, *above*) before departure, are sold individually and in packets for as many nights as needed and offer savings of up to 50%. Summer bargains for foreign tourists may also be available.

M
MAIL

The letter rate for Norway is NKr 3.50, NKr4 for the other

Nordic countries, NKr4.50 for Europe, and NKr5.50 for outside Europe for a letter weighing up to 20g (¾ ounce).

No one plans to get sick while traveling, but it happens, so **consider signing up with a medical assistance company.** These outfits provide referrals, emergency evacuation or repatriation, 24-hour telephone hot lines for medical consultation, dispatch of medical personnel, relay of medical records, cash for emergencies, and other personal and legal assistance.

The unit of currency in Norway is the krone (plural: kroner), which translates as "crown." In this book currency is abbreviated NKr (Norwegian kroner). In Norway, you may see prices indicated with Kr only, and you may see exchange rates in banks quoted for NOK. One krone is divided into 100 øre, and coins of 10 and 50 øre, 1, 5, 10, and 20 kroner are in circulation, although 10 øre are no longer in production. Bills are issued in denominations of 50, 100, 200, 500, and 1,000 kroner. In summer 1995, the exchange rate was NKr6.53 to U.S.$1, NKr10.33 to £1, and NKr4.79 to C$1. These rates fluctuate, so be sure to check them when planning a trip.

ATMS

Cirrus, Plus and many other networks connecting automated-teller machines operate internationally. Chances are that you can **use your bank card at ATMs** to withdraw money from an account and get cash advances on a credit-card account if your card has been programmed with a personal identification number, or PIN. Before leaving home, **check in on frequency limits** for withdrawals and cash advances. Also **ask whether your card's PIN must be reprogrammed** for use in Norway. Four digits are commonly used overseas. Note that Discover is accepted only in the United States.

On cash advances you are charged interest from the day you receive the money, whether from a teller or an ATM. Although transaction fees for ATM withdrawals abroad may be higher than fees for withdrawals at home, Cirrus and Plus exchange rates are excellent because they are based on wholesale rates only offered by major banks.

COSTS

Costs are high in Norway. Basic sample prices are: Cup of coffee, from NKr12 in a cafeteria to NKr25 or more in a restaurant; a 20-pack of cigarettes, NKr50; a half-liter of beer, NKr30–NKr50; the smallest hot dog (with bun plus *lompe*—a Norwegian tortilla-like bread—mustard, ketchup, and fried

onions) at a convenience store, NKr15; cheapest bottle of wine from a government store, NKr60; the same bottle at a restaurant, NKr120–NKr200; urban transit fare in Oslo, NKr15; soft drink, from NKr20 in a cafeteria to NKr35 in a better restaurant; one adult movie ticket, NKr45; shrimp or roast beef sandwich at a cafeteria, NKr40; one-mile taxi ride, NKr30–NKr50 depending upon time of day. Be aware that sales taxes can be steep, but foreigners can get some refunds by shopping at tax-free stores (*see* Taxes, *below*). City cards can save you transportation and entrance fees in many of the larger cities.

You can **reduce the cost of food by planning.** Breakfast–usually a fairly big meal with a selection of crusty bread, herring, cold meat, and cheese–is frequently included in your hotel bill; if not, you may wish to buy fruit, sweet rolls, and a beverage for a picnic breakfast. Restaurant lunches are often significantly less expensive than dinner. Instead of beer or wine, **drink tap water**—liquor can cost four times the price of the same brand in a store—but do specify tap water, as the term "water" can refer to soft drinks and bottled water, which are also expensive. Throughout Norway, the tip is included in the cost of your meal.

Local liquor laws arouse almost obsessional

interest among Norwegians. In most of the country, liquor and strong beer (over 3% alcohol) can be purchased only in state-owned shops, at very high prices, during weekday business hours, usually 9:30 to 6. A 70- or 75-centiliter bottle of whiskey, for example, can easily cost NKr250 (about $35). (When you visit relatives in Norway, a bottle of liquor or fine wine bought duty-free on the trip over is often a much-appreciated gift.)

EXCHANGING CURRENCY

For the most favorable rates, **change money at banks.** You won't do as well at exchange booths in airports, rail, and bus stations, or in hotels, restaurants, and stores, although you may find their hours more convenient. To avoid lines at airport exchange booths, **get a small amount of currency before you leave home.**

TAXES

One way to beat high prices is to **take advantage of tax-free shopping.** Throughout Norway, you can make major purchases free of tax if you have a foreign passport. Value-added tax, MVA for short, but called *moms* all over Scandinavia, is a hefty 23% on all services and purchases except books; it is included in the prices of goods. All purchases of consumer goods totaling over NKr300 (approximately $45) for export by nonresidents are eligible for value-added tax refunds.

Shops subscribing to "Norway Tax-Free Shopping" provide customers with vouchers, which they must present together with their purchases upon departure in order to receive an on-the-spot refund of 16.25% of the tax.

Shops that do not subscribe to this program have slightly more detailed forms, which must be presented to the Norwegian Customs Office along with the goods to obtain a refund by mail. This refund is closer to the actual amount of the tax.

It's essential to have both the forms and the goods available for inspection upon departure. Make sure the appropriate stamps are on the voucher or other forms before leaving the country.

Be aware that limits for EU tourists are higher than for those coming from outside the EU.

TIPPING

Tipping is kept to a minimum in Norway because service charges are added to most bills. It is, however, handy to have a supply of NKr5 or 10 coins for less formal service. Tip only in local currency.

Airport and railroad porters (if you can find them) have fixed rates per bag, so they will tell you how much they should be paid. Tips to doormen vary according to the type of bag and the distance carried: NKr5–NKr10 each, with similar tips for porters carrying bags to the room.

Room service usually has a service charge included already, so tipping is discretionary.

Round off a taxi fare to the next round digit, or tip anywhere from NKr5 to NKr10, a little more if the driver has been particularly helpful with luggage.

All restaurants include a service charge, ranging from 12% to 15%, in the bill. It is customary to add an additional 5% for exceptional service, but it is not obligatory. Maitre d's are not tipped, and coat checks have flat rates, ranging from NKr5 to NKr10 per person.

TRAVELER'S CHECKS

Whether or not to buy traveler's checks depends on where you are headed; **take cash to rural areas and small towns, traveler's checks to cities.** The most widely recognized are American Express, Citicorp, Thomas Cook, and Visa, which are sold by major commercial banks for 1% to 3% of the checks' face value—it pays to **shop around.** Both American Express and Thomas Cook issue checks that can be counter-signed and used by you or your traveling companion, and they both provide checks, at no extra charge, denominated in various non-U.S. currencies. So you won't be left with excess foreign currency, **buy a few checks in small denominations** to cash toward the end of your trip. Record the numbers of the checks, cross them off as you spend them, and keep this information separate from your checks.

WIRING MONEY

You don't have to be a cardholder to send or receive funds through MoneyGram[SM] from American Express. Just go to a MoneyGram agent, located in retail and convenience stores and in American Express Travel Offices. Pay up to $1,000 with cash or a credit card, anything over that in cash. The money can be picked up within 10 minutes in the form of U.S. dollar traveler's checks or local currency at the nearest Money-Gram agent, or, abroad, the nearest American Express Travel Office. There's no limit, and the recipient need only present photo identification. The cost runs from 3% to 10%, depending on the amount sent, the destination, and how you pay.

You can also send money using Western Union. Money sent from the United States or Canada will be available for pickup at agent locations in 100 countries within 15 minutes. Once the money is in the system, it can be picked up at any one of 25,000 locations. Fees range from 4% to 10%, depending on the amount you send.

P
PACKAGES
AND TOURS

A package or tour to Norway can make your vacation less expensive

and more convenient. Firms that sell tours and packages purchase airline seats, hotel rooms, and rental cars in bulk and pass some of the savings on to you. In addition, the best operators have local representatives to help you out at your destination.

A GOOD DEAL?

The more your package or tour includes, the better you can predict the ultimate cost of your vacation. Make sure you know exactly what is included, and **beware of hidden costs.** Are taxes, tips, and service charges included? Transfers and baggage handling? Entertainment and excursions? These can add up.

Most packages and tours are rated deluxe, first-class superior, first class, tourist, or budget. The key difference is usually accommodations. If the package or tour you are considering is priced lower than in your wildest dreams, **be skeptical.** Also, **make sure your travel agent knows the hotels** and other services. Ask about location, room size, beds, and whether it has a pool, room service, or programs for children, if you care about these. Has your agent been there or sent others you can contact?

BUYER BEWARE

Each year consumers are stranded or lose their money when operators go out of business—even very large ones with excel-

lent reputations. If you can't afford a loss, take the time to **check out the operator**—find out how long the company has been in business, and ask several agents about its reputation. Next, **don't book unless the firm has a consumer-protection program.** Members of the United States Tour Operators Association and the National Tour Association are required to set aside funds exclusively to cover your payments and travel arrangements in case of default. Nonmember operators may instead carry insurance; look for the details in the operator's brochure—and the name of an underwriter with a solid reputation. Note: When it comes to tour operators, **don't trust escrow accounts.** Although there are laws governing those of charter-flight operators, no governmental body prevents tour operators from raiding the till.

Next, **contact your local Better Business Bureau and the attorney general's office** in both your own state and the operator's; have any complaints been filed? Last, **pay with a major credit card.** Then you can cancel payment, provided that you can document your complaint. Always **consider trip-cancellation insurance** (*see* Insurance, *above*).

BIG VS. SMALL➤ An operator that handles several hundred thousand travelers annually can use its purchasing power to give you a good price. Its high volume may also indicate financial stability. But some small companies provide more personalized service; because they tend to specialize, they may also be experts on an area.

USING AN AGENT

Travel agents are an excellent resource. In fact, large operators accept bookings only through travel agents. But it's good to **collect brochures from several agencies**, because some agents' suggestions may be skewed by promotional relationships with tour and package firms that reward them for volume sales. If you have a special interest, **find an agent with expertise in that area;** the American Society of Travel Agents can give you leads in the United States. (Don't rely solely on your agent, though; agents may be unaware of small-niche operators, and some special-interest travel companies only sell direct).

SINGLE TRAVELERS

Prices are usually quoted per person, based on two sharing a room. If traveling solo, you may be required to pay the full double occupancy rate. Some operators eliminate this surcharge if you agree to be matched up with a roommate of the same sex, even if one is not found by departure time.

PACKING FOR NORWAY

Pack light and **take half of what you think you'll need.** A light suitcase

with wheels is a real joy, although most airports have luggage carts that are free for international travelers. Be sure, too, to leave room for the bulky sweaters, handblown glass, and wood bowls that you may bring home from Norwegian shops.

Also **bring a warm sweater, socks, and slacks even in summer** wherever you travel in Norway. Fresh summer days become cool evenings, and the wind is often brisk, particularly on the water, if you plan to travel by boat. Don't forget to **bring a bathing suit even in winter,** as many hotels have pools.

Take a folding umbrella, but be prepared for gusty winds that can destroy even the sturdiest. Also take a lightweight raincoat, as it can double as a windbreaker. You will probably find yourself taking them with you every day, everywhere you go, as it is common for the sky to be clear at 9 AM, rainy at 11 AM, and clear again in time for lunch. Don't forget that your feet get wet as well: An extra pair of walking shoes that dry quickly will come in handy. Except in summer, you'll be glad to have waterproof boots to keep you cozy.

Perhaps because of the climate, Norwegians tend to be practical and resilient, and fashion follows suit. It is safe to generalize that most Norwegians dress more casually than their Continental brethren in

Germany and Italy. Slacks and comfortable shoes are almost always acceptable attire. That said, don't forget to bring one nice outfit for your visit to a fine restaurant or the theater.

If you can't sleep when it is light and you are traveling during summer, bring a comfortable eye mask so you won't wake up automatically at the 4 AM sunrise. Because of the far-northern latitude, the sun slants at angles unseen elsewhere on the globe, and a pair of dark sunglasses can help prevent eyestrain. Sunscreen is a good idea during summer and for winter skiing.

Bug repellent is a good idea if you plan to venture away from the capital cities. Large mosquitoes can be a real nuisance on summer evenings, especially in the far-northern reaches.

Bring an extra pair of eyeglasses or contact lenses in your carry-on luggage, and if you have a health problem, **pack enough medication** to last the trip or have your doctor write a prescription using the drug's generic name, because brand names vary from country to country (you'll then need a prescription from a local doctor). **Don't put prescription drugs or valuables in luggage to be checked,** for it could go astray. To avoid problems with customs officials, carry medications in original packaging. Also don't forget the addresses of offices that handle refunds of lost traveler's checks.

ELECTRICITY

To use your U.S.-purchased electric-powered equipment, **bring a converter and an adapter.** The electrical current in Norway is 220 volts, 50 cycles alternating current (AC); wall outlets take continental-type plugs, with two round prongs.

If your appliances are dual voltage, you'll need only an adapter. Hotels sometimes have 110-volt outlets for low-wattage appliances marked "For Shavers Only" near the sink; don't use them for high-wattage appliances like blow-dryers. If your laptop computer is older, carry a converter; new laptops operate equally well on 110 and 220 volts, so you need only an adapter.

LUGGAGE

Free airline baggage allowances depend on the airline, the route, and the class of your ticket; ask in advance. In general, on domestic flights and on international flights between the United States and foreign destinations, you are entitled to check two bags—neither exceeding 62 inches, or 158 centimeters (length + width + height), or weighing more than 70 pounds (32 kilograms). A third piece may be brought aboard; its total dimensions are generally limited to less than 45 inches (114 centimeters), so it will fit easily under the seat in front

of you or in the overhead compartment. In the United States, the Federal Aviation Administration gives airlines broad latitude to limit carry-on allowances and tailor them to different aircraft and operational conditions. Charges for excess, oversize, or overweight pieces vary.

If you are flying between two foreign destinations, note that baggage allowances may be determined not by piece but by weight—generally 88 pounds (40 kilograms) in first class, 66 pounds (30 kilograms) in business class, and 44 pounds (20 kilograms) in economy. If your flight between two cities abroad *connects* with your transatlantic or transpacific flight, the piece method still applies.

SAFEGUARDING YOUR LUGGAGE➤ Before leaving home, **itemize your bags' contents** and their worth, and label them with your name, address, and phone number. (If you use your home address, cover it so that potential thieves can't see it.) Inside your bag, **pack a copy of your itinerary.** At check-in, **make sure that your bag is correctly tagged** with the airport's three-letter destination code. If your bags arrive damaged or not at all, file a written report with the airline before leaving the airport.

PASSPORTS AND VISAS

If you don't already have one, **get a pass-**

port. While traveling, **keep one photocopy of the data page** separate from your wallet and leave another copy with someone at home. If you lose your passport, promptly call the nearest embassy or consulate, and the local police; having the data page can speed replacement.

U.S. CITIZENS

All U.S. citizens, even infants, need a valid passport to enter Norway for stays of up to three months. New and renewal application forms are available at any of the 13 U.S. Passport Agency offices and at some post offices and courthouses. Passports are usually mailed within four weeks; allow five weeks or more in spring and summer.

CANADIANS

You need a valid passport to enter Norway for stays of up to three months. Application forms are available at 28 regional passport offices as well as post offices and travel agencies. Whether for a first or a renewal passport, you must apply in person. Children under 16 may be included on a parent's passport but must have their own to travel alone. Passports are valid for five years and are usually mailed within two to three weeks of application.

U.K. CITIZENS

Citizens of the United Kingdom need a valid passport to enter Norway. Applications for new and renewal passports are available from main post offices as well as at the passport offices, located in Belfast, Glasgow, Liverpool, London, Newport, and Peterborough. You may apply in person at all passport offices, or by mail to all except the London office. Children under 16 may travel on an accompanying parent's passport. All passports are valid for 10 years. Allow a month for processing.

R

RAIL TRAVEL

NSB, the Norwegian State Railway System, has five main lines originating from the **Oslo S Station.** The longest runs north to Trondheim, then extends onward as far as Fauske and Bodø. The southern line hugs the coast to Stavanger, while the western line crosses some famous scenic territory on the way to Bergen. An eastern line through Kongsvinger to Stockholm links Norway with Sweden.

Trains are clean, comfortable, and punctual. The prices are reasonable, and the network is extensive, allowing passengers to go wherever they wish, either by train or by links to local bus networks, which are coordinated with train schedules. Trains, though they take longer, are often cheaper than flying, you see more of the country, and an overnight train costs less than many Norwegian hotels.

Most have special compartments for travelers with disabili-

ties and for families with children under two years of age, and they also offer special smoking and quiet sections, plus bunk beds for overnight trips. Both seat and sleeper reservations are required on express and overnight rains. **Reserve a few days ahead in the summer, during major holidays, and for Friday and Sunday trains.**

To save money, **look into rail passes** (*see* Important Contacts A to Z, *above*). But be aware that if you don't plan to cover many miles, you may come out ahead by buying individual tickets. If you are over 60 or traveling with children, ask about discounts whenever you buy single-trip train tickets, as special prices are available in many places on many routes.

Many travelers assume that rail passes guarantee them seats on the trains they wish to ride. Not so. You need to **book seats ahead even if you are using a rail pass.**

RENTING A CAR

CUTTING COSTS

To get the best deal, **book through a travel agent and shop around.** When pricing cars, **ask where the rental lot is located.** Some off-airport locations offer lower rates—even though their lots are only minutes away from the terminal via complimentary shuttle. You may also want to **price local car-rental companies,** whose rates may be lower still, although service and maintenance

standards may not be up to those of a national firm. Also **ask your travel agent about a company's customer-service record.** How has it responded to late plane arrivals and vehicle mishaps? Are there often lines at the rental counter, and, if you're traveling during a holiday period, does a confirmed reservation guarantee you a car?

Always **find out what equipment is standard** at your destination before specifying what you want; **do without automatic transmission or air-conditioning** if they're optional. In Europe, manual transmissions are standard and air-conditioning is rare and often unnecessary.

Also in Europe, **look into wholesalers—** companies that do not own their own fleets but rent in bulk from those that do and often offer better rates than traditional car-rental operations. Prices are best during low travel periods, and rentals booked through wholesalers must be paid for before you leave the United States. If you use a wholesaler, **know whether the prices are guaranteed** in U.S. dollars or foreign currency, and if unlimited mileage is available; find out about required deposits, cancellation penalties, and drop-off charges; and confirm the cost of any required insurance coverage.

INSURANCE

When you drive a rented car, you are generally responsible for

THE GOLD GUIDE / SMART TRAVEL TIPS

any damage or personal injury that you cause as well as damage to the vehicle. Before you rent, **see what coverage you already have** by means of your personal auto-insurance policy and credit cards. For about $14 a day, rental companies sell insurance, known as a collision damage waiver (CDW), that eliminates your liability for damage to the car; it's always optional and should never be automatically added to your bill.

REQUIREMENTS

Norway requires drivers to be over 20 years old, but some car-rental companies require that drivers be at least 25; be sure to ask. Your own driver's license is acceptable in Norway. An International Driver's Permit, available from the American or Canadian Automobile Association, is a good idea.

SURCHARGES

Before picking up the car in one city and leaving it in another, **ask about drop-off charges or one-way service fees,** which can be substantial. Note, too, that some rental agencies charge extra if you return the car before the time specified on your contract. To avoid a hefty refueling fee, **fill the tank just before you turn in the car.**

S
SENIOR-CITIZEN DISCOUNTS

To qualify for age-related discounts, **mention your senior-citizen status up front** when booking hotel reservations, not when checking out, and before you're seated in restaurants, not when paying your bill. Note that discounts may be limited to certain menus, days, or hours. When renting a car, **ask about promotional car-rental discounts**—they can net lower costs than your senior-citizen discount.

Travelers over 60 can buy a **SeniorRail Card** for NKr150 (about $27) in Norway. It gives 30% discounts on train travel in 21 European countries for a whole year from purchase.

SHOPPING

Prices in Norway are never low, but quality is high, and specialties are sometimes less expensive here than elsewhere. Good buys include handicrafts, handknitted sweaters, yarn, embroidery kits, textiles, pewter, rustic ironwork, silverware, wooden bowls and spoons, hand-dipped candles, and Christmas ornaments made from natural materials. *Husfliden* (homecraft) outlets are located in almost every city. **Keep an eye out for sales, called *tilbud* in Norwegian.**

Norwegian rustic antiques may not be exported. Even the simplest corner shelf or dish rack valued at $50 is considered a national treasure if it is known to be over 100 years old.

STUDENTS ON THE ROAD

To save money, **look into deals available through student-ori-**ented travel agencies. To qualify, you'll need to have a bona fide student I.D. card. Members of international student groups also are eligible. *See* Students in Important Contacts A to Z, *above.*

T
TELEPHONES

The telephone system in Norway is modern and efficient; international direct service is available throughout the country. Phone numbers consist of 6 digits throughout the country, plus a 2-digit area code.

LOCAL CALLS

Local calls cost NKr2 or NKr3 from a pay phone and about NKr3 from hotel phones.

INTERNATIONAL CALLS

Dial the international access code, 00, then the country code, and number. All telephone books list country code numbers including the United States and Canada (1), Great Britain (44), and Australia (61). Norway's code is 47. For operator-assisted calls, dial 117 for domestic calls and 115 for international calls. All international operators speak English.

INFORMATION

Dial 180 for information for Norway, 181 for other international telephone numbers.

W
WHEN TO GO

The Norwegian tourist season peaks in June, July, and August, when daytime temperatures are often in the 70s (21°C to 26°C) and sometimes rise into the 80s (27°C to 32°C). A temperature chart for Oslo appears below. In general, the weather is not overly warm, and a brisk breeze and brief rainstorms are possible anytime. Nights can be chilly, even in summer.

Truly delightful are the incredibly long summer days. In June, the sun rises in Oslo at 4 AM and sets at 11 PM, and daylight lasts even longer farther north, making it possible to extend your sightseeing into the balmy evenings. Many attractions extend their hours during the summer, and some shut down altogether in winter. Fall, spring, and even winter are pleasant, despite the area's reputation for gloom. The days become shorter quickly, but the sun casts a golden light one does not see farther south. On dark days, fires and candlelight will warm you indoors.

The Gulf Stream warms the western coast of Norway, making winters in these areas similar to those in London. Even the harbor of Narvik, far to the north, remains ice-free year-round. Away from the protection of the Gulf Stream, however, central Norway experiences very cold, clear weather that attracts skiers.

CLIMATE

The following are average daily maximum and minimum temperatures for Oslo.

Climate in Oslo

Jan.	28F	– 2C	**May**	61F	16C	**Sept.**	60F	16C
	19	– 7		43	6		46	8
Feb.	30F	– 1C	**June**	68F	20C	**Oct.**	48F	9C
	19	– 7		50	10		38	3
Mar.	39F	4C	**July**	72F	22C	**Nov.**	38F	3C
	25	– 4		55	13		31	– 1
Apr.	50F	10C	**Aug.**	70F	21C	**Dec.**	32F	0C
	34	1		54	12		25	– 4

1 Destination: Norway

NORWEGIAN LANDSCAPES

JUST NORTH OF LILLEHAMMER lives a Norwegian family on the banks of the Mjøsa Lake. Every year they pack their bags and drive to their holiday retreat, where they bask in the warmth of the long, northern sun for four full weeks—then they pack up and drive the 100 yards back home again.

While most Norwegians vacation a bit farther from home, their sentiments—attachment to, pride in, and reverence for their great outdoors—remain the same as the feelings of those who only journey across the street. Whether in the verdant dales of the interior, the brooding mountains of the north, or the carved fjords and archipelagoes of the coast, their ubiquitous *hytter* (cabins or cottages), dot even the most violent landscapes. It's a question of perspective: To a Norwegian, it's not a matter of whether or not to enjoy the land, but how to enjoy it at this very moment.

In any kind of weather, blasting or balmy, inordinate numbers are out of doors, to fish, bike, ski, hike, and, intentionally or not, strike the pose many foreigners regard as larger-than-life Norwegian: ruddy-faced, athletic, reindeer-sweatered. And all—from cherubic children to decorous senior citizens—bundled up for just one more swoosh down the slopes, one more walk through the forest.

Although it's a modern, highly industrialized nation, vast areas of the country (up to 95%) remain forested or fallow; and Norwegians intend to keep them that way—in part by making it extremely difficult for foreigners, who may feel differently about the land, to purchase property.

When discussing the size of their country, Norwegians like to say that if Oslo remained fixed and the northern part of the country were swung south, it would reach all the way to Rome. Perched at the very top of the globe, this northern land is long and rangy, 2,750 kilometers (1,700 miles) in length, with only 4 million people scattered over it—making it the least densely populated land in Europe except for Iceland. Knuckled by snow-topped mountains, and serrated by Gulf Stream–warmed fjords, this country has an abundance of magnificent views. No matter how or where you approach, if you fly above the clean ivory mountains of Tromsø in the winter, or tear by in a heart-stopping train north of Voss in the spring, getting there is often as eye-popping as arriving.

Thanks to the Gulf Stream, the coastal regions enjoy a moderate, temperate climate in winter, keeping the country green, while the interior has a more typical northern climate. Of course, throughout the land, winter temperatures can dip far below zero, but that doesn't thwart the activities of the Norwegians. As one North Caper put it, "We don't have good weather or bad weather, only a lot of weather."

Norwegians are justifiably proud of their native land, and of their ability to survive the elements and foreign invasions. The first people to appear on the land were reindeer hunters and fisherfolk who were migrating north, following the path of the retreating ice. By the Bronze Age, settlements began to appear and, as rock carvings show (and modern school children are proud to announce), the first Norwegians began to ski—purely as a form of locomotion—some 4,000 years ago.

The Viking Age has perhaps left the most indelible mark on the country. The Vikings' travels and conquests took them to Iceland, England, Ireland (they founded Dublin in the 840s), and North America. Though they were famed as plunderers, their craftsmanship and fearlessness is revered by modern Norwegians, who place ancient Viking ships in museums, cast copies of thousand-year-old silver designs into jewelry, and adventure across the seas in sailboats to prove the abilities of their forefathers.

Harald I, better known as Harald the Fairhaired, swore he would not cut his hair until he united Norway, and in the 9th century he succeeded in doing both. But a millennium passed between that great era and Norwegian independence. Between the Middle Ages and 1905, Norway remained under the rule of either Denmark or Sweden, even after the constitution was written in 1814.

The 19th century saw the establishment of the Norwegian identity and a blossoming of culture. This romantic period produced some of the nation's most famous individuals, among them composer Edvard Grieg, dramatist Henrik Ibsen, expressionist painter Edvard Munch, polar explorer Roald Amundsen, and explorer/humanitarian Fridtjof Nansen. Vestiges of nationalist lyricism spangle the buildings of the era with Viking dragonheads and scrollwork, all of which symbolize the rebirth of the Viking spirit.

FAITHFUL TO THEIR democratic nature, Norwegians held a referendum to choose a king in 1905, when independence from Sweden became reality. Prince Carl of Denmark became King Haakon VII. His baby's name was changed from Alexander to Olav, and he, and later his son, presided over the kingdom for more than 85 years. When King Olav V died in January 1991, the normally reserved Norwegians stood in line for hours to write in the condolence book at the Royal Palace. Rather than simply sign their names, they wrote personal letters of devotion to the man they called the "people's king." Thousands set candles in the snow outside the palace, transforming the winter darkness into a cathedral of ice and flame.

Harald V, Olav's son, is now king, with continuity assured by his own young-adult son, Crown Prince Haakon. Norwegians continue to salute the royal family with flag-waving and parades on May 17, Constitution Day, a spirited holiday of independence that transforms Oslo's main boulevard, Karl Johans Gate, into a massive street party as people of all ages, many in national costume, make a beeline to the palace.

During both World Wars, Norway tried to maintain neutrality. World War I brought not only casualties and a considerable loss to the country's merchant fleet, but also financial gain through the repurchase of major companies, sovereignty over Svalbard (the islands near the North Pole), and the reaffirmation of Norway's prominence in international shipping. At the onset of World War II, Norway once again proclaimed neutrality and appeared more concerned with Allied mine-laying on the west coast than with national security. A country of mostly fisherfolk, lumber workers, and farmers, it was just beginning to realize its industrial potential when the Nazis invaded. Five years of German occupation and a burn-and-retreat strategy in the north finally left the nation ravaged. True to form, however, the people who had been evacuated returned to the embers of the north to rebuild their homes and villages.

In 1968, oil was discovered in the North Sea, and Norway was transformed from a fishing and shipping outpost to a highly developed industrial nation. Though still committed to a far-reaching social system, Norway developed in the next 20 years into a wealthy country, with a per capita income and standard of living among the world's highest, as well as long life expectancy.

Stand on a street corner with a map, and a curious Norwegian will show you the way. Visit a neighborhood, and within moments you'll be the talk of the town. As a native of Bergen quipped, "Next to skiing, gossip is a national sport." With one foot in modern, liberal Scandinavia and the other in the provincial and often self-righteous countryside, Norway, unlike its Nordic siblings, is clinging steadfastly to its separate and distinct identity within Europe. Famous for its social restrictiveness—smoking is frowned upon, liquor may not be served before 3 PM (and never on Sunday), and violence, even among cartoon characters, is closely monitored—Norway is determined to repel outside interference, so much so that a national referendum in November 1994 chose to reject membership in the European Union for the second time. The next few years will show if prosperous Norway will pay an economic price for its proud assertion of independence.

— Melody Favish and Karina Porcelli
Updated by Fiona Smith

WHAT'S WHERE

Norway, roughly 155,000 square miles, is about the same size as California. Approximately 30 percent of this long, narrow country is covered with clear lakes, lush forests, and rugged mountains. Western Norway, bordered by the Norwegian Sea and the Atlantic Ocean, is the fabled land of the fjords—few places on earth can match the power and splendor of this land. The magnificent **Sognefjord,** the longest inlet in Western Norway, is only one of many fjords found here, including the Hardangerfjord, the Geirangerfjord, the Lysefjord, and the Nordfjord.

Bergen, often hailed as the "Fjord Capital of Norway," is the second largest city in the country. The cobblestone streets, the well-preserved buildings at the Bryggen, and the seven mountains that surround the city all add to its storybook charm.

Eastern Norway, bordered by Sweden (and Finland and Russia to the North), has rolling hills, abundant valleys, and fresh lakes—much more subdued than the landscape of the west. Near Gudbrandsdalen (the Gudbrands valley) you'll find **Lillehammer,** the sight of the 1994 Winter Olympics. Almost directly south, rising from the shores of the Oslofjord, is the capital of Norway—**Oslo.** With a population of about half a million, Oslo is a friendly, manageable city.

If you follow the coast south, you'll come to **Kristiansand,** one of Sørlandet's (the Southland's) leading cities. Sørlandet is known for its long stretches of unspoiled, uncrowded beach. Stavanger, further west, is one of the most cosmopolitan cities in Scandinavia—its oil and gas industry draws people from around the globe.

Halfway between Oslo and Bergen lies **Hardangervidda** (Hardanger plateau), Norway's largest national park. At the foot of the plateau is Geilo, one of the country's most popular ski resorts. Almost directly north is bustling city of Trondheim.

From here, a thin expanse of land stretches up to the **Nordkapp** (North Cape). Known as the "Land of the Midnight Sun" (the display of the northern lights in the winter is pretty amazing, too), this area has exquisite views: glaciers, fjords, and rocky

coasts. Narvik, a major Arctic port, is the gateway to the **Lofoten Islands,** where puffins and penguins can be seen. Even further north is the home of one of Norway's major universities, Tromsø, which is the lifeline to settlements and research centers at the North Pole. At the very top of Norway is the county of Finnmark, where many Samis live. Access to the area is primarily through **Hammerfest,** Europe's northernmost city, where the sun is not visible from November 21 to January 21, but is uninterrupted May 17 through July 29.

PLEASURES & PASTIMES

Beaches
Although Norway is better known for its craggy coastlines, the region does have some lovely beaches. This fact is not lost on landlocked Germans, who surge northward in such numbers every summer that many shopkeepers advertise their wares in English and German as well as Norwegian. The beaches around **Mandal** in the south and **Jaeren's Ogna, Brusand,** and **Bore** closer to Stavanger, are the country's best, with fine white sand. The western fjords are warmer and calmer than the open beaches of the south, and inland freshwater lakes are chillier still than Gulf Stream-warmed fjords. Topless bathing is common, and there are nude beaches all along the coast.

Biking
Biking is pleasurable, although hilly, throughout Norway. Bikers' clubs (see Important Contacts A to Z) publish maps with information in English about local biking routes and camping places.

Dining
For centuries, Norwegians regarded food as fuel, and their dining habits still bear traces of this.

Breakfast is a fairly big meal, usually with a selection of crusty bread, jams, herring, cold meat, and cheese. *Geitost* (a sweet, caramel-flavored whey cheese made wholly or in part from goats' milk) and Norvegia, a Norwegian Gouda-type cheese, are on virtually every table. They are eaten in thin slices, cut with a cheese plane or slicer, a Norwegian invention, on buttered wheat or rye bread.

Lunch is a simple, usually open-faced sandwiches. Most businesses have only a 30-minute lunch break, so unless there's a company cafeteria, most people eat home-packed sandwiches. Big lunchtime buffet tables, *koldtbord*, where one can sample most of Norway's special dishes all at once, are primarily for special occasions and visitors.

Dinner, the only hot meal of the day, is early–from 1 to 4 in the country, 3 to 7 in the city–so many cafeterias serving home-style food close by 6 or 7 in the evening.

Traditional, home-style Norwegian food is stick-to-the-ribs fare, served in generous portions and blanketed with gravy. One of the most popular meals is *kjøttkaker* (meat cakes), which resemble small Salisbury steaks, served with boiled potatoes, stewed cabbage, and brown gravy. Almost as popular are *medisterkaker* (mild pork sausage patties), served with brown gravy and caraway-seasoned sauerkraut, and *reinsdyrkaker* (reindeer meatballs), served with cream sauce and lingonberry jam. Other typical meat dishes include *fårikål*, a great-tasting lamb and cabbage stew, and *steik* (roast meat), always served well done. Fish dishes include poached *torsk* (cod) or *laks* (salmon), served with a creamy sauce called Sandefjord butter, *seibiff* (fired pollack and onions), and *fiskegrateng*, something between a fish soufflé and a casserole, usually served with carrot slaw.

Norway is known for several eccentric, often pungent fish dishes, but these are not representative–both *rakørret* and *raklaks* (fermented trout and salmon) and *lutefisk* (dried cod soaked in lye and then boiled) are acquired tastes, even for natives.

Traditional desserts include the ubiquitous *karamellpudding* (crème caramel), and *rømmegrøt* (sour cream porridge served with cinnamon-sugar) and a glass of *saft* (raspberry juice). The porridge, a typical farm dish, tastes very much like warm cheesecake batter–delicious. It's often served with *fenalår* (dried leg of mutton) and *lefsekling*, a thin pancake made with sour cream and potatoes, buttered and coated

with sugar. Christmastime brings with it a delectable array of light, sweet, and buttery pastries. The *bløtkake* (layered cream cake with custard, fruit, and marzipan) is a favorite for Christmas and special occasions but can be purchased in bakeries year-round.

Norwegian restaurant food has undergone major changes during the past few years. Until recently, fine restaurants were invariably French, and fine food usually meant meat. Today seafood and game have replaced beef and veal. Fish, from common cod and skate to the noble salmon, have a prominent place in the new Norwegian kitchen, and local capelin roe, golden caviar, is served instead of the imported variety. Norwegian lamb, full of flavor, is now in the spotlight, and game, from birds to moose, is prepared with sauces made from the wild berries that are part of their diet. These dishes are often accompanied by root vegetables.

Desserts, too, often feature fruit and berries. Norwegian strawberries and raspberries ripen in the long early summer days and are sweeter and more intense than those grown farther south. Red and black currants are also used. Two berries native to Norway are *tyttebær* (lingonberries), which taste similar to cranberries but are much smaller, and *multer* (cloudberries), which look like orange raspberries but have an indescribable taste. These wild berries grow above the tree line and are a real delicacy. Multe are often served as *multekrem* (in whipped cream) as a dessert, while tyttebær preserves often accompany traditional meat dishes.

Fishing

Whether it's fly-fishing for salmon or trout in western rivers or deep-sea fishing off the northern coast, Norway has all kinds of angling possibilities. Before you cast a line anywhere, check with the local tourism office to find out what the licensing requirements are.

Orienteering

One of Norway's most popular mass-participation sports is based on running or hiking over territory with a map and compass to find control points marked on a map. Special cards can be purchased at sports shops to be punched at control points found during a season. It's an enjoyable, inexpensive family sport, and gear can be purchased at any sports shop.

Sailing

Sailing is a sport dear to many Scandinavian hearts. One excellent route leads you up the western coast of Norway. Be aware that the weather can change suddenly and dangerously, the water is cold enough for swimmers to get numb quickly, and you must be able to navigate using sea charts to avoid going aground or getting lost; these waters are not for beginners. Boats can be chartered in major cities and harbors.

Shopping

Prices in Scandinavia are never low, but quality is high, and specialties are sometimes less expensive here than elsewhere. Norwegian furs are just some of the items to look for.

Skating

Norway had one of the first indoor rinks in the world in the early 20th century. Outdoor rinks, *kunstisbane*, with public opening hours can be found in the larger cities. Some rinks have a few hours of public figure skating on weekends and just about every school in the country floods its playground in winter.

Skiing

The ski is Norway's contribution to the world of sports. In 1994 the Winter Olympics were held in Lillehammer, which, along with other Norwegian resorts, regularly hosts World Cup competitions and world skiing championships.

Skiing—downhill, cross-country, and trekking—is excellent much of the year; snow in Norway often lasts as late as May and is present year-round in some areas. Disadvantages in winter include short days and bitter cold, as low as −35°C (any temperature below −10°C makes the danger of frostbite great enough to prohibit skiing, advises one experienced Scandinavian skier). It is a good idea to ski here in fall or spring, when the days are longer and warmer—November and March are preferable.

Most areas in Norway are suited for cross-country skiing. The neighboring Geilo and Ustaoset resorts are known for their downhill skiing but also have over 81 miles of marked cross-country trails. In ad-

dition to downhill and cross-country, the 100-year-old **Telemark style** is enjoying a revival across the country. It involves a characteristic deep-knee bend in the turns and traditional garb, including heavy boots, attach to the skis only at the toe.

Voss, only an hour from Bergen, has both giant slalom and slalom runs. Lillehammer has downhill and cross-country skiing, as well as night skiing, a bobsleigh and luge track, and dog-sledding.

FODOR'S CHOICE

Dining

★ **Bagatelle, Oslo.** One of the best restaurants in Europe features the Franco-Norwegian cuisine of internationally known owner-chef Eyvind Hellstrøm. **$$$$**

Lodging

★ **Kvikne's Hotel, Balestrand.** This huge wooden gingerbread house at the edge of the Sognefjord has been a landmark since 1915. **$$**

Museums

★ **Munchmuseet (Munch Museum), Oslo.** Edvard Munch, one of Scandinavia's leading artists, bequeathed thousands of his works to Oslo when he died in 1944.

★ **Norsk Folkemuseum (Norwegian Folk Museum), Bygdøy, Oslo.** Some 140 structures from all over the country have been reconstructed on the museum grounds.

Special Moments

★ **Eating dinner in a Sami tent,** with your reindeer parked outside

★ **People-watching along Oslo's Karl Johans Gate**

FESTIVALS AND SEASONAL EVENTS

WINTER

December 1: The Christmas tree at University Square in Oslo is lit.

December 10: The **Nobel Peace Prize** is awarded in Oslo.

December: Christmas concerts, fairs, and crafts workshops are held at museums and churches throughout the country. The **Oslo Jazz Festival** provides entertainment for jazz enthusiasts.

January: The **Holmenkollen Ski Festival** in Oslo is a festival of international Nordic events, including ski jumping. **Northern Light Festival,** Tromsø, features classical, contemporary, and chamber music.

March: The **Birkebeiner Race** commemorates a centuries-old cross-country ski race from Lillehammer to Rena. **The Finnmark Race,** Europe's largest dogsled competition, follows old mail routes across Finnmarksvidda. At the **Voss Jazz Festival** major European and American performers play.

SPRING

April: The **Karasjok Easter Festival** features traditional Sami entertainment and folklore and reindeer racing.

May 17: Constitution Day brings out every flag in the country and crowds of marchers for the parade in Oslo.

May: The **Grete Waitz Race,** a 5-kilometer (3-mile) street marathon in Oslo is open to women only. The annual **Bergen International Festival** features a world-class program of music, drama, ballet, and folklore. One of the largest festivals in Scandinavia, it is customarily opened by the king.

SUMMER

June: The **North Norwegian Cultural Festival** at Harstad includes plays, concerts, ballet, and art exhibitions. The **North Cape March** brings hikers from around the world to walk the 70 kilometers from Honingsvåg to the North Cape and back. The **Great Endurance Test** is a bicycle race (560 km/347 mi) from Trondheim to Oslo.

June 23: Midsummer Eve, called "Sankt Hans Afton," is celebrated nationwide with bonfires, fireworks, and outdoor dancing.

June and July: The annual **Emigration Festival** in Kvinesdal provides an opportunity to meet fellow Norwegian Americans and Norwegians.

July: The **Bislett Games** attract the best international track and field stars

to Bislett Stadium. The **Molde International Jazz Festival** is Norway's best-known jazz festival. The **Traditional Dance Music Festival** in Røros features top Norwegian performers.

Late July: The **Stiklestad Festival** and the **Olavsfestdagene** in Trondheim honor Olav the Holy (Haraldsson) with outdoor theater performances and concerts.

Mid-August: The **European Sea Fishing Championships** are held at Tananger, outside Stavanger.

August: Oslo Chamber Music Festival draws participants from around the world, as does the **Oslo Rock Festival. Norway Cup,** the world's largest youth soccer tournament, attracts 1,000 teams from around the world. During the **Peer Gynt Festival,** in Lillehammer, there are art exhibits, music, and open-air performances of Henrik Ibsen's *Peer Gynt.*

AUTUMN

September: Oslo Marathon, 42 kilometers (26 miles) through the streets of Oslo, draws men and women.

2 Oslo

ALTHOUGH IT IS ONE OF THE WORLD'S largest capital cities in area, Oslo has only about 475,000 inhabitants. Nevertheless, in recent years the city has taken off: Shops are open late; pubs, cafés, and restaurants are crowded at all hours; and theaters play to full houses every night of the week.

Even without nightlife, Oslo has a lot to offer—parks, water, trees, hiking and skiing trails (2,600 kilometers/1,600 miles in greater Oslo), and above all, spectacular views. Starting at the docks opposite City Hall, right at the edge of the Oslo Fjord, the city sprawls up the sides of the mountains that surround it, providing panoramic vistas from almost any vantage point but no definable downtown skyline. A recent building spree has added a number of modern towers, particularly in the area around the Central Railway Station, which clash painfully with the neoclassical architecture in the rest of the city.

Oslo has been Norway's center of commerce for about 500 years, and most major Norwegian companies are based in the capital. The sea has always been Norway's lifeline to the rest of the world: The Oslo Fjord teems with activity, from summer sailors and shrimpers to merchant ships and passenger ferries heading for Denmark and Germany.

Oslo is an old city, dating from the mid-11th century. All but destroyed by fire in 1624, it was redesigned with wide boulevards and renamed Christiania by Denmark's royal builder, King Christian IV. An act of Parliament finally changed the name back to Oslo, its original Viking name, in 1925.

EXPLORING

Karl Johans Gate, starting at Oslo S Station and ending at the Royal Palace, forms the backbone of downtown Oslo. Many of Oslo's museums and most of its historic buildings lie between the parallel streets of Grensen and Rådhusgata. Just north of the center of town is a historic area with a medieval church and old buildings. West of downtown is Frogner, the residential area closest to town, with embassies, fine restaurants, antiques shops, galleries, and the Vigeland sculpture park. Farther west is the Bygdøy Peninsula, with five museums and a castle. Northwest of town is Holmenkollen, with beautiful houses, a famous ski jump, and a restaurant. On the east side, where many new immigrants live, are the Munch Museum and the botanical gardens.

Numbers in the margin correspond to points of interest on the Oslo map.

Tour 1: Downtown, from the Royal Palace to the Harbor

Although the city is huge (454 square kilometers/175 square miles), downtown Oslo is compact, with shops, museums, historic sights, restaurants, and clubs concentrated in a small, walkable center—brightly illuminated at night.

❶ Oslo's main promenade street, Karl Johans Gate, runs from **Slottet** (the Royal Palace) through town. The neoclassical palace, completed in 1848, is closed to visitors, but the garden is open to the public. An equestrian statue of Karl Johan, king of Sweden and Norway and the street's namesake, stands in the square in front of the palace. The changing of the guard happens every day at 1:30.

❷ Down the incline and to the left are the three buildings of the old **Universitet** (university), which remains one of Norway's premier educational centers. The great hall of the center building is decorated with murals by Edvard Munch, and is the site of the Nobel Peace Prize award ceremony. *Aulaen, Karl Johans Gt. 47,* ☏ *22/85–93–00, ext. 756.* ☛ *Free.* ⊘ *July, weekdays noon–2.*

❸ Around the corner from the university, with access from Universitetsgata, is the newly refurbished **Nasjonalgalleriet** (National Gallery). There are some excellent pieces in the 19th- and early 20th-century Norwegian rooms. The collection also includes many works by Scandinavian impressionists, called the "Northern Light" artists, who have recently been discovered by the rest of the world. The gallery also has an extensive Munch collection. It was from here that Edvard Munch's famous painting *The Scream* was stolen during the 1994 Winter Olympics. It was recovered and is back, with added security. *Universitetsgt. 13,* ☏ *22/20–04–04.* ☛ *Free.* ⊘ *Mon., Wed., Fri., and Sat. 10–4; Thurs. 10–8; Sun. 11–3.*

❹ Back-to-back with the National Gallery, across a parking lot, is a big cream-brick Art Nouveau–style building housing the **Historisk Museum** (Historical Museum). In addition to Asian and African ethnographic exhibits, the museum displays a collection of Viking and medieval artifacts, including many intricately carved stave church portals. *Frederiksgt. 2,* ☏ *22/41–63–00.* ☛ *Free.* ⊘ *Mid-May–mid-Sept., Tues.–Sun. 11–3; mid-Sept.–mid-May, Tues.–Sun. noon–3.*

❺ Continue along Frederiksgate to the university and cross Karl Johans Gate to the **Nationaltheatret** (National Theater) and **Studenterlunden Park**. In front of the theater are statues of Norway's great playwrights, Bjørnstjerne Bjørnson (who wrote the words to the national anthem and won a Nobel Prize for his plays) and Henrik Ibsen, author of *A Doll's House, Hedda Gabler,* and *The Wild Duck.*

Across the street on the other side of the theater is the **Hotel Continental,** owned by the same family since it was built in 1900. Take a quick tour around the lobby bar to see the collection of Munch graphics. The hotel's Theatercafeen is one of Oslo's most fashionable restaurants.

★ ❻ Turn right on Universitetsgata to reach the redbrick **Rådhuset** (City Hall), a familiar landmark with its two block towers, dedicated during Oslo's 900th-year jubilee celebrations in 1950. It took 17 years to build because construction was interrupted by World War II. Many sculptures outside, as well as murals inside, reflect the artistic climate in Norway in the 1930s—socialist modernism in its highest form. *Rådhuspl.,* ☏ *22/86–16–00.* ☛ *Free.* ⊘ *May–Aug., Mon.–Sat. 9–5, Sun. noon–4; Sept.–April, Mon.–Sat. 9–3:30, Sun. noon–4. Guided tours year round, weekdays 10, noon, and 2.*

Return to Stortingsgata, turn right, and walk past Tordenskioldsgate to Rosenkrantz' Gate, both lined with specialty shops. Cross over Stortingsgata and along the short end of the park back to Karl Johans Gate. On the left is a refurbished news kiosk from the early years of this century. Across the street is the **Grand Hotel,** where many Norwegians check in on Constitution Day, May 17, in order to have a room overlooking the parades. The Grand Café was a favorite with Ibsen, who began his mornings with a brisk walk followed by a stiff drink here, in the company of local journalists.

TIME OUT   Inside the Grand Hotel, in the informal **Palmen,** salads and light meals are served, as well as pastries and cakes.

Walk past the Lille Grensen shopping area and once again across Karl Johan to **Stortinget** (Parliament), which was built in the middle of the 19th century. Its a classical building, magnificently perched on the top of the hill, and becomes a people-watching spot at night, with vendors, promenaders, and students. *Karl Johans Gt. 22,* ☎ *22/31–30–50.* ☛ *Free. Public gallery open weekdays 11–1. Guided tours in July and August.*

Turn left on Kongens Gate from Karl Johans Gate to reach **Stortorvet,** Oslo's main square. On the right as you enter the square is **Oslo Domkirke** (cathedral), completed in 1697, which has an intricately carved Baroque pulpit. *Stortorvet 1,* ☎ *22/41–27–93.* ☛ *Free.* ☉ *June–Aug., weekdays 10–3, Sat. 10–1; Sept.–May, weekdays 10–3.*

Behind the cathedral is a semicircular arcade, called **Kirkeristen** or Basarhallene, housing many small artisans' shops. The building was constructed in the middle of the 19th century but was inspired by medieval architecture.

TIME OUT Order a cup of hot, foamy **cappuccino** at the **café** of the same name in the inner arcade. A copy of the *International Herald-Tribune* hangs from a rod inside for anyone to read.

From the cathedral, follow Kirkegata left past Karl Johan to Bankplassen and the 1902 Bank of Norway building, since 1990, the **Museet for Samtidskunst** (Museum of Contemporary Art). The building, a good example of geometric Norwegian Art Nouveau, houses a fine collection of international and Norwegian pieces, mostly in small rooms built around a large core. *Bankpl. 4,* ☎ *22/33–58–20.* ☛ *Free.* ☉ *Tues.–Fri. 11–7, weekends 11–4.*

Turn left onto Myntgata to reach Nedre Slottsgate, Oslo's oldest neighborhood, where the half-timber buildings on the left stable police horses. At the corner of Nedre Slottsgate and Rådhusgata is the Old City Hall, housing the 354-year-old **Gamle Rådhus** restaurant. Upstairs is the **Teatermuseet** (Theater Museum), a collection of old pictures and costumes, which sometimes holds an open house at which children can try on costumes and have makeup applied. The first public theater performance in Oslo took place here. *Nedre Slottsgt. 1,* ☎ *22/41–81–47.* ☛ *NKr15 adults, NKr5 children.* ☉ *Wed. 10–3, Sun. noon–4.*

Diagonally across Rådhusgata are two 17th-century buildings that house art galleries and a café. Turn left on Rådhusgata and walk over the grassy hill to the entrance of **Akershus Slott** (castle). It's a climb, but the views from the top are worth it. The oldest part of the castle was built around 1300 and includes an "escape-proof" room built four centuries later for a thief named Ole Pedersen Høyland. In fact he broke out of this cell, robbed the Bank of Norway, was caught, and brought back to jail. With no possibility of a second escape, he killed himself here. Today some of the building is used for state occasions, but a few rooms, including the chapel, are open to the public. *Akershus Slott, Festningspl.,* ☎ *22/41–25–21.* ☛ *Castle grounds and concerts free.* ☉ *Daily 6 am–9 pm; concerts, mid-May–mid-Oct., Sun. at 2.* ☛ *Castle: NKr15 adults; NKr5 children, students, and senior citizens.* ☉ *May–mid-Sept., Mon.–Sat. 10–4; year-round, Sun. 12:30–4. Guided tours May–Sept., Mon.–Sat. 11, 1, and 3; Sun. 1 and 3.*

The castle became the German headquarters during the occupation of Norway in World War II, and many members of the Resistance were executed on the castle grounds. Their memorial has been erected at the site, across the bridge at the harbor end of the castle precinct. In a build-

Oslo

KEY

i Tourist Information

— Rail Lines

Akershus Slott, **11**
Fram-Museet, **23**
Gamle Aker Kirke, **14**
Historisk Museum, **4**
Holmenkollbakken, **18**
Kon-Tiki Museum, **24**
Kunstindustri-
museet, **13**
Munchmuseet, **19**
Museet for
Samtidskunst, **9**

Nasjonalgalleriet, **3**
Nationaltheatret, **5**
Norsk
Folkemuseum, **21**
Oscarshall Slott, **20**
Oslo Domkirke, **8**
Rådhuset, **6**
Skogbrand
Insurance, **12**
Slottet, **1**

Stortinget, **7**
Teatermuseet, **10**
Tryvannstårnet, **17**
Universitet, **2**
Vigelandsparken, **15**
Vigelandsmuseet, **16**
Vikingskiphuset, **22**

ing next to the castle, at the top of the hill, is the **Norges Hjemme-frontmuseum** (Norwegian Resistance Museum), which documents events that took place during the German occupation (1940–45). *Norges Hjemmefrontmuseum, Akershus Festning,* ☎ *22/40–31–38.* ☛ *NKr15 adults, NKr5 children, students, senior citizens.* ⊘ *Oct.–mid-Apr., Mon.–Sat. 10–3, Sun. 11–4; mid-Apr.–mid-June and Sept., Mon.–Sat. 10–4 and Sun. 11–4; mid-June –Aug., Mon.–Sat. 10–5, Sun. 11–5.*

⑫ Walk back to Rådhusgata to see another interesting building, **Skog-brand Insurance** (Rådhusgt. 23B), in the block above the retaining wall. Architects Jan Digerud and Jon Lundberg have won awards for their innovative 1985 vertical addition to this 1917 building. Continue along to the harborside, where you can buy shrimp from one of the boats docked opposite City Hall and enjoy them on a bench overlooking the water.

Tour 2: St. Olavs Gate to Damstredet

This quiet, old-fashioned district just north of the city center is particularly well preserved. It features artisans' shops and Oslo's most historic cemetery.

⑬ At the corner of St. Olavs Gate and Akersgata is the **Kunstindustrimuseet** (Decorative Arts Museum), which houses a superb furniture collection as well as an entire floor of Norwegian decorative art. The most interesting collection is on the top floor—royal clothing, including Queen Maud's jewel-encrusted, wasp-waist coronation gown from 1904—clothes worthy of any fairytale. *St. Olavs Gt. 1,* ☎ *22/20–35–78.* ☛ *NKr20 adults, NKr10 children, students, and senior citizens.* ⊘ *Tues.– Fri. 11–3, weekends noon–4.*

Across Akersgata is St. Olavs Kirke. Up the hill, on the right, is **Vår Frelsers Gravlund** (Our Savior's Cemetery), where many of Norway's famous, including Ibsen and Munch, are buried. At its northeastern

⑭ corner is **Gamle Aker Kirke** (Old Aker Church), the city's only remaining medieval church, a stone basilica that has undergone many changes since it was constructed around 1100. *Akersvn. 25,* ☎ *22/69–35–82.* ☛ *Free.* ⊘ *Mon.–Sat. noon–2.*

Tour 3: Frogner, Holmenkollen, and the Munch Museum

Catch the No. 2 "Majorstuen og Frogner" *trikk* (as the Norwegians fondly call the streetcars), which stops on Stortingsgate at Nationaltheatret and runs along the Drammensveien side of the Royal Palace.

Opposite the southwestern end of the palace grounds is the triangular **U.S. Embassy,** designed by Finnish-American architect Eero Saarinen and built in 1959. At Solli Plass, the trikk turns right onto Frognerveien.

Stay on the trikk and ride to Frogner Park or walk the seven short blocks, following Balders Gate to Arno Bergs Plass with its central fountain. Turn left on Gyldenløves Gate (street of the golden lion) and walk through one of the city's most stylish neighborhoods. Most of the buildings were constructed in the early years of this century, and many have interesting sculptural decoration and wrought ironwork. Gyldenløves Gate ends at Kirkeveien. Turn right, past the Dutch Embassy, and cross the street at the light, which is next to the trikk stop. Frogner Park is just ahead.

★ ⑮ There's nothing anywhere else in the world quite like **Vigelandsparken** in Frogner Park. Sculptor Gustav Vigeland began his career as a wood-carver, and his talent was quickly appreciated and supported by the townspeople of Oslo. In 1921 they provided him with a free house and studio, in exchange for which he began to chip away at his life's work, which he would ultimately donate to the city. He worked through World War II and the German occupation, and after the war the work was unveiled, to the combined enchantment and horror of the townsfolk. Included was the 470-ton monolith that is now the highlight of the park, as well as hundreds of writhing, fighting, and loving sculptures representing the varied forms and stages of human life. The figures are nude, but they're more monumental than erotic—bullet-headed, muscular men and healthy, solid women with flowing hair.

TIME OUT Just before the sculpture bridge, on the left, is the park's outdoor restaurant, **Herregårdskroen,** where during the summer you can enjoy anything from a buffet lunch to a three-course dinner, depending on the time of day. It's a prime place for people-watching.

Frogner Park is a living part of the city—people walk dogs on the green and bathe chubby babies in the fountains, and they jog, ski, and sunbathe throughout. The park complex also includes the City Museum, a swimming pool, an ice rink and skating museum (☎ 22/43-49–20), several playgrounds, and a restaurant. *Middlethunsgt.* ☛ *Free.*

⑯ **Vigelandsmuseet** (the Vigeland Museum), across from the park, displays many of the plaster models for the sculptures, Vigeland's woodcuts and drawings, and mementoes of his life. *Nobelsgt. 32,* ☎ *22/ 44–11–36.* ☛ *NKr20 adults, NKr10 children, students, and senior citizens.* ☉ *May–Sept., Tues.–Sat. 10–6, Sun. noon–7; Oct.–Apr., Tues.–Sat. noon–4, Sun. noon–6.*

Continue on Kirkeveien to the Majorstuen underground station, up the steps on the left, and take the Holmenkollen line to Frognerseteren, a 15-minute ride.

TIME OUT **Frognerseteren Restaurant,** built in the national romantic style, dates from 1909, when newly independent Norway sought inspiration from its earlier history. (*See* Dining, *below.*)

⑰ As if the view from Frognerseteren weren't spectacular enough, the **Tryvannstårnet** TV tower, offering the best panoramic view of Oslo, is only a 15-minute, signposted walk away. *Kongevn 5,* ☎ *22/14–67–11.* ☛ *NKr50 adults, NKr25 children, students, and senior citizens. May and Sept., daily 10–7; June, daily 10-7; July, daily 9 –10; Aug., daily 9–8; Jan.–Apr., weekdays 10–3, weekends 11–4.*

★ ⑱ Downhill is the **Holmenkollbakken** (Holmenkollen Ski Museum and Ski Jump), which can be seen from many points in the city. The 1892 jump was rebuilt for the 1952 Winter Olympics. At the base of the jump, turn right, past the statue of the late King Olav V on skis, to enter the museum. It displays equipment from the Nansen and Amundsen polar voyages and a model of a ski-maker's workshop, in addition to a collection of skis, the oldest dating from pre-Viking times. You can also climb (or ride the elevator) to the top of the jump tower. It's intimidating enough with a firm grip on the rail, but on skis and snow, it's mind-boggling. *Kongevn. 5,* ☎ *22/92–32–00.* ☛ *NKr50 adults, NKr25 children, students, and senior citizens.* ☉ *July, daily 9 am–10 pm; June and Aug., daily 9–8; May and Sept., daily 10–5; Jan.–Apr., weekdays 10–3, weekends 11–4.*

To catch the train back to town, walk downhill to Holmenkollen Station, less than a mile away. Leave the train at Majorstuen, cross the street, and catch Bus 20, marked "Galgeberg," which runs east to the

★ ⑲ **Munchmuseet** (Munch Museum). Edvard Munch, one of Scandinavia's leading artists, bequeathed an enormous collection of his work (about 1,100 paintings, 4,500 drawings, and 18,000 graphic works) to the city when he died in 1944. It languished in warehouses for nearly 20 years, until the city built a museum to house it in 1963. For much of his life Munch was a troubled man, and his major works, dating from the 1890s, with such titles as *The Scream* and *Vampire*, reveal his angst, but he was not without humor. His extraordinary talent as a graphic artist emerges in the print room, with its displays of lithograph stones and wood blocks. *Tøyengt. 53,* ☎ *22/67–37–74.* ☛ *NKr40 adults, NKr15 children, students, and senior citizens.* ☉ *June–Sept., daily 10–6, mid-Sept.–May, Tues.–Sat. 10–4, Thurs.,Sun. 10–6.*

You can walk downhill from the Munch Museum to Tøyen Senter shopping area to catch the subway back downtown.

Tour 4: Bygdøy

Oslo's most important historic sights are concentrated on Bygdøy Peninsula. From May to September you can catch a ferry from the Rådhuset to Bydøy. Times vary so check with Nortra (*see* Important Addresses and Numbers, *below*) for schedules. Another alternative is to take Bus 30, marked "Bygdøy," from Stortingsgate at Nationaltheatret along Drammensveien to Bygdøy Allé, a wide avenue lined with chestnut trees. The bus passes Frogner Church and several embassies on its way to Olav Kyrres Plass, where it turns left, and soon left again, onto the peninsula. If you see some horses on the left, they come from the king's stables (the dark red building with the monogram); the royal family's current summer residence, actually just a big white frame house, is on the right. Get off at the next stop, "Norsk Folkemuseum." Backtrack until you come to the narrow Oscarshallveien, which

⑳ leads to **Oscarshall Slott,** an eccentric neo-Gothic palace built in 1852 for King Oscar I as a site for picnics and other summer pursuits. *Oscarshallvn.,* ☎ *22/43–77–49.* ☛ *NKr15 adults, NKr5 children.* ☉ *Mid-May–mid-Oct., Tues., Thurs. noon–6. Groups catered for upon request.*

★ ㉑ Next is the **Norsk Folkemuseum** (Norwegian Folk Museum), which consists of some 140 structures from all over the country that have been reconstructed on site. The best-known and most important building is the **Gol Stavkirke** (Gol Stave Church), constructed around 1200. In summer and on weekends year-round, guides in the buildings demonstrate various home crafts, such as weaving tapestries, sewing national costumes, and baking flatbread. Indoor collections in the main building include toys, dolls and dollhouses, a Sami (Lapp) collection, national costumes, and Ibsen's actual study. On one side of this museum is a reconstructed 19th-century village, with shops and houses. Among its exhibits are a pharmaceutical museum and a dentist's office, complete with turn-of-the-century braces—a real mouthful of springs and bands. The museum puts on a summer calendar of special events, including daily activities from folk dancing to concerts with instruments from the museum's collection. *Museumsvn. 10,* ☎ *22/43–70–20.* ☛ *Summer, NKr 50 adults, NKr25 students and senior citizens, NKr10 children; winter, NKr20, NKr15, and NKr5.* ☉ *Mid-May–mid-Sept., daily 11–7; mid-Sept.–mid-May, daily noon–4.*

★ ㉒ Around the corner to the right is the **Vikingskiphuset** (Viking Ship Museum), one of Norway's best-known attractions. It looks like a cathedral from the outside, and inside the feeling of reverence is very real. It's hard to believe that the three ships on display, all found buried along the Oslo Fjord, are nearly 1,200 years old. The richly carved *Oseberg* ship, thought to have been the burial chamber for Queen Åse, is the most decorative, while the *Gokstad* ship is a functional longboat, devoid of ornament. The small *Tune* ship has been left unrestored. Items found with the ships, including sleds with intricately carved decoration, tools, household goods, and a tapestry, are also on view. *Huk Aveny 35,* ☎ *22/43–83–79.* ☛ *NKr20 adults, NKr10 students, senior citizens, and children.* ◑ *May–Aug., daily 9–6; Sept., daily 11–5; Apr. and Oct., daily 11–4; Nov.–Mar., daily 11–3.*

TIME OUT Besides a collection of model ships and small boats, the nearby **Maritime Museum** has an outdoor café, **Najaden,** overlooking the Oslo Fjord.

★ ㉓ Just beyond the Maritime Museum is the **Fram-Museet,** an A-frame structure in the shape of a traditional Viking boathouse. This museum, with its matter-of-fact displays of life on board ship, vividly depicts the history of polar exploration. The *Fram* was constructed in 1892 by Scottish-Norwegian shipbuilder Colin Archer. Fridtjof Nansen led the first *Fram* expedition across the ice surrounding the North Pole; the ship's most famous voyage took Roald Amundsen to Antarctica, the first leg of his successful expedition to the South Pole in 1911. Visitors board the ship by gangplank and are allowed to walk all over the vessel. *Bygdøynes,* ☎ *22/43–83–70.* ☛ *NKr20 adults, NKr10 students, children, and senior citizens.* ◑ *Late May–Aug., daily 9–5:45; early May and Sept., daily 10–4:45; Mar., Apr., Oct., Nov., weekdays 11–2:45, weekends 11–3:45.*

★ ㉔ Across the parking lot from the *Fram* is the older **Kon-Tiki Museum,** which houses the famous raft, along with the papyrus boat *Ra II.* Thor Heyerdahl continued the Norwegian tradition of exploration in his 1947 voyage from Peru to Polynesia on the *Kon-Tiki,* a balsa raft, to confirm his theory that the first Polynesians originally came from Peru. The *Kon-Tiki,* now showing its age, is suspended on a plastic sea. The *Ra II* sailed from Morocco to the Caribbean in 1970. *Bygdøynesvn. 36,* ☎ *22/43–80–50.* ☛ *NKr 25, adults, NKr10 students, children, and senior citizens.* ◑ *Oct.–Mar., daily 10:30–4; Apr.–May and Sept., daily 10:30–5; mid-May–Aug., daily 9–6.*

You can get a ferry back to the City Hall docks from the dock in front of the *Fram.* Before catching a ferry back to the center of Oslo, try a snack at **Lanternen Kro,** which overlooks the entire harbor. **Rodeløkken Kafé,** a short walk from the museum, has coffee and homemade heart-shaped waffles served with cream and preserves.

Short Excursions from Oslo

Numbers in the margin correspond to points of interest on the Oslo Excursions map.

Henie-Onstad Center

Sonja Henie died in 1969, but she still skates her way through many a late-night movie. The three-time Olympic gold medal winner was the first to realize the potential of the ice show, and her technical assistant, Frank Zamboni, has been immortalized in skating rinks around the world by the ice-finishing machine he developed just for her, the Zamboni. Henie had a shrewd head for money and marriage, and her third, to Norwegian shipping magnate Niels Onstad, resulted in the

❶ **Henie-Onstad Kunstsenter,** about 12 kilometers (7 miles) from Oslo.

Oslo Excursions

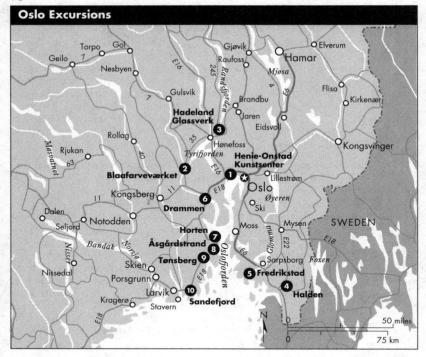

They put together a fine collection of early 20th-century art, with important works by Leger, Munch, Picasso, Bonnard, and Matisse.

Buses 151, 152, and 251 from Oslo S Station stop near the entrance to the museum grounds. To drive, follow E18 (toward Drammen) 12 kilometers (about 7 miles) from Oslo. *1311 Høvikodden,* ☎ *67/54–30–50.* ☛ *NKr40 adults, NKr15 students and senior citizens, NKr20 children.* ☉ *Mon. 9–5, Tues.–Fri. 9–9; also June–Aug., weekends 11–7 and Sept.–May, weekends 11–5.*

Cobalt Works

❷ The **Blaafarveværket** (Cobalt Works), founded in 1773 to extract cobalt from the Modum mines, is about 70 kilometers (45 miles) from Oslo, in Åmot i Modum. The mineral was used to make dyes for the world's glass and porcelain industries, but today the complex is a museum and a national park. The main building houses a one-person show of works by a different Scandinavian artist every year. There is also a permanent collection of old cobalt-blue glass and porcelain. For children there's a petting farm. Up the hill from the art complex is **Haugfossen,** the highest waterfall in eastern Norway. Beside the falls is an old-fashioned country store. Restaurants serve Norwegian country dishes. Outdoor concerts are held on the grounds throughout the summer.

Take E18 to Drammen, then Route 11 west to Hokksund, and Route 35 to Åmot, turning onto Route 287 to Sigdal. The bus to Modum leaves from the old university on Karl Johans Gate at 9:45 AM on Tuesday, Thursday, and Saturday. ☎ *32/78–49–00.* ☛ *Special exhibitions, NKr50 adults, NKr 10 children; cobalt works, NKr40 adults, children free with adults.* ☉ *Late May–Sept. 10–6 daily.*

Hadeland

A day trip to **Hadeland** combines a drive along the Tyrifjord, where you can see some of the best fjord views in eastern Norway, with a visit to a glass factory that has been in operation since 1762. **Hadeland Glassverk** (Rte. 241, toward Jevnaker, ☎ 61/31–10–00) produces both practical table crystal and one-of-a-kind art glass. You can watch artisans blowing glass and buy their handiwork (first quality and seconds) at the gift shop. The museum and gallery have a collection of 15,000 items, with about 800 on display. Take E18 west to Sandvika, turn right onto E16 and follow the signs to Hønefoss. At the Route 241 intersection, take the road to Jevnaker, which passes the glass factory. You can also take Bus 71, marked "Hønefoss," which leaves from the university on Karl Johan at seven minutes after the hour. Change in Hønefoss for the Jevnaker bus (no number). The total trip takes about two hours. ✪ *June–Aug., Mon.–Sat. 9–6; Sun. 11–6; Sept.–May, weekdays 9–4, Sat. 10–3, Sun. noon–5.*

What to See and Do with Children

Bygdøy (*see* Tour 4, *above*) is a good place to take children. The Viking Ship, *Fram*, and *Kon-Tiki* museums are all good choices there; the **Norsk Folkemuseum** has special exhibitions of old toys and dollhouses. Live events, changing daily all summer, include old-fashioned bicycle races and sheep shearing.

The **Barnekunstmuseet** (Children's Art Museum) was the brainchild of Rafael Goldin, a Russian immigrant who has collected children's drawings from more than 150 countries. Materials are provided for children to create on the spot. *Lille Frøensvn. 4,* ☎ *22/46–85–73.* ☛ *NKr30 adults, NKr15 children, students, and senior citizens.* ✪ *Late June–mid-Aug., Tues.–Thurs., Sun. 11–4; early Sept.–mid-Dec., late Jan.–mid-June, Tues.–Thurs. 9:30–2, Sun. 11–4.*

One stop closer to town on the subway is the **Sporveismuseet** (Transport Museum), with old buses and trains, including a horse-drawn streetcar. Take the subway or the trikk to Majorstuen. *Gardevn. 15,* ☎ *22/60–94–09.* ☛ *NKr10 adults, NKr5 children.* ✪ *May.–Sept., weekends only noon–3; Oct.–May., Sun. noon–3.*

Oslo is proud of its **Teknisk** (Technical) **Museum,** about 20 minutes north of the city on trikk line 11, marked "Kjelsås." Exhibits include the first airplane to fly over the North Sea, classic cars and motorcycles, and the development of computers, waterpower, and communication, all accompanied by demonstrations and films. *Kjelsåsvn. 143,* ☎ *22/22–25–50.* ☛ *NKr30 adults, NKr15 children.* ✪ *Late June–late Aug., Tues–Sun. 10–8, Mondays in July 10–6; late Aug.–Dec. and Jan–mid-June, Tues. 10–9, Wed–Sat 10–4, Sun. 10–5.*

Everyone enjoys **Norgesparken Tusenfryd,** Oslo's amusement park, a 20-minute ride east of the city. There are carnival rides, such as a merry-go-round, a Ferris wheel, and a roller coaster with a loop, and a water slide. Tusenfryd's newest neighbor is the theme park "Vikinglandet" which brings you back 1,000 years to experience the Viking lifestyle, from shipbuilding to burial mounds. There's a separate entrance fee of NKr90 for adults and NKr80 for children, but both parks are under the same management. A free shuttle bus departs from Oslo City Hall daily. *Vinterbro,* ☎ *64/94–63–63.* ☛ *NKr60.* ✪ *June–mid-Aug., daily 10:30–8; late April–May and mid-Aug.–Sept., weekends only 10:30–8.*

Off the Beaten Path

Oslo was founded by Harald Hårdråde (Hard Ruler) in 1048, and the earliest settlements were near what is now Bispegata, a few blocks behind Oslo S Station. The ruins at **Minneparken** are all that is left of the city's former spiritual center: the **Korskirken** (Cross Church; Egedes Gate 2), a small stone church dating from the end of the 13th century; **Olavs Kloster** (St. Halvards plass 3), built around 1240 by Dominican monks; and the foundations of **St. Halvards Kirke,** named for the patron saint of the city and dating from the early 12th century. The latter remained the city's cathedral until 1660. Stones from its walls were used to build Akershus Slott. Take trikk 9, marked "Ljabru," to Bispegata, where signs point to the various ruins.

The oldest traces of human habitation in Oslo are the 5,000-year-old carvings on the runic stones near **Ekebergsletta** Park. They are across the road from the park on Karlsborgveien and are marked by a sign reading FORTIDSMINNE. At the other end of the park, down Oslogate and then Bispegata, is **Oslo Ladegård,** which has scale models of 16th–18th-century Oslo on the site of the 13th-century Bispegard (Bishop's Palace). *St Hallvards Pl., Oslogt. 13,* ☎ *22/19–44–68.* ☛ *NKr20 adults, NKr10 children.* ☉ *May–Sept.; guided tours on Wed. at 6 and Sun. at 1.*

Once you have your fill of history, you can get in touch with something a bit more corporeal at the **Emanuel Vigeland Museum.** Although he never gained the fame of his brother Gustav, the creator of Vigeland Park, the younger Emanuel is an artist of some notoriety. His alternately saucy, natural, and downright erotic frescoes make even the sexually liberated Norwegians blush. Take subway line 15 to Slemdal. *Grimelundsvn. 8,* ☎ *22/14–93–42.* ☛ *Free.* ☉ *Sun. noon–3.*

SHOPPING

Oslo is the best place for buying anything Norwegian. Prices of handmade articles, such as knitwear, are controlled, making comparison shopping unnecessary. Otherwise shops have both sales and specials—look for the words *salg* and *tilbud*. Sales of seasonal merchandise, combined with the value-added tax refund, can save you more than half the original price. Norwegians do like au courant skiwear, so there are plenty of bargains in last season's winter sportswear.

Two shopping districts stand out—downtown, in the area around **Karl Johans Gate;** and **Majorstuen,** starting at the subway station with the same name and proceeding down Bogstadveien to the Royal Palace. **Vikaterrassen,** near **Aker Brygge** (*see below*) is a pleasant shopping street with small exclusive stores, and from there if you wander up Bygdøy Allé, you'll find modern and antique furniture stores as well as some interior design shops and specialty clothing stores.

Shopping Centers
Aker Brygge, Norway's first major shopping center, is right on the water across from the Tourist Information Office at Vestbanen. Shops are open until 8 most days, and some even on Sundays. **Oslo City,** at the other end of downtown, with access to the street from Oslo S Station (Stenersgt. 1E, ☎ 22/44–44–44), is the largest indoor mall, but the shops are run-of-the-mill, and the food is mostly fast. **Paleet** (Karl Johans Gt. 39–41, between Universitetsgt. and Rosenkrantz' Gt., ☎ 22/42–70–58), the newest downtown development, opens up into a grand atrium lined with supports of various shades of black and gray marble. Up-

stairs are familiar chain stores and specialty shops; the basement houses a food court.

Department Stores

Christiania GlasMagasin (Stortorvet 9, ☎ 22/11–63–50) is not a true department store, but it has a much more extensive selection of merchandise than a specialty shop does. The best buys are glass and porcelain: Hadeland, Magnor, Randsfjord, and Severin glass, and Porsgrunn and Figgjo porcelain and stoneware. Christmas decorations reflecting Norway's rural heritage are easily packed. There is also a wide selection of pewter ware. **Steen & Strøm** (Kongens Gt. 23, ☎ 22/41–68–00) consists of several individual shops. **Årstidene,** which offers a fine selection of Norwegian souvenirs, can be found there.

Street Markets

The best flea market is on Saturday at **Vestkanttorvet,** near Frogner Park at Amaldus Nilsens Plass at the intersection of Professor Dahlsgate and Eckerberg Gate. Check the local paper for others.

Specialty Stores

ANTIQUES

Norwegian rustic antiques cannot be taken out of the country, but just about anything else can with no problem. **Kaare Berntsen** (Universitetsgt. 12, ☎ 22/20–34–29) sells paintings, furniture, and small items, all very exclusive, and priced accordingly. **Blomqvist Kunsthandel** (Tordenskiolds Gt. 5, ☎ 22/41–26–31) has a good selection of small items and paintings, with auctions six times a year. **West Sølv og Mynt** (Niels Juels Gt. 27, ☎ 22/55–75–83) has the largest selection of silver, both old and antique, in town. The Frogner district is dotted with antiques shops, especially Skovveien and Thomas Heftyes Gate between Bygdøy Allé and Frogner Plass. **Esaias Solberg** (Dronningens Gt. 27, ☎ 22/42–41–08), behind Oslo Cathedral, has exceptional small antiques.

BOOKS

Tanum Libris (Karl Johans Gt. 37, ☎ 22/41–11–00) and **Erik Qvist** (Drammensvn. 16, ☎ 22/44–52–69) have the best selections of English books in Oslo. **Bjørn Ringstrøms Antikvariat** (Ullevålsvn. 1, ☎ 22/20–78–05), across the street from the Museum of Decorative Art, has a wide selection of used books and records. **Pocketboka** (Ole Vigs Gt. 25, ☎ 22/69–00–18) at Majorstuen has new and used paperbacks.

EMBROIDERY

Husfliden (*see* Handicrafts, *below*) sells embroidery kits, including do-it-yourself *bunader* (national costumes), and traditional yarn shops also sell embroidery. **Randi Mangen** (Jac Aalls Gt. 17, ☎ 22/60–50–59), near Majorstuen, sells only embroidery.

FOOD

Buy a smoked salmon or trout for a special treat. Most grocery stores sell vacuum-packed fish. **W. Køltzow,** at Aker Brygge (Stranden 3, ☎ 22/83–00–70), specializes in fish and can arrange for just about anything to be packed for export.

FUR

Look for the Saga label for the best-quality farmed Arctic fox and mink. **Studio H. Olesen** (Karl Johans Gt. 31, enter at Rosenkrantz' Gt., ☎ 22/33–37–50, and Universitetsgt. 20, ☎ 22/42–99–49) has the most exclusive designs. **Hansson Pels** (Kirkevn. 54, ☎ 22/69–64–20), near Majorstuen is another shop with an excellent selection.

FURNITURE

Norway is well known for both rustic furniture and orthopedic yet well-designed chairs. **Tannum** (Stortingsgt. 28, ☎ 22/83–42–95) is a good starting point. Drammensveien and Bygdøy Allé have a wide selection of interior design stores.

GLASS, CERAMICS, AND PEWTER

If there's no time to visit a glass factory (*see* Short Excursions from Oslo, *above*), department stores are the best option. **Christiania Glas-Magasin** (Stortorvet 9, ☎ 22/11–63–50) stocks both European and Norwegian designs. **Norway Designs** (Stortingsgt. 28, ☎ 22/83–11–00) specializes in Norwegian and Scandinavian glass. The shops at Basarhallene behind the cathedral also sell glass and ceramics. **Abelson Brukskunst** (Skovvn. 27, ☎ 22/55–55–94), behind the Royal Palace, is crammed with the best modern designs.

HANDICRAFTS

Heimen Husflid AS (Rosenkrantz' Gt. 8, ☎ 22/41–40–50, enter at Rosenkrantzgt.) has small souvenir items and a specialized department for Norwegian national costumes. **Husfliden** (Møllergt. 4, ☎ 22/42–10–75) has an even larger selection, including pewter, ceramics, knits, handwoven textiles, furniture, handmade felt boots and slippers, hand-sewn loafers, sweaters, national costumes, wrought-iron accessories, and Christmas ornaments, all made in Norway. **Format Kunsthandverk** (Vestbanepl. 1, ☎ 22/83–73–12) has beautiful, yet pricey, individual pieces. **Basarhallene,** the arcade behind the cathedral, is also worth a browse.

JEWELRY

Gold and precious stones are no bargain, but silver and enamel jewelry, along with reproductions of Viking pieces, are. Some silver pieces are made with Norwegian stones, particularly pink thulite. **David-Andersen** (Karl Johans Gt. 20, ☎ 22/41–69–55), is Norway's best-known goldsmith. **Oslo City** (☎ 22/17–09–34) also has a wide selection of jewelry. **Heyerdahl** (Stortingsgt. 18, ☎ 22/41–59–18), near City Hall, is a good jeweler. **ExpoArte** (Drammensvn. 40, ☎ 22/55–93–90), specializes in custom pieces. (*See also* Antiques, *above*.)

KNITWEAR AND CLOTHING

Norway is famous for its handmade, multicolored ski sweaters, but even mass-produced models are of top quality. The prices are regulated, so buy what you like when you see it. **Husfliden** (*see* Handicrafts, *above*) stocks sweaters in the traditional style, many of which are handmade. **Maurtua** (Fr. Nansens Pl. 9, ☎ 22/41–31–64), near City Hall, has a huge selection of sweaters and blanket coats. **Oslo Sweater Shop** (SAS Scandinavia Hotel, Tullinsgt. 5, ☎ 22/11–29–22) has one of the city's widest selections. **Siril** (Rosenkrantz' Gt. 23, ☎ 22/41–01–80), near City Hall, is a small shop with attentive staff. **Rein og Rose** (Ruseløkkvn. 3, ☎ 22/83–21–39) has a good selection of knitwear, yarn, and textiles. **William Schmidt** (Karl Johans Gt. 41, ☎ 22/42–02–88), founded in 1853, is Oslo's oldest shop specializing in sweaters and souvenirs.

SPORTSWEAR

Look for the Helly-Hansen brand. The company makes everything from insulated underwear to rainwear, snow gear, and great insulated mittens. **Sportshuset** (Ullevålsvn. 11, ☎ 22/20–11–21, and Frognervn. 9C, ☎ 22/55–29–57) has the best prices. **Gresvig** (Storgt. 20, ☎ 22/17–39–80) is a little more expensive, but has a good selection. **Sigmund**

Ruud (Kirkevn. 57, ☎ 22/69–43–90) also has a comprehensive stock of quality sportswear.

WATCHES

For some reason, Swiss watches are much cheaper in Norway than in many other countries. **Bjerke** (Karl Johans Gt. 31, ☎ 22/42–20–44, and Prinsensgt. 21, ☎ 22/42–60–50) has the largest selection in town.

SPORTS AND FITNESS

Surrounding Oslo's compact center are a variety of lovely and unspoiled landscapes, including forests, farmland, and, of course, the fjord. Just 15 minutes north of the city center by tram is the **Oslomarka,** where locals ski in winter and hike in summer. The area is dotted with 27 small hytter, which can be reserved through the **Norske Turistforening** (Stortingsgt. 28, ☎ 22/83–25–50), which has maps of the *marka* (fields and land), surrounding Oslo as well. The **Oslo Archipelago** is also a favorite with sunbathing urbanites, who hop ferries to their favorite isles.

Bicycling

Den Rustne Eike (The Rusty Spoke, Vestbanepl. 2, ☎ 22/83–72–31) rents bikes and equipment, including helmets (required by law). **Sykkeldelisk** (Fridtjof Nansens Pl. 7, ☎ 22/42–60–20) and **Oslo Sykkelutleie** (Kjelsåsvn. 145, ☎ 22/22–13–46) also rent a full range of bikes. The latter are located just on the edge of Oslomarka, and they specialize in arranging routes covering that territory. **Syklistenes Landsforening** (National Organization of Cyclists; Maridalsvn. 60, ☎ 22/71–92–93) sells books and maps for cycling holidays in Norway and abroad and gives friendly, free advice.

Fishing

A national fishing license (NKr60, available in post offices) and a local fee (NKr60 from local sports shops) are required in order to fish in the Oslo Fjord and the surrounding lakes. Ice fishing is also popular in the winter, but you'll have a hard time finding an ice drill—truly, you may want to bring one from home.

Golf

Oslo's international-level golf course, **Oslo Golfklubb** (Bogstad, ☎ 22/50–44–02) is private, and heavily booked, but will admit members of other golf clubs if space is available. There are also one 18-hole and several 9-hole courses with expansions planned.

Hiking and Jogging

Head for the woods surrounding Oslo, the **marka,** for jogging or walking; there are thousands of kilometers of trails, hundreds of them lit. Frogner Park has many paths, and you can jog or hike along the Aker River, but a few unsavory types may be about late at night or early in the morning. Or you can take the Sognsvann trikk to the end of the line and walk or jog along the Sognsvann stream. The Norske Turistforening (*see above*) has many maps of trails around Oslo and can recommend individual routes.

Skiing

The **Skiforeningen** (Kongevn. 5, ☎ 22/92–32–00) can provide tips on the multitude of cross-country trails. Among the floodlit trails in the Oslomarka are the **Bogstad** (3.5 kilometers/2.1 miles, marked for the disabled and blind), the **Lillomarka** (about 25 kilometers/15.6 miles), and the **Østmarken** (33 kilometers/20.6 miles).

For downhill, which usually lasts from mid-December to March, there are 15 local city slopes, and organized trips to several outside slopes, including **Norefjell** (☎ 32/14–94–00), 100 kilometers (66 miles) north of the city, are also available.

The Skiforeningen also offers cross-country classes for young children (3- to 7-year-olds), downhill for older children (7- to 12-year-olds) and both, in addition to Telemark-style and racing techniques, for adults. For details, call the Skiforeningen.

Swimming
Tøyenbadet (Helgesensgt. 90, ☎ 22/67–18–87) and **Frogner Park** have large outdoor swimming pools that are open from May 18 through August 20 (weekdays 11–5:45, weekends 10–5). Tøyenbadet also has an indoor pool (open weekdays 10–7, weekends 10–2:30). All pools cost NKr35 adults, NKr15 children.

DINING

Food once was an afterthought in Oslo, but no longer. The city's chefs are winning contests all over the world, and Norwegian cuisine, based on the products of its pristine waters and countryside, is firmly in the culinary spotlight. Eating out is a luxury for many Norwegians. In Oslo, bad food is expensive and good food doesn't necessarily cost more—it's just a matter of knowing where to go.

For price-category definitions, *see* How to Use this Book *in* On the Road with Fodor's.

$$$$ **Bagatelle.** Oslo's best restaurant is a short walk from downtown. Paint-
★ ings by contemporary Norwegian artists accent the otherwise subdued interior, but the food is the true show here. Internationally known chef-owner Eyvind Hellstrøm's cuisine is modern Norwegian with French overtones. His grilled scallops with a saffron-parsley sauce, and the marinated salmon tartare with an herbed crème fraîche sauce are extraordinary. Bagatelle has a wine cellar to match its food. ✕ *Bygdøy Allé 3/5,* ☎ *22/44–63–97. Reservations advised. Jacket and tie. AE, DC, MC, V. Closed Sun., 1 week at Christmas and Easter. Dinner only.*

$$$$ **D'Artagnan.** Freddie Nielsen's restaurant, right off Karl Johans Gate, recently underwent a facade refurbishment, but inside it's still the same. The stairs lead to a comfortable lounge, while another floor up is the dining room. The decor is eclectic, but the food is classic and pure. The saffron-poached pike with asparagus is a good way to start a meal, while the boned fillet of salmon with lobster-cream sauce seasoned with dill is attractive and flavorful. The dessert cart is loaded with jars of fruit preserved in liqueurs, which are served with various sorbets and ice creams. This spot also serves game in season, such as roasted reindeer or moose with cowberry sauce. ✕ *Øvre Slottsgt. 16,* ☎ *22/41–50–62. Reservations advised. AE, DC, MC, V. Closed weekends and July. Dinner only.*

$$$$ **De Fem Stuer.** Near the famous Holmenkollen ski jump, in the historic
★ Holmenkollen Park Hotel, this restaurant has first-rate views and food. Chef Frank Halvorsen's modern Norwegian dishes have strong classic roots. Well worth trying is the three-course "A Taste of Norway," with salmon, reindeer, and cloudberries. ✕ *Holmenkollen Park Hotel, Kongevn. 26,* ☎ *22/14–60–90. Reservations advised. Jacket and tie. AE, DC, MC, V.*

$$$$ **Feinschmecker.** The name is German, but the food is modern Scandinavian. The atmosphere is friendly and intimate, with green rattan chairs, yellow tablecloths, and floral draperies. Owners Lars Erik Underthun, one of Oslo's foremost chefs, and Bengt Wilson, one of Scandinavia's leading food photographers, make sure the food looks as good as it tastes. The roast rack of lamb with crunchy fried sweetbreads on tagliatelle and the chocolate-caramel teardrop with passion-fruit sauce are two choices on a menu that also makes fascinating reading. ✗ *Balchensgt. 5,* ☎ *22/44–17–77. Reservations required. AE, DC, MC, V. Closed Sun., 1 week Christmas and Easter, last 3 weeks of July. Dinner only.*

$$$ **Ambassadeur.** This cozy restaurant serving modern Scandinavian food is in the cellar of the Ambassadeur Hotel. Huge swaths of fabric, dark colors, and baroque-style paintings of food create a plush, cocoonlike ambience. The food itself stands in contrast to the decor—it's light, in both concept and color. The seafood salad in a light vinaigrette with plump mussels and shrimp is a winner, while the scallops in lemon buerre blanc are delicate and subtle. The bar, one of Oslo's best, is comfortable and well stocked. ✗ *Hotel Ambassadeur, Camilla Collets vei 15,* ☎ *22/44–18–35. Reservations advised. AE, DC, MC, V. Closed weekends and July. Dinner only.*

$$$ **Babette's Gjestehus.** This tiny restaurant is hidden in the shopping arcade by City Hall. Chef Ortwin Kulmus and his friendly staff know how to make their guests feel welcome—bright blue walls, starched white tablecloths, and lace curtains against paned windows also contribute to the rustic, homey feel. The food is Scandinavian with a French touch. Try the garlic-marinated rack of lamb in rosemary sauce or pan-fried breast of duck with creamed spring cabbage. Dishes vary according to season, but are always well prepared. ✗ *Rådhuspassasjen, Roald Amundsensgt. 6,* ☎ *22/41–64–64. Reservations required. AE, DC, MC, V. Closed Sun. Dinner only.*

$$$ **Hos Thea.** This old-fashioned-looking gem with blue-and-beige decor has only 36 seats. It's located at the beginning of Embassy Row, a short distance from downtown. Owner Sergio Barcilon, originally from Spain, is one of the pioneers of the new Scandinavian cooking. The small menu offers four or five choices in each category, but every dish is superbly prepared, from the venison in a sauce of mixed berries to the sherbets and fruitcake. Noise and smoke levels can be high late in the evening. ✗ *Gabelsgt. 11, entrance on Drammensvn.,* ☎ *22/44–68–74. Reservations required. AE, DC, MC, V. Closed 1 week at Christmas and Easter. Dinner only.*

$$$ **Le Canard.** This oasis in Frogner is furnished with antiques and Oriental rugs; fresh, white crocheted tablecloths and silver candlesticks contrast with the somber stone walls. The specialty is, of course, duck, from beef with duck-liver in Madeira sauce to sautéed breast of duck with horseradish and cognac sauce. But chef Lucien Mares is known to conjure up other sumptuous treats for his guests too. The wine list is extensive. ✗ *Oscars Gt. 81,* ☎ *22/43–40–28. Reservations advised. AE, DC, MC, V. Closed Sun., Christmas, Easter. No lunch in winter.*

$$$ **Theatercafeen.** This Oslo institution, on the ground floor of the Hotel
★ Continental, is jammed day and night. Built in 1900, the last Viennese-style café in northern Europe retains its Art Nouveau character. The menu is small and jumbled, with starters and main dishes interspersed; the only hint of the serving size is the price column. From 1 to 7, there's a reasonably priced two-course "family dinner." Pastry chef Robert Bruun's *konfektkake* (a rich chocolate cake) and apple tart served with homemade ice cream are reasons enough to visit. ✗ *Stortingsgt. 24–26,* ☎ *22/33–32–00. Reservations advised. AE, DC, MC, V.*

$$ **A Touch of France.** At this clean, inviting brasserie where the tables sit
★ close together, the French ambience is further accented by the waiters' long, white aprons. The tempting menu includes a steaming hot bouil-

Oslo Dining and Lodging

KEY

🛈 Tourist Information
—— Rail Lines

Dining
A Touch of France, **27**
Ambassadeur, **11**
Babette's
Gjestehus, **16**
Bagatelle, **9**
D'Artagnan, **27**
De Fem Stuer, **3**
Den Grimme
Ælling, **20**
Det Gamle
Raadhus, **28**
Dinner, **26**
Dionysos Taverna, **32**

Feinschmecker, **5**
Frognerseteren, **4**
Hos Thea, **8**
Kaffistova, **24**
Kastanjen, **6**
Le Canard, **10**
Lofotstua, **2**
Quatro Amigos, **15**
Shalimar, **34**
Theatercafeen, **17**
Tysk City Grill, **30**
Vegeta, **14**

Lodging
Ambassadeur, **11**
Bondeheimen, **24**
Bristol, **21**
Cecil, **19**
Gabelshus, **7**
Grand Hotel, **25**
Gyldenløve, **12**
Haraldsheim, **33**
Holmenkollen Park
Hotel Rica, **3**
Hotel Continental, **17**

Munch, **23**
Oslo Plaza, **31**
Rica Victoria, **18**
Royal Christiania, **29**
SAS Park Royal, **1**
SAS Scandinavia
Hotel, **13**
Stefan, **22**

labaisse. ✕ *Øvre Slottsgt. 16*, ☎ *22/42–56–97. Reservations advised weekends. AE, DC, MC, V.*

$$ Dinner. Though its name is not the best for a restaurant specializing in ★ Szechuan-style cuisine, this is the place for Chinese food, both spicy and not so pungent. The mango pudding for dessert is wonderful. Don't bother with the other Chinese restaurants. ✕ *Arbeidergt. 2*, ☎ *22/42–68–90. Reservations advised. AE, DC, MC, V. Dinner only.*

$$ Dionysos Taverna. Nicola Murati gives his guests a warm welcome in ★ this unpretentious little Greek restaurant. The hors d'oeuvre platter, which includes stuffed vine leaves, meatballs, feta cheese, tzatziki, tomatoes, and cucumbers, is a meal in itself. The souvlaki and moussaka are authentically prepared, as are the more unusual casserole dishes. A bouzouki duo provides live music on Friday and Saturday. ✕ *Calmeyersgt. 11*, ☎ *22/60–78–64. AE, MC, V. Dinner only.*

$$ Frognerseteren. Just above the Holmenkollen Ski jump, this restaurant, specializing in fish, reindeer, and venison, looks down on the entire city. Be sure not to miss the house specialty—scrumptious apple cake. The newly renovated upstairs room has the same view as the more expensive panorama veranda, and there is also an outdoor café. Take the Holmenkollbanen to the end station and then follow the signs downhill to the restaurant. ✕ *Voksenkollen*, ☎ *22/14–37–36. AE, DC, MC, V.*

$$ Det Gamle Raadhus. Oslo's oldest restaurant, which celebrated its 350th birthday in 1991, is in the Old City Hall. Don't let the beer signs and dirty windows put you off. The dining room is straight out of Ibsen, with dark brown wainscoting, deep-yellow painted walls, old prints, and heavy red curtains. Famous for its *lutefisk*, a Scandinavian specialty made from dried fish that has been soaked in lye and then poached, the restaurant's menu allows ample choice for the less daring. Try the fresh cod in season. ✕ *Nedre Slottsgt. 1*, ☎ *22/42–01–07. Dinner reservations advised. AE, DC, MC, V. Closed Sun.*

$$ Kastanjen. This casual Frogner bistro is the kind every neighborhood ★ needs. The style of food is new traditional—modern interpretations of classic Norwegian dishes. The three-course meal is good value for the money, but check out the "dish of the day" at an unbeatable price. ✕ *Bygdøy Allé 18*, ☎ *22/43–44–67. Reservations advised. AE, DC, MC, V. Closed Sun., 1 week at Christmas and Easter.*

$$ Shalimar. This Pakistani restaurant is off the beaten track, about 15 minutes from the center of the city near Carl Berners Plass, but well worth the trip. The food, prepared by chefs imported from Karachi, is delectable. Try the tandoori mixed grill, which includes chicken, lamb, and kebab, or the chicken biryani with aromatic rice. Vegetarians have ample choices, and the nan bread is addictive. ✕ *Konghellegt. 5*, ☎ *22/37–47–68. AE, DC, MC, V. Dinner only.*

$ Den Grimme Ælling. Dane Bjarne Hvid Pedersen is well established with his popular Copenhagen restaurant in the food court at Paleet. His *smørbrød* are the best buy in town: lots of meat, fish, or cheese on a small piece of bread. He also has daily dinner specials, such as homemade *hakkebøf* (Danish Salisbury steak) with gravy, onions, and potatoes. ✕ *Paleet, Karl Johans Gt. 41B*, ☎ *22/42–47–83. No credit cards.*

$ Kaffistova. Norwegian country cooking is served, cafeteria style, at this ★ downtown restaurant. Everyday specials include soup and a selection of entrées, including a vegetarian dish. *Kjøttkaker* (meat cakes) served with creamed cabbage is a Norwegian staple, and the steamed salmon with Sandefjord butter is as good here as in places where it costs three times as much. Low-alcohol beer is the strongest drink served. ✕ *Rosenkrantz' Gt. 8*, ☎ *22/42–95–30. AE, DC, MC, V.*

$ **Lofotstua.** This rustic fish restaurant has a cozy atmosphere and personal service right out of Norway's far north. Fresh cod and seafood from Lofoten are among the good, moderately priced food served here. ✗ *Kirkevn. 40,* ☎ *22/46–93–96. Reservations advised. AE, DC, MC, V. Closed Sat.*

$ **Quatro Amigos.** A favorite among the young crowd, this simple restaurant is the place to hit when you crave spicy Mexican fare and big portions. The menu has all the standards, including enchiladas, tacos, and burritos, which are served alongside rice, black beans, and salad. ✗ *Stortingsgt. 16,* ☎ *22/42–48–30. AE, MC, V. Dinner only.*

$ **Tysk City Grill.** In the midst of the Oslo City shopping mall's food court
★ is a tiny, authentic German restaurant, complete with oompah music. The grilled bratwurst (with real German mustard and curry ketchup) with homemade potato salad is the most filling cheap meal in town, while the Eisbein and the pea soup, both homemade, are hearty fare. ✗ *Stenersgt. 1,* ☎ *22/17–05–12. No credit cards.*

$ **Vegeta.** Next to the Nationaltheatret bus and streetcar station, this no-smoking restaurant is a popular spot for hot and cold vegetarian meals and salads. The all-you-can-eat specials offer top value. ✗ *Munkedamsvn. 3B,* ☎ *22/83–40–20. No reservations. No credit cards.*

LODGING

Most hotels are centrally located, a short walk from Karl Johans Gate, the main street. The newest hotels are in the area around Oslo S Station, at the bottom end of Karl Johan. For a quiet stay, choose a hotel in Frogner, the elegant residential neighborhood just minutes from downtown.

Lodging in the capital is expensive. Prices for downtown accommodations are high, even for bed-and-breakfasts, although just about all hotels have weekend, holiday, and summer rates (25% to 50% reductions). Taxes, service charges, and, unless otherwise noted, a buffet breakfast are included.

Oslo usually has enough hotel rooms to go around, but it's always a good idea to reserve a room at least for the first night of your stay, especially if you will be arriving late. The hotel accommodations office at Oslo S Station is open from 8 AM to 11 PM and can book you in anything from a luxury hotel to a room in a private home for a fee of NKr20 adults, NKr10 children, plus 10% of the room rate, which is refunded when you check in.

If you are interested in renting an apartment, contact **Bed & Breakfast** (Stasjonsvn. 13, Blommenholm, 1300 Sandvika, ☎ 67/54–06–80, FAX 67/54–09–70; open weekdays 8:30–4). Most are located in Bærum, 15 to 20 minutes from downtown Oslo. All addresses provided by the group are no more than a 10-minute walk from public transport.

For price-category definitions, *see* How to Use this Book *in* On the Road with Fodor's.

$$$$ **Grand Hotel.** Located right in the center of Karl Johans Gate, the Grand
★ has been Oslo's premier hotel since it opened in 1874. Ibsen and Munch were regular guests, and since their time the Grand has hosted many famous people and all recipients of the Nobel Peace Prize. The lobby gives no idea of the style and flair of the rooms. Even standard rooms are large, looking more like guest quarters in an elegant house than hotel rooms. Those in the new wing are smaller, cheaper, and not

as nice. ☎ *Karl Johans Gt. 31, 0159,* ☎ *22/42–93–90,* FAX *22/42–12–25. 289 rooms with bath, 60 suites. 3 restaurants, 2 bars, health club, indoor pool, meeting rooms. AE, DC, MC, V.*

$$$$ **Holmenkollen Park Hotel Rica.** The magnificent 1894 building in the national romantic style commands an unequaled panorama of the city and is worth a visit even if you don't lodge there. The rather ordinary guest rooms are in a newer structure (1982) behind it. The ice-covered snowflake sculpture in the lobby is appropriate for a hotel that's a stone's throw from Holmenkollen ski jump. Ski and walking trails are just outside. ☎ *Kongevn. 26, 0390,* ☎ *22/92–20–00,* FAX *22/14–61–92. 191 rooms with bath. 2 restaurants, bar, pool, sauna, nightclub, convention center. AE, DC, MC, V.*

$$$$ **Hotel Continental.** The Brockmann family, owners since 1900, have succeeded in combining the rich elegance of the Old World with modern, comfortable living. The Theatercafeen (*see* Dining, *above*) is a landmark, and the newest addition, Lipp, a restaurant, café, and bar in one, is among Oslo's "in" places. Dagligstuen (The Sitting Room) is a wonderful place in which to start or end the evening with an appetizer or nightcap. Munch graphics from the family's own collection adorn the walls. ☎ *Stortingsgt. 24–26, 0161,* ☎ *22/41–90–60,* FAX *22/42–96–89. 158 rooms with bath, 12 suites. 3 restaurants, 2 bars, nightclub. AE, DC, MC, V.*

$$$$ **Oslo Plaza.** Northern Europe's largest hotel, built in 1990, is a three-minute walk from Karl Johans Gate. Modern, decorated in Scandinavian style, it is favored by business travelers, who tend toward the pricier, deluxe suites in the tower. Below the 27th floor the standard rooms are decorated in red tones and have ample marble baths. The hotel has one of the city's best Japanese restaurants, and the rooftop nightclub offers spectacular views of the city. ☎ *Sonja Henies Pl. 3, 0134,* ☎ *22/17–10–00,* FAX *22/17–73–00. 662 rooms with bath, 20 suites. 3 restaurants, 2 bars, nightclub, health club, indoor pool, shops, convention center. AE, DC, MC, V.*

$$$$ **Royal Christiania.** It started out as bare-bones housing for 1952
★ Olympians. The original exterior has been retained, but inside it's a whole new hotel, built around a central atrium. The emphasis here is on discreet comfort—the large rooms are decorated in soft colors with light-color furniture. The restaurant, La Trattoria, serves up delicious, traditional Italian fare. ☎ *Biskop Gunnerus' Gt. 3, 0106,* ☎ *22/42–94–10,* FAX *22/42–46–22. 451 rooms with bath, 73 suites. 3 restaurants, 3 bars, health club, indoor pool, nightclub, convention center. AE, DC, MC, V.*

$$$$ **SAS Scandinavia Hotel.** Oslo's leading downtown business hotel, built in 1974, is getting some competition, but it can still hold its own: There's a business-class airline check-in in the lobby; the lower-level shopping arcade features high-fashion clothing and leather-goods shops. Rooms come in four different styles, from high-tech to Asian. Standard rooms are spacious and light. The SAS is across the street from the palace grounds (but don't walk through them at night). ☎ *Holbergs Gt. 30, 0166,* ☎ *22/11–30–00,* FAX *22/11–30–17. 494 rooms with bath, 3 large suites. 2 restaurants, 2 bars, nightclub, disco, health club, pool, business center, shopping arcade. AE, DC, MC, V.*

$$$ **Ambassadeur.** This comfortable and elegant hotel hides behind a pale
★ pink facade with wrought-iron balconies in a stylish residential area behind the Royal Palace, a few minutes from downtown. Originally built in 1889 as an apartment hotel, the Ambassadeur has practically no lobby, but the rooms make up for that. Apart from several singles, each room is individually furnished with thematic decors and

Norwegian art. The small, professional staff doesn't bother with titles because everyone does whatever task presents itself, from laundering a shirt on short notice to delivering room service. ☎ *Camilla Colletts vei 15, 0258,* ☎ *22/44–18–35,* FAX *22/44–47–91. 41 rooms with bath, 8 suites. Restaurant, bar, pool, sauna, conference room. AE, DC, MC, V.*

$$$ Bristol. In the past few years, the Bristol has begun catering to people who want a dignified hotel in the center of town. The lobby, decorated in the 1920s with a Moorish theme, is a tribute to style, and the library bar is Oslo's most comfortable. Some of the rooms are decorated with lightly colored painted Scandinavian furniture, while others have a Regency theme. The banquet rooms have true Old World elegance, and at the restaurant, the Bristol Grill, red meat has not gone out of style. ☎ *Kristian IV's Gt. 7, 0164,* ☎ *22/82–60–00,* FAX *22/82–60–01. 141 rooms with bath, 4 suites. 2 restaurants, 2 bars, nightclub, convention center AE, DC, MC, V.*

$$$ Rica Victoria. Opened in May 1991, the hotel occupies a contemporary structure built around a center atrium. The rooms are elegant and very stylish, furnished with Biedermeier reproductions and textiles in bold reds and dark blues. Rooms with windows on the atrium may be claustrophobic for some. ☎ *Rosenkrantz' Gt. 13, 0160,* ☎ *22/42–99–40,* FAX *22/41–06–44. 197 rooms with bath or shower, 4 suites. Restaurant, bar. AE, DC, MC, V.*

$$$ SAS Park Royal. Oslo Fornebu Airport's only hotel is somewhat anonymous, with long, narrow corridors and standard American-style hotel rooms. There are excellent business facilities, including a business-class airline check-in, and the airport bus stops right outside. The restaurant serves modern Scandinavian food such as dill-marinated salmon, monkfish, fillet of pork, and tasty cloudberries and cream for dessert. ☎ *Fornebuparken, Box 185, 1324 Lysaker,* ☎ *67/12–02–20,* FAX *67/12–00–11. 254 rooms with bath, 14 suites. Restaurant, bar, tennis court, health club, business services. AE, DC, MC, V.*

$$$ Stefan. This hotel makes every aspect of a stay a positive experience, from hot welcome drinks for late arrivals to breakfast tables complete with juice boxes and plastic bags for packing a lunch. The top-floor lounge has books and magazines in English. The Stefan's kitchen still creates the best buffet lunch in town—but it's only open to guests. ☎ *Rosenkrantz' Gt. 1, 0159,* ☎ *22/42–92–50,* FAX *22/33–70–22. 130 rooms with bath or shower. Restaurant, meeting rooms. AE, DC, MC, V.*

$$ Bondeheimen. Founded in 1913 for country folk visiting the city, Bondeheimen, which means "farmers' home," still gives discounts to members of Norwegian agricultural associations. (International groups would be free to negotiate, however.) The lobby and rooms are decorated with pine furniture, handwoven rag rugs, soft blue textiles, and modern Norwegian graphics, just the way a Norwegian country home should look. Bondeheimen serves no alcohol, and the staff has a squeaky-clean look. ☎ *Rosenkrantz' Gt. 8, 0159,* ☎ *22/42–95–30,* FAX *22/41–94–37. 76 rooms with shower. Café, meeting room. AE, DC, MC, V.*

$$ Cecil. ★ This hotel, one block from Stortinget, was built in 1989. The second floor opens onto an atrium: the hotel's activity center. In the morning it's a breakfast room, with one of Oslo's best buffets, but in the afternoon it becomes a lounge, serving coffee, juice, and fresh fruit, with newspapers available in many languages. The single rooms have double beds, while doubles have queen-size beds. ☎ *Stortingsgt. 8, 0130,* ☎ *22/42–70–00,* FAX *22/42–26–70. 110 rooms with bath, 2 suites. AE, DC, MC, V.*

$$ Gabelshus. With only a discreet sign above the door, this ivy-covered brick house in a posh residential area is one of Oslo's most personal hotels. It has been owned by the same family for almost 50 years. The lounges are filled with antiques, some in the national romantic style, but the rooms are plain. It's a short walk to several of Oslo's best restaurants and a short trikk ride to the center of town. The Ritz Hotel, across the parking lot, is owned by the same family and takes the overflow. ☎ *Gabels Gt. 16, 0272,* ☎ *22/55–22–60,* FAX *22/44–27–30. 45 rooms with bath (plus 42 rooms with bath in Ritz). Restaurant. AE, DC, MC, V.*

$ Gyldenløve. Nestled among the many shops and cafés on Bogstadveien, this hotel is one of the city's most reasonable bed-and-breakfast establishments. It is within walking distance of Vigeland Park, and the trikk stops just outside the door. Reproductions of city scenes from old Christiania (Oslo) hang in every room. ☎ *Bogstadvn. 20, 0355,* ☎ *22/60–10–90,* FAX *22/60–33–90. 169 rooms with shower. AE, DC, MC, V.*

$ Haraldsheim. Oslo's hilltop youth hostel is one of Europe's largest. Most of the rooms have four beds, and those in the new wing have showers. Bring your own sheet or sleeping bag or rent one here. It is 4 kilometers (2½ miles) from the city center—take Tram 1 or 7 or trikk 11 or 12 (marked Kjelsås) to Sinsen. Nonmembers of the International Youth Hostel organization pay a surcharge. Breakfast is included in the price. ☎ *Haraldsheimvn. 4, 0409,* ☎ *22/15–50–43,* FAX *22/34–71–97. 264 beds. No credit cards.*

$ Munch. This modern bed-and-breakfast, about a 10-minute walk from Karl Johans Gate, is unpretentious, well run, clean, and functional. The rooms, renovated in 1994, are of a decent size and painted in pastels or blue with floral curtains. The lobby, with Chinese rugs and leather couches, contrasts with the rest of the hotel. ☎ *Munchsgt. 5, 0165,* ☎ *22/42–42–75,* FAX *22/20–64–69. 180 rooms with shower. Breakfast room. AE, DC, MC, V.*

THE ARTS AND NIGHTLIFE

The Arts

The monthly *Oslo Guide* lists cultural events in Norwegian, as does section four of *Aftenposten,* Oslo's (and Norway's) leading newspaper. The Wednesday edition of *Dagbladet,* Oslo's daily liberal tabloid, also gives an exhaustive preview of the week's events. The information number at **Oslo Spektrum** congress and concert complex (☎ 22/17–80–10) gives a rundown of all scheduled events. Tickets to virtually all performances in Norway, from classical or rock concerts to hockey games, can be purchased at any post office.

Nationaltheatret (Stortingsgt. 15, ☎ 22/41–27–10) performances are in Norwegian: bring along a copy of the play in translation, and you're all set.

Det Norske Teater (Kristian IV's Gt. 8, ☎ 22/42–43–44) is a showcase for pieces in Nynorsk, musicals, and guest artists from abroad. Musicals and dance events play at **Bryggeteatret** (Aker Brygge, ☎ 22/83–88–20), Oslo's newest theater.

The **Norwegian Philharmonic Orchestra,** under the direction of Mariss Janssons, is among Europe's leading ensembles. Its house, **Konserthuset** (Munkedamsvn. 14, ☎ 22/83–32–00), was built in 1977 in marble, metal, and rosewood. **Den Norske Opera** (Storgt. 21, ☎ 22/42–94–75 for information; 22/42–77–24 to order tickets between

10 and 1 on the day of the performance) and the ballet perform at Youngstorvet.

Oslo Spektrum (Sonja Henies Pl. 2, ☎ 22/17–80–10), a rounded brick building sprinkled with glazed-tile mosaics, is the most interesting piece of architecture in the area around Oslo S Station. The Spektrum is used as a conference center, a sports stadium, and a concert hall.

All **films** are shown in the original language with subtitles, except for some children's films, which are dubbed. If you plan to take children to see a film, check the age limits first. Norwegian film censors set high and strictly enforced age limits on films they consider to be violent.

Nightlife
For the past few years Oslo has been the nightlife capital of Scandinavia. At any time of the day or night, people are out on Karl Johan, and many clubs and restaurants in the central area stay open until 4 or 5 AM. Night-lifers can pick up a copy of the free monthly paper *Natt og Dag,* which lists rock, pop, and jazz venues and contains a "barometer" listing the city's cheapest and most expensive places for a beer—a necessary column in a city where a draft, on the average, costs NKr33. The listings are in Norwegian but some ads are in English.

BARS AND LOUNGES
Churchill Wine Bar (Fr. Nansens Pl. 6, ☎ 22/33–53–43) and **Fridtjof's** (Fr. Nansens Pl. 7, ☎ 22/33–40–88) are yuppie favorites for pricey after-work imbibing. Both are near City Hall. For the serious beer connoisseur, **Oslo Mikrobryggeri** (Bogstadvn. 6, ☎ 22/56–97–76) is the place, with beer brewed on the premises; for variety, go to **Lorry** (Parkvn. 12, ☎ 22/69–69–04). Filled with a cast of grizzled old artists, the place advertises 81 brews, but don't be surprised if not all of them are in stock. **Barbeint** (Drammensvn. 20,☎ 22/44–59–74) has a lively atmosphere and is popular with students and media folk. **Studenten Bryggeri** (Karl Johans Gt. 45, ☎ 22/42–56–80), another microbrewery, has a piano player. If you're more partial to lounging than drinking, try the English-style bar at the **Bristol Hotel** (Kristian IV's Gt. 7, ☎ 22/41–58–40).

CAFÉS
Many cafés are open for cappuccino and a quiet conversation practically around the clock, and they're the cheapest eateries as well. In the trendy area around Frogner and Homansbyen, try **Onkel Oswald** (Hegdehaugsvn. 34, ☎ 22/69–05–35), **Broker Cafe** (Bogstadvn. 27, ☎ 22/69–36–47), or **Clodion Art Café** (Bygdøy Allé 63, ☎ 22/44–97–26). Downtown, **Kafe Celsius** (Rådhusgt. 19, 22/42–45–39) in a half-timber building from 1626, attracts an arty crowd, while **Sjakk Matt** (Haakon VII's Gt. 5, ☎ 22/83–41–56) appeals to a very hip set. **Nichol & Son** (Olavs Gt. 1, ☎ 22/83–19–60) a must for Jack Nicholson fans, is an ambient spot to relax with a newspaper.

DISCOS AND NIGHTCLUBS
Most discos open late, and the beat doesn't really start until near midnight. There's usually an age limit, and the cover charge is around NKr50. Thursday is student disco night at **Snorre-Kompagniet** (Rosenkrantz' Gt. 11, ☎ 22/33–52–60). Oslo's beautiful people congregate at **Barock** (Universitetsgt. 26, ☎ 22/42–44–20) and **Lipp** (Roald Amundsensgt. 2, ☎ 22/41–44–00), a restaurant, nightclub, and bar. **Kristiania** (Kristian IV's Gt. 12, ☎ 22/42–56–60), another hot spot, has a live jazz club, a disco, and a bar filling up its three art-bedecked floors. Most of the big hotels have discos that appeal to the over-30 crowd. **Sky Bar,**

on the top floor of the Oslo Plaza (Sonja Henies Pl. 3, ☎ 22/17–10–00), is the most bizarre, accessible only from the glass elevator outside. **Grotten** (Wergelandsvn. 5, ☎ 22/20–96–04) is popular with well-heeled and well-dressed singles over 30.

GAY BARS

For information about gay and lesbian activities in Oslo, you can read *Blikk*, the gay newsletter. **LLH** (The Union for Lesbian and Gay Liberation), the nationwide gay association, has offices at St. Olavs Pl. 2, and operates **Molina Pub and Eatery** at the same address. **Andy Capp Pub** (Fr. Nansens Pl. 4, ☎ 22/41–41–65) is popular with gays (later at night), but it reeks of old smoke. **London Bar og Pub** (C. J. Hambros Pl. 5, ☎ 22/42–99–15) is packed on weekends. **Den Sorte Enke** (the Black Widow, Møllergt. 23, ☎ 22/11–05–60), **Coco Chalet** (Øvre Slottsgt. 8, ☎ 22/33–32–66), and **Recepten Bar** (Prinsensgt. 22, ☎ 22/42–65–00) are also popular meeting places for lesbians and gays. For a more refined venue, go to **3 Brødre** (Øvre Slottsgt. 14, ☎ 22/42–39–00), with a beer and wine bar at street level and 1890s-style wall paintings of forest maidens and cherubs on the ceiling.

JAZZ CLUBS

Norwegians love jazz, and every summer the Oslo Jazz Festival, with a list of major international artists, attracts big crowds. **Oslo Jazzhus** (Stockholmsgt. 12, ☎ 22/38–59–63) is in an out-of-the-way location and is open only Thursday through Saturday, but the music is worth the journey. **Stortorvets Gjæstgiveri** (Grensen 1, ☎ 22/42–88–63) often presents New Orleans and ragtime bands. **Gamle Christiania** (Grensen 1, ☎ 22/42–74–93) is the home of the New Orleans Jazz Workshop. **Smuget** (Rosenkrantz' Gt. 22, ☎ 22/42–52–62) has live jazz, blues, and rock every evening.

ROCK CLUBS

At Oslo's numerous rock clubs, the cover charges are low, the crowds young and boisterous, and the music loud. **Rockefeller** (Torggt. 16, ☎ 22/20–32–32) presents a good mix of musical styles, from avant-garde to salsa; Thursday is student disco night. Its only real competitor is **Sentrum Scene** (Arbeidersamfunnets Pl. 2, ☎ 22/20–60–40). There's always music at **Cruise Café** (Aker Brygge 1, ☎ 22/83–64–30). **Blue Monk** (St. Olavs Gt. 23, ☎ 22/20–22–90) has live music on Wednesdays, Fridays and Saturdays—and the beer is surprisingly cheap. In the basement you'll find the boisterous Sub Pub which airs punk and 80's classics. If your taste leans toward reggae and calypso, try the **Afro International Night Club** (Brennerivn. 5, ☎ 22/36–07–53), which has frequent Caribbean evenings.

OSLO ESSENTIALS

Arriving and Departing

BY BOAT

Several ferry lines connect Oslo with the United Kingdom, Denmark, Sweden, and Germany. **Color Line** (☎ 22/83–60–10) sails to Kiel, Germany, and Hirtshals, Denmark; **DFDS Scandinavian Seaways** (☎ 22/41–90–90) to Copenhagen; and **Stena Line** (☎ 22/41–22–10) to Frederikshavn, Denmark.

BY BUS

The terminal, **Bussterminalen** (☎ 22/17–01–66), is located under Galleri Oslo, across from the Oslo S Station. Tickets for **Nor-Way Bussekspress** (long-distance routes ☎ 22/17–52–90, FAX 22/17–59–22) can be purchased here or at travel agencies. Buy local bus tickets at the terminal or on the bus. For local traffic information, call 22/17–70–30.

BY CAR

Route E18 connects Oslo with Göteborg, Sweden (by ferry between Sandefjord and Strömstad, Sweden), Copenhagen, Denmark (by ferry between Kristiansand and Hirtshals, Denmark), and Stockholm directly overland. The land route from Oslo to Göteborg is the E6. All streets and roads leading into Oslo have toll booths a certain distance from the city center, forming an "electronic ring." The toll is NKr11 and was implemented to reduce pollution downtown. If you have the correct amount in change, drive through one of the lanes marked "Mynt." If you don't, or if you need a receipt, use the "Manuell" lane.

BY PLANE

Oslo Fornebu Airport, 20 minutes west of the city, has international and domestic services under the same roof. Nevertheless the walks between international arrivals, baggage claim, and passport control are long.

SAS (☎ 810/03–300) is the main carrier, with both international and domestic flights. **Braathens SAFE** (☎ 67/59–70–00) and **Widerøe** (☎ 22/73–66–00) are the main domestic carriers.

Other major airlines serving Fornebu include **British Airways** (☎ 22/33–16–00), **Air France** (☎ 22/83–56–30), **Delta Air Lines** (☎ 22/41–56–00), **Finnair** (☎ 22/42–58–56), **Icelandair** (☎ 22/42–39–75), **KLM** (☎ 67/58–38–00), and **Lufthansa** (☎ 22/83–65–65).

Gardermoen Airport, 50 kilometers (30 miles) north of Oslo, is used primarily for charter traffic.

BETWEEN THE AIRPORT AND DOWNTOWN

Oslo Fornebu Airport is a 15–20-minute ride from the center of Oslo at off-peak hours. At rush hour (7:30–9 AM from the airport and 3:30–5 PM to the airport), the trip can take more than twice as long. None of the downtown hotels provides free shuttle service, although some outside the city do.

By Bus: Flybussen (☎ 67/59–62–20; NKr35 adults, children 15 and under free; weekdays 6 AM–9:45 PM, Sat. 6 AM–8:30 PM, Sun. 6 AM–9:45 PM) departs from its terminal under Galleri Oslo shopping center every 10 minutes and reaches Fornebu approximately 20 minutes later. Another bus departs from the SAS Scandinavia Hotel 10 minutes after and 20 minutes before the hour and costs the same. A third bus leaves from the bus stop near Nationaltheatret. Another alternative is Suburban Bus 31, marked "Snarøya," which stops outside the Arrivals terminal. On the trip into town it stops on the main road opposite the entrance to the airport. The cost is NKr20.

By Taxi: There is a taxi line to the right of the Arrivals exit. The fare to town is about NKr130. All taxi reservations should be made through the **Oslo Taxi Central** (☎ 22/38–80–80) no less than 20 minutes before pickup time.

BY TRAIN

Long-distance trains arrive at and leave from **Oslo S Station** (☎ 22/17–40–00), while most suburban commuter trains use **Nationaltheatret** or **Oslo S.** Commuter cars reserved for monthly pass holders are marked with a large black "M" on a yellow circle. Trains marked "IC," or InterCity, offer such upgraded services as breakfast and "office cars" with phones and power outlets, for an added fee.

Getting Around

The **Oslo Card** offers unlimited travel on all public transport in greater Oslo as well as free admission to museums, theaters, sightseeing attractions, the amusement park Tusenfryd, and racetracks, and discounts at various stores, cinemas (May, June, July), sports centers, and hotels. The three-day adult card gives a 30% discount for trains to and from Oslo. A one-day Oslo Card costs NKr110, a two-day card NKr190, and a three-day card NKr240. For children, the cost is NKr55, NKr80, and NKr110, respectively. It can be purchased at tourist information offices, hotels, and central post offices.

Tickets on all public transportation within Oslo cost NKr16 without transfer, while tickets that cross communal boundaries have different rates. It pays to buy a pass or a multiple travel card, which includes transfers. A one-day "Tourist Ticket" pass costs NKr35 and a seven-day pass costs NKr130. A Flexicard is good for 10 trips with free transfer within one hour and costs NKr130. Children 15 and under and senior citizens pay half-price. These cards can be purchased at post offices, tourist information offices, subway stations, and on some routes. **Trafikanten** (Jernbanetorget, ☎ 22/17–70–30), the information office for public transportation, is open weekdays 7 AM–11 PM, weekends 8–11.

Most public transportation starts running by 5:30 AM, with the last run just after midnight. On weekends there is night service on certain routes.

BY BUS

About 20 bus lines, including 6 night buses on weekends, serve the city. Most stop at **Jernbanetorget** opposite Oslo S Station. Tickets can be purchased from the driver.

BY CAR

Oslo Card holders can park for free at all parking places run by the city (P-lots), but pay careful attention to time limits. Parking is very difficult in the city—many places have one-hour limits and can cost up to NKr17 per hour. Instead of individual parking meters in P-lots, you'll find one machine that dispenses validated parking tickets to display in your car windshield. Travelers with disabilities with valid parking permits from their home country are allowed to park free and with no time limit in spaces reserved for the handicapped.

If you plan to do any amount of driving in Oslo, buy a copy of the *Stor Oslo* map, available at book stores and gasoline stations.

BY FERRY

A ferry to **Hovedøya** and other islands in the harbor basin leaves from **Vippetangen,** behind Akershus Castle (take Bus 29 from Jernbanetorget). From April through September, ferries run between **Rådhusbrygge 3,** in front of City Hall, and **Bygdøy,** the western peninsula.

BY SUBWAY

Oslo has seven subway lines, which converge at **Stortinget** station. The four eastern lines all stop at **Tøyen** before branching off, while the four western lines run through **Majorstuen** before emerging above ground for the rest of their routes to the northwestern suburbs. Tickets can be purchased at the stations.

BY TAXI

All city taxis are connected with the central dispatching office (☎ 22/38–80–90), which can take up to 30 minutes to send one during peak hours. Cabs can be ordered from 20 minutes to 24 hours in advance

(☎ 22/38–80–80). Special transport, including vans and cabs equipped for the people with disabilities, can also be ordered (☎ 22/38–80–80). Taxi stands are located all over town, usually alongside Narvesen kiosks, and are listed in the telephone directory under "Taxi" or "Drosjer."

It is possible to hail a cab on the street, but cabs are not allowed to pick up passengers within 100 meters of a stand. A cab with its roof light on is available. Rates start at NKr8 for hailed or rank cabs, NKr30 to NKr40 for ordered taxis, depending upon the time of day.

BY TRIKK/STREETCAR
Five *trikk* lines serve the city. All stop at **Jernbanetorget** opposite Oslo S Station. Tickets can be purchased from the driver.

Guided Tours
Tickets for all tours are available from Tourist Information at Vestbanen and at the Oslo S Station. Tickets for bus tours can be purchased on the buses. All tours, except H.M.K.'s Oslo Highlights tour (*see below*), operate only during the summer.

ORIENTATION
H.M.K. Sightseeing (Hegdehaugsvn. 4, ☎ 22/20–82–06) offers four bus tours. **Båtservice Sightseeing** (Rådhusbryggen 3, ☎ 22/20–07–1 5) offers one bus tour, five cruises, and one combination tour.

All bus tours leave from the harborside entrance to City Hall (**Rådhuset**); combination boat-bus tours depart from Rådhusbrygge 3, the wharf in front of City Hall.

PERSONAL GUIDES
Tourist Information at Vestbanen can provide an authorized city guide for your own private tour. **OsloTaxi** (Trondheimsvn. 100, ☎ 22/38–80–90) also offers private sightseeing.

WALKING
Organized walking tours are listed in *What's on in Oslo,* available from Tourist Information and at most hotels.

SPECIAL-INTEREST
Dogsled Tours: For a faster and more exciting experience, tour the marka by dogsled. Both lunch and evening tours are available. Contact **Norske Sledehundturer** (Einar Kristen Aas, 1500 Moss, ☎ 69/27–56–40, FAX 69/27–37–86).

Forest Tours: Tourist Information at Vestbanen can arrange four- to eight-hour motor safaris through the forests surrounding Oslo (☎ 22/83–00–50).

Sailing: Norway Yacht Charter (H. Heyerdahls Gt. 1, ☎ 22/42–64–98) can arrange sailing or yacht tours for groups of 5 to 200 people.

Skiing: Tomm Murstad Skiskole (Tommkleiva, Øvresetertjern, ☎ 22/14–46–65), is a ski school where you can rent skis, located five minutes away from Voksenkollen station. From Christmas to Easter you can learn either downhill or cross-country skiing. There are daytime and evening classes.

Sleigh Rides: During the winter it is possible to ride an old-fashioned sleigh through Oslomarka, the wooded area surrounding the city. **Vangen Skistue** (Laila and Jon Hamre, Fjell, 1404 Siggerud, ☎ 64/86–54–81) can arrange this for you. In the summertime, they switch from sleighs to horses and buggies.

Street Train: Starting at noon and continuing at 45-minute intervals until 10 PM, the **Oslo Train** (☎ 22/42−23−64), which looks like a chain of dune buggies, leaves Aker Brygge for a 30-minute ride around the center of town. The train runs daily June 23−September 15.

Important Addresses and Numbers

BOOKSTORES
The best selection of English books can be found at **Tanum Libris** (Karl Johans Gt. 37−41, ☎ 22/41−11−00) and at **Erik Qvist** (Drammensvn. 16, ☎ 22/44−03−26 or 22/44−52−69).

DENTISTS
Oslo Kommunale Tannlegevakt (Kolstadgt. 18, ☎ 22/67−30−00) is at Tøyen Senter. **Oslo Private Tannlegevakt** (Hansteens Gt. 3, ☎ 22/44−46−36) is a private clinic.

DOCTORS
Volvat Medisinske Senter (Borgenvn. 2A, ☎ 22/95−75−00) is Norway's largest private clinic, located near the Borgen underground station. **Oslo Akutten** (N. Vollgt. 8, ☎ 22/41−24−40) is an emergency clinic downtown, near Stortinget.

EMBASSIES
U.S. Embassy, Drammensvn. 18, ☎ 22/44−85−50. **Canadian Embassy,** Oscars Gt. 20, ☎ 22/46−69−55. **U.K. Embassy,** Thomas Heftyes Gt. 8, ☎ 22/55−24−00.

EMERGENCIES
Police: ☎ 112 or 22/66−90−50. **Fire:** ☎ 111 or 22/66−90−50. **Ambulance:** ☎ 113 or 22/11−70−70. **Car Rescue:** ☎ 22/23−20−85.

Oslo Legevakt (Storgt. 40, ☎ 22/11−70−70), the city's public and thus less expensive hospital, is near the Oslo S Station and is open 24 hours.

TRAVEL AGENCIES
American Express/Winge Reisebureau (Karl Johans Gt. 33/35, ☎ 22/41−20−30); **Bennett Reisebureau** (Pilestredet 35, ☎ 22/94−36−00); **Berg-Hansen** (agent for Thomas Cook, Arbiensgt. 3, ☎ 22/55−19−01); and **Kilroy Travels Norway** (Universitetssenteret, Blindern, ☎ 22/85−32−00), for student travel.

24-HOUR PHARMACY
Jernbanetorgets Apotek (Jernbanetorget 4B, ☎ 22/41−24−82), across from Oslo S Station, is open 24 hours.

VISITOR INFORMATION
The main tourist office (**Norway Information Center,** ☎ 22/83−00−50), located in the old Vestbanen railway station, is open weekdays 9−6 (9−8 in summer); weekends 9−4. The office at the main railway station, **Sentralstasjonen** (Jernbanetorget, ☎ 22/17−11−24) is open daily 8 AM−11 PM. Look for the big round blue-and-green signs marked with a white **i.** Information about the rest of the country can be obtained from **NORTRA** (Nortravel Marketing, Postboks 499, Sentrum, 0150 Oslo, ☎ 22/92−52−00, FAX 22/56−05−05).

WHERE TO CHANGE MONEY
After normal banking hours money can be changed at the following places: The bank at **Oslo S Station** is open June−Sept., daily 8 AM−11 PM; otherwise, weekdays 8 AM−8:30 PM, Saturday 8−2. The bank at **Oslo Fornebu Airport** is open weekdays 6:30 AM−9 PM, Saturday 7−5, Sunday 7 AM−8 PM. All post offices exchange money. **Oslo Central Post Office** (Dronningensgt. 15) is open weekdays 8−8, Saturday 9−3.

EXCURSIONS FROM OSLO

Halden and Fredrikstad

Numbers in the margin correspond to points of interest on the Oslo Excursions map in the Short Excursions from Oslo section (see above).

Exploring Halden and Fredrikstad

❹ **Halden** is practically at the Swedish border, a good enough reason to fortify the town. **Fredriksten Festning** (Fredriksten Fort, ☎ 69/17–50–50), built on a French star-shaped plan in the late 17th century, is perched on the city's highest point. Norwegians and Swedes had ongoing border disputes, and the most famous skirmish at Fredriksten resulted in the death of King Karl XII in 1718. Few people realize that slavery existed in Scandinavia, but until 1845 there were up to 200 slaves at Fredriksten, mostly workers incarcerated and sentenced to a lifetime of hard labor for trivial offenses. Inside the fort itself is **Fredriksten Kro,** a good, old-fashioned inn with outdoor seating. ☎ 69/17–52–32. ☛ *NKr25 adults, NKr10 children.* ⊙ *Mid-May–mid-Sept. Mon.–Sat. 10–5, Sun. 10–6.*

❺ North of Halden is **Fredrikstad,** at the mouth of the Glomma, Norway's longest river. The country's oldest fortified city, it has bastions and a moat that date from the 1600s. The Old Town has been preserved and has museums, art galleries, cafés, artisans' workshops, antiques shops, and old bookstores, as well as the **Fredrikstad Museum,** which documents town history. ☎ 69/39–43–82. ☛ *NKr20.* ⊙ *May–Sept. weekdays 11–5, Sun., noon–5.*

Just east is **Kongsten Festning** (Kongsten Fort), which mounted 200 cannons and could muster 2,000 men at the peak of its glory. ☎ 69/32–05–32. ☛ *Free.* ⊙ *May–Sept., 24 hours.*

A 5-kilometer (3-mile) ride outside **Moss,** at **Jeløy,** is **Galleri F15,** an art center set in an old farm. ☎ 69/27–10–33. ☛ *NKr20.* ⊙ *Jun.–Sept., Tues.–Sun. 11–7; Oct.–May, Tues.–Sat. 11–5, Sun. 11–7.*

For price-category definitions, *see* Lodging *in* Norway Essentials, *below.*

Dining and Lodging

$$$ **Refsnes Gods.** The main building dates from 1770, when it was a fam-
★ ily estate, but it did not become a hotel until 1938. In the back is a long, tree-lined promenade extending to the shores of the Oslo Fjord. The recently renovated rooms are airy and pretty; they are painted in blue and beige and have light-wood furnishings. Refsnes has one of Norway's best kitchens and a wine cellar with some of the oldest bottles of Madeira in the country. Chef Oddmund Haarsaker utilizes the fjords' resources and adds a French touch to traditional Norwegian seafood. ✉ *Box 236, 1502 Moss,* ☎ *69/27–04–11,* FAX *69/27–25–42. 60 rooms. Restaurant, pool, sauna, beach, boating, meeting rooms. AE, DC, MC, V.*

Drammen, Tønsberg, and Sandefjord

The towns lining the western side of the Oslo Fjord are some of Norway's oldest and wealthiest, their fortunes derived from whaling and lumbering. Although these activities no longer dominate, their influence remains in the monuments and in the wood architecture. This is summer-vacation country for many Norwegians, who retreat to cabins on the water during July.

Numbers in the margin correspond to points of interest on the Oslo Excursions map in the Short Excursions from Oslo section (see above).

Exploring Drammen, Tønsberg, and Sandefjord

❻ **Drammen,** an industrial city of 50,000 situated on the Simoa River at its outlet to a fjord, was a timber town and port for 500 years; it was the main harbor for silver exported from the Kongsberg mines. Today cars are imported into Norway through Drammen. The city's main attraction, the **Spiralen** (Spiral), is a corkscrew road tunnel that makes six complete turns before emerging about 600 feet above, on Skansen Ridge. It's open year-round and is free. The entrance is behind the hospital by way of a well-marked road.

Drammens Museum, on the grounds of Marienlyst Manor (which dates from 1750), is across the river. Its new addition looks like a small temple set in the manor garden. This county museum includes displays of glass from the Nøstetangen factory, which was in operation between 1741 and 1777, and a collection of rustic painted pieces. *Konnerudgt. 7,* ☎ *32/83–89–48.* ☞ *NKr30 adults, NKr20 senior citizens and students, NKr10 children.* ☉ *May–Oct., Tues. 11–7, Wed.–Sat. 11–3, Sun. 11–5; Nov.–Apr., Tues.–Sat, 11–5, Sun. 11–3.*

❼ Off the main route south, toward the coast, is **Horten,** which has some distinctive museums. The town was once an important naval station and still retains the officers' candidates school. **Marinemuseet** (the Royal Norwegian Navy Museum), built in 1853 as a munitions warehouse, displays relics from the nation's naval history. Outside is the world's first torpedo boat, from 1872, plus some one-person submarines from World War II. Mistletoe thrives in the trees, but don't pick it: It's protected by law. *Karl Johans Vern,* ☎ *33/04–20–81, ext. 452.* ☞ *Free.* ☉ *May–Oct., weekdays 10–4, weekends noon–4; Oct.– May, weekdays 10–4, Sun. noon–4.*

The **Redningsselskapets Museum** (Museum of the Sea Rescue Association) traces the history of ship-rescue operations. The organization has rescued more than 320,000 people since it was founded more than 100 years ago. *Strandpromenaden 8, Horten Tourist Office,* ☎ *33/04–33– 90.* ☞ *NKr10 adults, NKr5 children.* ☉ *Apr.–Sept., Fri.–Sun. 10–4.*

The **Preus Fotomuseum** houses one of the world's largest photographic collections. Exhibits include a turn-of-the-century photographer's studio and a tiny camera that was strapped to a pigeon for early aerial photography. *Langgt. 82,* ☎ *33/04–70–66.* ☞ *NKr15.* ☉ *Weekdays 10–2, Sun. noon–2.*

❽ Just beyond the town, between the road and the sea, is a Viking grave site, **Borrehaugene,** with five earth and two stone mounds. Continue past the 12th-century Borre church to **Åsgårdstrand,** which was an artists' colony for outdoor painting at the turn of the century. Edvard Munch painted *Girls on the Bridge* here and earned a reputation as a ladies' man. He spent seven summers at **Munchs lille hus** (little house), now a museum. *Munchsgt., no* ☎ ☞ *NKr10.* ☉ *May–Sept., weekends 1– 7; Jun.–Aug, daily 1–7.*

Continuing south, you'll pass the site where the Oseberg Viking ship, dating from around AD 800 and now on display at Vikingskiphuset in Oslo, was found at **Slagen,** on the road to Tønsberg, 105 kilometers (64 miles) from Oslo. Look for a mound where it was buried as you pass Slagen's church.

❾ According to the sagas, **Tønsberg** is Norway's oldest settlement, founded in 871. Little remains of its early structures, although the ruins at **Slotts-**

fjellet (Castle Hill), by the train station, include parts of the city wall, the remains of a church from around 1150, and a 13th-century brick citadel, the **Tønsberghus.** Other medieval remains are below the cathedral and near Storgata 17. Tønsberg's fortunes took a turn for the worse after the Reformation, and the city did not recover until shipping and whaling brought it into prominence in the 18th century.

The **Vestfold Fylkesmuseum** (county museum), north of the railroad station, houses a small Viking ship, several whale skeletons, and some inventions. There's an open-air section, too. *Farmannsvn. 30,* ☏ *33/ 31–29–19.* ☞ *NKr15 adults, NKr8 groups over 10, children free.* ☉ *Mid-May–mid-Sept., daily 10–5; mid-Sept.–mid-May, weekdays 10– 2; inquire at office for other opening hours.*

TIME OUT Take a break at **Seterkafe,** the museum's restaurant. Try *spekemat* (dried cured meats) served with sour cream and/or potato salad.

⑩ Continue 25 kilometers (16 miles) south of Tønsberg to **Sandefjord,** which, in 1900, was the whaling capital of the world and possibly Norway's wealthiest city. Now the whales are gone and all that remains of that trade is a monument to it. Thanks to shipping and other industries, however, the city is still rich.

Kommandør Christensens Hvalfangstmuseum (Commander Christensen's Whaling Museum) traces the development of the industry from small primitive boats to huge floating factories. An especially arresting display chronicles whaling in the Antarctic. *Museumsgt. 39,* ☏ *33/46–32–51.* ☞ *NKr20 adults, NKr10 children and senior citizens.* ☉ *May–Sept., daily 11–5; Oct.–Apr., Fri.–Sun. noon–4.*

Dining

$$–$$$ **Edgar Ludl's Gourmet.** It took an Austrian chef to show the Norwe-
★ gians that there's more in the sea than cod and salmon. Ludl is a champion of the local cuisine, and a "catch of the day" platter may include salmon, ocean catfish, stuffed sole, a fish roulade, and lobster. Ludl's desserts are equally good, especially the cloudberry marzipan basket. ✕ *Rådhusgt. 7, Sandefjord,* ☏ *33/46–27–41. Reservations advised. AE, DC, MC, V.*

$$ **Spiraltoppen Café.** At the top of Bragernes Hill, this café offers excellent views as well as good food. The specialties are Norwegian food in generous portions. Try the meatballs with stewed cabbage, a Norwegian specialty, or the open-face sandwiches. ✕ *Bragernesåsen, Drammen,* ☏ *32/83–78–15. No reservations. AE, DC, MC, V.*

Lodging

$$–$$$$ **Rica Park Hotel.** It *looks* formal for a hotel built right on the water in a resort town, but there's no dress code. The older rooms are nicer than the newer ones. The decor is 1960s style, but it doesn't seem passé. Summer rates make the Park more affordable. ⌑ *Strandpromenaden 9, 3200 Sandefjord,* ☏ *33/46–55–50,* ⊠ *33/46–79–00. 174 rooms with bath, 8 suites. 2 restaurants, bar, indoor pool, health club, dock, nightclub, convention center. AE, DC, MC, V.*

$$ **Rica Park.** This comfortable hotel in the center of Drammen has well-equipped rooms and two good restaurants, a bar, and a nightclub. As with all Rica hotels, the atmosphere is comfortable and button-down. *Gamle Kirkepl. 3, 3012 Drammen,* ☏ *32/83–82–80,* ⊠ *32/89–32– 07. 103 rooms with bath or shower. 2 restaurants, 2 bars, nightclub. AE, DC, MC, V.*

$–$$$ **Atlantic Home.** The Atlantic Home was built in 1914, when Sandefjord was a whaling center. The history of whaling is traced in exhibits in glass cases and in pictures throughout the hotel. There's no restaurant, but the hotel provides *aftens*, a supper consisting of bread and cold cuts plus hot soup and light beer, as part of the room rate. A coffeemaker and waffle iron are at your disposal at all times. *Jernbanealleen 33, 3200 Sandefjord,* ☎ *33/46–80–00,* FAX *33/46–80–20. 72 rooms with bath. Lobby lounge, sauna. AE, DC, MC, V.*

Oslo Excursions Essentials

Halden and Fredrikstad

ARRIVING AND DEPARTING

By Car: Follow Route E18 southeastward from Oslo and turn south at Mysen to reach Halden. Route E6 takes you north to Sarpsborg, where you can turn left to Fredrikstad.

By Train: Trains for Halden leave from Oslo S Station and take two hours to make the 136-kilometer (85-mile) trip, with stops in Moss, Fredrikstad, and Sarpsborg.

VISITOR INFORMATION

Fredrikstad: Fredrikstad Turistkontor (Turistsentret v/Østre Brohode, 1632 Gamle Fredrikstad, ☎ 69/32–03–30). **Halden:** Halden Reiselivskontor (Box 167, 1751 Halden, ☎ 69/17–48–40). **Moss:** Moss Turistkontor (Fleischersgt. 17, 1531 Moss, ☎ 69/25–32–95).

Drammen, Tønsberg, and Sandefjord

ARRIVING AND DEPARTING

By Boat: The most luxurious and scenic way to see the region is by boat: There are guest marinas at just about every port.

By Bus: Because train service to these towns is infrequent, bus travel is the best alternative to cars. Check with Nor-Way Bussekspress (☎ 22/33–08–62) for schedules.

By Car: Route E18 south from Oslo follows the coast to the towns of this region. Sandefjord is 125 kilometers (78 miles) south of Oslo.

By Train: Drammen is about 40 kilometers (25 miles) from Oslo. Take a suburban train from Nationaltheatret or trains from Oslo S Station to reach Horten, Tønsberg, and Sandefjord.

VISITOR INFORMATION

Drammen: Drammen Kommunale Turistinformasjonskontor (Rådhuset, 3017 Drammen, ☎ 32/80–62–10). **Sandefjord:** Sandefjord Reiselivsforening (Torvet, 3200, ☎ 33/46–05–90). **Tønsberg:** Tønsberg og Omland Reiselivslag (Nedre Langgt. 36 B, 3110, ☎ 33/31–02–20).

3 Sørlandet

THE COAST BORDERING THE SKAGERAK, the arm of the North Sea separating Norway and Denmark, is lined with small communities stretching from Oslo as far as Lindesnes, which is at the southernmost tip. Sørlandet (Southland) towns are often called "pearls on a string," and in the dusk of a summer evening, reflections of the white-painted houses on the water have a silvery translucence.

This is a land of wide beaches toasted by the greatest number of sunny days in Norway, waters warmed by the Gulf Stream, and long, fertile tracts of flatland. Not a people to pass up a minute of sunshine, the Norwegians have sprinkled the south with their hytter and made it their number-one domestic holiday spot. Nonetheless, even at the height of summer, you can sail to a quiet skerry or take a solitary walk through the forest.

The two chief cities of Norway's south, Kristiansand on the east coast and Stavanger on the west coast, differ sharply. Kristiansand is a resort town, scenic and relaxed, while Stavanger, once a fishing center, is now the hub of the oil industry and Norway's most cosmopolitan city. Between the two is the coastal plain of Jæren, dotted with prehistoric burial sites and the setting for the works of some of the country's foremost painters.

EXPLORING

Numbers in the margin correspond to points of interest on the Sørlandet map.

Tour 1: The Coast

❶ Larvik is the last of the big whaling towns, 19 kilometers (12 miles) south of Sandefjord. It's still a port, but now the traffic is made up of passengers to Fredrikshavn, Denmark. Near the ferry quays is **Kong Olavs Kilde** (King Olav's Spring), also called Farris Kilde (Farris Spring), Norway's only natural source of mineral water. A spa was built here in 1880, but people now drink the water rather than bathe in it. *Fjellvn., ☎ 33/18–20–00. Guided tours June 20–Aug. 5.*

Larvik is the site of **Herregården,** a large estate once owned by the noble Gyldenløve family. The main building was finished in 1677. Inside, the furnishings are masterful examples of trompe l'oeil: Scandinavian nobility had to make do with furniture painted to look like marble or carving rather than the real thing. *Herregaardssletta 1, ☎ 33/13–04–04. ☛ NKr20 adults, NKr10 children. ☉ June 20–Aug. 20, daily noon–5; May 21–Sept. 3, Sun. noon–5; Apr.–Oct., open on request. Call to confirm times.*

The **Maritime Museum** is located in the former customs house and chronicles Larvik's seafaring history. There's heavy coverage of Thor Heyerdahl's voyages, with models of *Kon-Tiki* and *Ra II.* ☛ *Charges and opening times vary; check with the tourist office.*

From Larvik, it's only 8 kilometers (5 miles) along the coast to **Stavern,** a popular sailing center. On the water east of town is **Fredriksvern,** which was Norway's main naval station between 1750 and 1850, named for King Fredrik V. The church is a fine example of Scandinavian Rococo. Its pews were designed so their backs could be folded down to make beds in case the church had to be used as a field hos-

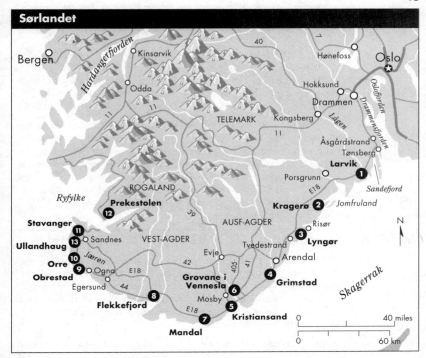

pital in time of war. *Stavern Church,* ☏ *33/19–99–75. Guided tours by appointment.*

② Farther down the coast about 62 kilometers (45 miles) comes **Kragerø,** a picturesque town with its own small archipelago. **Theodor Kittelsen** (1857–1914), famous for his drawings of trolls and illustrations of Norwegian fairy tales, lived in Kragerø, and his birthplace is now a museum. *Th. Kittelsens vei. 5,* ☏ *35/98–23–88.* ☞ *NKr20 adults, NKr10 children.* ☉ *Mid-June–mid-Aug., weekdays 11–3.*

The next pearl on the southern string is **Risør,** east from E18 on the coast. On the first weekend in August the town holds a festival that fills the harbor with beautiful antique boats.

③ **Lyngør,** on four tiny rocky islands off the coast, was recently chosen Europe's best-preserved village by an association of European travel professionals. In winter the population is 110, but every summer thousands descend upon it. Hardly changed since the days of sailing ships, it's idyllic and carless, lined with rows of white-painted houses bearing window boxes filled with pink and red flowers. You'll find white houses all along the southern coast, a tradition that began about 100 years ago, when Dutch sailors traded white paint for wood. Until that time, only red paint was available in Norway. To get to Lyngør follow E18 to the sign for Sørlandsporten (Gateway to the South). Turn off just after the sign and drive 26 kilometers (16 miles) to Lyngørfjorden Marina, where you can take a five-minute watertaxi ride (☏ 37/16–68–00, Cost: 80 NKr) to the island. The only hotel books most of its rooms by the year to large firms, so don't count on staying overnight.

TIME OUT In a historic late-19th-century white house with blue trim, **Den Blå Lanterne** (☏ 37/16–64–80, open May–Sept., reservations advised), is

Lyngør's only restaurant. Although it's pricey, you can eat as much of the famous fish soup as you like, and there's often live music.

Arendal, a little farther south, has more tidy white houses. On the island of **Merdøy,** a 30-minute boat ride from Arendal's Langbrygga (wharf), is an early 18th-century sea captain's home, now a museum, **Merdøgaard.** ☎ 37/08–52–43. ☛ NKr10 adults, NKr5 children. ⊙ Late June–mid-Aug., daily 11–5. Guided tours on the hour until 4.

❹   To the south is **Grimstad.** Its glory was also in the days of sailing ships—about the same time the 15-year-old Henrik Ibsen worked as an apprentice at the local apothecary shop. Grimstad Apotek is now a part of the **Ibsenhuset** (Ibsen House) and has been preserved with its 1837 interior intact. Ibsen wrote his first play, Catlina, here. Henrik Ibsensgt. 14, ☎ 37/04–46–53. ☛ NKr20 adults, NKr10 children and senior citizens. ⊙ Mid-Apr–mid-Sept., Mon.–Sat. 9–5, Sun. 1–5. Groups by appointment.

Tour 2: Kristiansand

❺   **Kristiansand,** with 67,000 inhabitants, is one of Sørlandet's leading cities and the domestic summer-vacation capital of Norway. According to legend, King Christian IV in 1641 marked the four corners of the city with his walking stick, and within that framework the grid of wide streets was drawn. The center of the city, called the **Kvadrat,** still retains the grid, even after numerous fires.

Start at the **Fisketorvet** (fish market) at the southern corner of the grid, right on the sea. Follow the Strandpromenaden (Beach Walk), past contemporary Norwegian artist Kjell Nupen's interpretation of Kristiansand's roots more than 350 years ago to **Christiansholm Festning** (fortress), on a promontory opposite Festningsgata. Completed in 1672, the circular building with 15-foot-thick walls has played more a decorative than a defensive role; it was used once, in 1807, to defend the city against British invasion. Now it contains art exhibits.

Six blocks inland is the Gothic Revival **Cathedral** from 1885. The third-largest church in Norway, it often hosts summertime concerts in addition to an annual week-long International Church Music Festival in mid-May (☎ 38/02–13–11 for information) that includes organ, chamber, and gospel music. Kirkegt., ☎ 38/02–11–88. ☛ Free. ⊙ June–Aug., daily 9–2.

Next, head north across the Otra River on Bus 22 or drive to Route E18 and cross the bridge over the Otra to Parkveien. Turn left onto Ryttergangen and drive to Gimleveien, where you'll turn right to **Gimle Gård** (Gimle Manor). Built by a wealthy merchant/shipowner around 1800 in the Empire style, it displays period furnishings, paintings, silver, and decoration, including hand-blocked wallpaper. Gimlevn. 23, ☎ 38/09–02–28. ☛ NKr20 adults, NKr10 children. ⊙ July–mid-Aug., Tues.–Sun. noon–4; May–June and mid-Aug.–Nov., Sun. noon–5.

Eastward on Route E18 is **Oddernes Church,** one of the oldest churches in Norway and dedicated to St. Olav. The runestone in the cemetery tells that Øyvind, godson of St. Olav, built this church in 1040 on property he inherited from his father. The altar and the pulpit are both in the Baroque style, and richly gilded. Oddernesvn., ☎ 38/09–01–87. ☛ Free. ⊙ May–Aug., Sun.–Fri. 9–2.

Continue to **Vest-Agder Fylkesmuseum** (County Museum), 4 kilometers (3 miles) east of Kristiansand on Route E18. Here you can visit two *tun*—farm buildings traditionally set in clusters around a common area, which suited the extended families. There are dwellings and workshops on a reconstructed city street. *Kongsgård,* ☎ *38/09–02–28.* ☛ *NKr20 adults, NKr10 children.* ۞ *Mid–June–mid-Aug., Mon.–Sat. 10–6; May 21–mid-Sept., Sun. noon–6; mid-Sept.–mid-May, Sun. noon–5; or by appointment.*

Once you've had your fill of museums, head back across the river and northwest of town to **Ravnedalen** (Raven Valley), a lush park, filled in spring with flowers. It's a favorite with hikers and strolling nannies. Wear comfortable shoes and you can hike the narrow, winding paths up the hills and climb 200 steps up to a 304-foot lookout.

East of town 11 kilometers (6 miles) is one of Norway's most popular attractions. **Kristiansand Dyrepark** is five separate parks, including a water park (bring bathing suits and towels), a forested park, an entertainment park, and a zoo, which contains an enclosure for Scandinavian wolves and Europe's (possibly the world's) largest breeding ground for Bactrian camels. Finally, the park contains **Kardemomme By** (Cardamom Town), named for a book by Norwegian illustrator and writer Thorbjørn Egner. His story comes alive here in a precisely replicated village, with actors playing townsfolk, shopkeepers, pirates, and a delightful trio of robbers. Families who are hooked can even stay overnight in one of the village's cozy apartments or nearby cottages (reserve at least a year in advance). *Kristiansand Dyrepark, 4609 Kardemomme by,* ☎ *38/04–97–00.* ☛ *NKr150 adults, NKr130 children; includes admission to all parks and rides.* ۞ *Jan.–mid-June, daily 10–3; mid-June–mid-Aug., daily 9–6; mid-Aug.–Dec., daily 10–3.*

Excursions from Kristiansand

❻ The **Setesdalsbanen** (Setesdal Railway) at **Grovane i Vennesla,** 20 kilometers (13 miles) north of Kristiansand, is a 4.7-kilometer-long (3-mile-long) stretch of narrow-gauge track on which a steam locomotive from 1894 and carriages from the early 1900s run. Follow Route 39 to Mosby, veer right onto 405, and continue to Grovane. *Vennesla Stasjon,* ☎ *38/15–55–08. Fare: NKr50 adults, NKr25 children (50% discount with Summerpass).* ۞ *Mid-June–Aug., daily at 1:30, Sun. at 11:30, 1:30, 3. Call for other times.*

Many rockhounds head for **Evje,** about 60 kilometers (36 miles) north of Kristiansand, to look for semiprecious stones. At **Evje Mineralsti,** you can hunt for blue-green amazonite. ☎ *37/93–14–00.* ☛ *NKr35, NKr70 family.* ۞ *Daily 10–5:30, mid-May–mid-Sept. At other times, visitors pay by honor system.*

You can also visit **Fennefoss Museum** just south of Evje in Hornnes and look at the mineral collection. ☎ *37/93–10–56.* ☛ *NKr15 adults, NKr5 children.* ۞ *Mid-June–mid-Aug., daily 10–4.*

Tour 3: The South

❼ From Kristiansand you can go 42 kilometers (28 miles) southwest to **Mandal,** Norway's most southerly town, famous for its historic core of well-preserved wooden houses and its beautiful long beach, Sjøsanden. **Mandal Kirke,** built in 1821, is Norway's largest Empire-style wooden church. ☎ *38/26–54–84.* ۞ *Daily 11–2.*

Lindesnes Fyr (☎ *38/25–88–51*), Norway's oldest lighthouse, was built on the southernmost point of the country. The old coal-fired light dates from 1822. For the next 40 kilometers (27 miles) or so west, the road climbs and weaves its way through steep, wooded valleys and then

⑧ descends to the fishing port of **Flekkefjord,** known for its **Hollender-byen,** a historic district with small, white-painted houses lining narrow, winding streets. Route E18 heads inland here to Stavanger, but it is more rewarding to follow the coast road (Route 44) past the fishing port of **Egersund,** 40 kilometers (25 miles) ahead, and a little farther to **Ogna,** known for the stretch of sandy beach that inspired so many Norwegian artists, among them Kitty Kjelland. (Here, Route 44 also connects with Route E18 by way of Route 504). Whichever road you choose, they both continue northward along the rich agricultural coastal plain of **Jæren.** Flat and stony, it is the largest expanse of level terrain in this mountainous country. The mild climate and the absence of good harbors mean that the population here turned to agriculture, and the miles of stone walls are a testament to their labor. Ancient monuments are still visible here, notably the **Hå gravesite** below the Hå

⑨ parsonage near the **Obrestad** light on coastal Route 44. It consists of about 60 mounds, including two star-shaped and one boat-shaped, dating from around AD 500, all marked with stones. **Hå Gamle Preste-gaard,** (Old Parsonage) built in the 1780s, is now a cultural center. ☛ *NKr20 adults, children free.* ⊙ *May–mid-Sept., weekdays 11–7, Sat. noon–5, Sun. noon–7; mid-Sept.–May, Sat. noon–5, Sun. noon–7.*

⑩ Continue northward on Route 507 to **Orre,** site of a medieval stone church. Near Orre pond, slightly inland, is a bird-watching station.

Tour 4: Stavanger

⑪ **Stavanger** has always prospered from the riches of the sea. During the 19th century, huge harvests of brisling and herring established it as the sardine capital of the world. A resident is still called a Siddis, from S(ta-vanger) plus *iddis,* which means "sardine label," and the city's symbol, fittingly enough, is the key of a sardine can.

During the past two and a half decades, a different product from the sea has been Stavanger's lifeblood—oil. Since its discovery in the late 1960s, North Sea oil has transformed both the economy and the lifestyle of the city. In the early days of drilling, expertise was imported from abroad, chiefly from the United States. Although Norwegians have now taken over most of the projects, foreigners constitute almost a tenth of the inhabitants, making Stavanger the country's most international city. Though the population hovers around 100,000, the city has all the agreeable bustle of one many times its size.

In the center, next to a small pond called Breiavatnet, is **Stavanger Domkirke** (Cathedral), a large, well-preserved medieval church. Construction was begun in 1125 by Bishop Reinald of Winchester, probably assisted by English craftsmen. Largely destroyed by fire in 1272, it was rebuilt to include a Gothic chancel, the result of which is that its once elegant lines are now festooned with macabre death symbols and airborne putti. The cathedral often hosts organ recitals, with coffee served afterward in the crypt. ☛ *Free.* ⊙ *Mid-May–mid-Sept., daily 9–6; mid-Sept.–mid-May, Mon.–Sat. 9–2, Sun. 1–8.*

Next to the cathedral is the **Kongsgård,** former residence of bishops and kings, but now a school and not open to visitors. On the other side of the pond, up the steep hill behind the Atlantic Hotel, is Eiganesveien, an old patrician residential district. As the road angles to the left, it's only one long block to **Breidablikk** manor house, built by a Norwegian shipping magnate. An outstanding example of what the Norwegians call "Swiss style" architecture, it has been perfectly preserved since the '60s and feels as if the owner has only momentarily slipped away. In spite of its foreign label, the house is uniquely Norwegian, inspired by national romanticism. *Eiganesvn. 40A, ☎ 51/52–60–35. ☛ NKr20 adults, children free. ☉ Mid-June–mid-Aug., daily 11–4; mid-Aug.–mid-June, Sun. 11–4.*

Across the road and through the park is **Ledaal,** a stately house built by the Kielland family in 1799 but now the residence of the royal family when they visit Stavanger. The second-floor library is dedicated to the writer Alexander Kielland, a social critic and satirist. *Eiganesvn. 45, ☎ 51/52–06–18. ☛ NKr20 adults, children free. ☉ Mid-June–mid-Aug., daily 11–4; mid-Aug.–mid-June, Sun. 11–4.*

Exit toward Alexander Kiellands Gate, turn right, and walk to the end of the stadium complex, turn left, and right again on Stokkaveien until you reach Øvre Strandgate. Along with Nedre Strandgate, this is the heart of old Stavanger, where you can wind down narrow cobblestone streets past small, white houses with many-paned windows and terra-cotta roof tiles.

Tucked between the neighborhood and the harbor is the fascinating, albeit obscure, **Norsk Hermetikkmuseum** (Canning Museum), housed in a former canning factory. Exhibits document the processing of brisling and sardines—the city's most important industry for nearly 100 years, thanks greatly to savvy turn-of-the-century packaging (naturally, the inventor of the sardine-can key was from Stavanger). Tuesdays and Thursdays from mid-June to mid-August, and the first Sunday of the month year-round, the museum holds canning and smoking demonstrations in which visitors are encouraged to participate. Taste tests are free; canned King Oscar sardine purchases in the tiny gift store are voluntary but a must for fish lovers. *Øvre Strandgt. 88A, ☎ 51/53–49–89. ☛ NKr20 adults, children free. ☉ Mid-June–mid-Aug., daily 11–4; early June and late Aug., Tues.–Fri. 11–3, Sun. 11–4; Sept.–May, Sun. 11–4.*

Walk along Strandkaien to the **Sjøfartsmuseet** (Maritime Museum), in the only two shipping merchants' houses that remain completely intact. The warehouses face the wharf, while the shops, offices, and apartments face the street on the other side. Inside, the house is just as it was a century ago, complete with office furniture, files, and posters, while the apartments show the standard of living for the mercantile class at that time. Although signs are only in Norwegian, an English-language guidebook and guided tours outside normal opening hours are available. *Nedre Strandgt. 17–19, ☎ 51/52–59–11. ☛ NKr20 adults, children free. ☉ Mid-June–mid-Aug., daily 11–4; early June and late Aug., Tues.–Fri. 11–3, Sun. 11–4; Sept.–May, Sun. 11–4.*

From all along the quay you can see **Valbergtårnet** (Valberget 4, ☎ 51/89–55–01), built on the highest point of the old city. Once a fire watchtower, it is now a crafts center.

If you are of Norwegian stock you can trace your roots at **Det Norske Utvandrersenteret** (Norwegian Emigrant Center). Bring along any information you have, especially where your ancestors came from in Norway and when they arrived in the United Kingdom, North America, or elsewhere. The center is located on the fourth floor of Tinghuset (the courthouse), a dull, brooding minimalist building close to the harbor. You can make arrangements via fax to have the center do research for you, but the wait for this service is long. *Bergjelandsgt. 30, 4012 Stavanger, ☎ 51/89–56–44, FAX 51/50–12–90. ☛ Free, but each written request costs NKr 180. ☉ Weekdays 9–3, Sat. 9–1.*

By Mosvannet, a lake just off the E18 highway at the northern end of downtown, is **Rogaland Kunstmuseum.** The museum, which opened in 1992, exhibits Norwegian art from the early 19th century to the present. It houses the country's largest collection of works by Lars Hertervig, a Romantic painter who is often considered the country's greatest after Edvard Munch. *Tjensvoll 6, Mosvannsparken,* ☎ *51/53–09–00.* ☛ *NKr30 adults, NKr15 students, children free.* ☉ *Tues.–Thurs. 10–2 and 6–9, Fri. 10–2, Sat. 11–3, Sun. 11–5.*

Excursions from Stavanger

Not a good choice if you suffer from vertigo, but great for a heart-stopping view is **Prekestolen** (Pulpit Rock), a huge cube of rock with a vertical drop of 2,000 feet. You can join a tour to get there (*see* Guided Tours, *below*) or you can do it on your own from June 16 to August 25 by taking the ferry from Fiskepiren across Hildefjorden to Tau. During these summer months a bus runs regularly from the ferry to the parking lot at the Pulpit Rock Lodge. It takes 1½ to two hours to walk from the lodge to the rock—the well-marked trail crosses some uneven terrain, so good walking shoes or boots are vital. Food and lodging are near the trail. The rock can also be reached by sightseeing boat.

Take your imagination farther back in time at **Ullandhaug,** a reconstruction of an Iron Age farm 5 kilometers (3 miles) west of Stavanger. Three houses have been built around a central garden, and guides wearing period clothing demonstrate the daily activities of 1,500 years ago, spinning thread on a spindle, weaving, and cooking over an open hearth. *Grannesvn., Ullandhaug,* ☎ *51/53–41–40.* ☛ *NKr20 adults, NKr10 children.* ☉ *Mid-June–Aug., daily noon–5; early May–mid-Sept., Sun. noon–4.*

You can see the place where what we know as Norway was founded by traveling 1 mile east on Grannesveien to the Harfsfjord. In 872, in the Battle of Harfsfjord, Harald Hårfagre (Harald the Fair-Haired), the warrior king from the eastern country of Vestfold, finally succeeded in quelling the resistance of local chieftains in Rogaland and was promptly declared king of all Norway. A memorial in the shape of three giant swords plunged halfway into the earth marks the spot.

About a half-hour drive to the north on coastal highway 1, through the world's second-longest undersea car tunnel, lies Mosterøy, and **Utstein Kloster.** Utstein Monastery was originally the palace of Norway's first king, Harald Hårfagre, and later the residence of King Magnus VI. It was used as a monastery from 1265 to 1537, when it reverted to the royal family. One of the best-preserved medieval monuments in Norway, the monastery opened to the public in 1965 and is today used to host classical and jazz concerts on Sunday afternoons during the summer. After the concert, try the *Får i kål* (mutton, potatoes, and cabbage boiled in a peppery juice, a Norwegian staple) at **Utstein Kloster Vertshus,** approximately 1 mile from the monastery along the water's edge. There is a toll of NKr75, plus NKr25 per passenger for the tunnel passage (free with the Stavanger Card). Buses depart from Stavanger at 12:15, returning from the monastery at 4:05, Monday through Friday. A special concert bus departs from Skagenkaien 1½ hours before each concert. *Mosterøy,* ☎ *51/51–47–05.* ☛ *NKr20 adults, NKr10 children ages 7–16, children age 6 and below free.* ☉ *May–mid-Sept., Tues.–Sat. 1–4, Sun. noon–5.*

What to See and Do with Children

Kristiansand
Kardemomme By (Cardamom Town) and **Dyrehaven** (*see* Tour 2, *above*) are the big draws in Kristiansand.

Stavanger
At the **Canning Museum** (*see* Tour 4, *above*), children can collect sardine-can labels and play marbles. **Kongeparken Amusement Park** has an 85-meter (281-foot) -long figure of Gulliver and a lifelike dinosaur exhibit as its main attractions, and plenty of rides. *4330 Ålgård,* ☎ *51/61–71–11.* ☞ *NKr110 adults, NKr90 children; rides and activities, NKr5–20.* ☉ *July, daily 11–5. Other spring and summer hours vary. Call the park for specific times.*

In **Sandnes,** 25 kilometers (16 miles) south of Stavanger, is **Havana Badeland,** Norway's largest indoor aquapark, complete with a 300-foot water slide, several whirlpool baths both for adults and children, saunas, a Turkish steambath, and massage parlors and solariums. *Hanaveien 17, 4300 Sandnes,* ☎ *51/62–92–00.* ☞ *NKr90 adults, NKr55 children.* ☉ *Mon.–Wed. 1–8, Thurs. 1–10, weekends 10–8.*

SHOPPING

Porsgrunn
Outside Porsgrunn, 27 kilometers (17 miles) west of Larvik, is **Porsgrunn Porselænfabrik** (porcelain factory; Porselensgt. 12, ☎ 35/55–00–40), where you can visit the seconds shop and take a factory tour Monday through Friday at 10, 11, or 1. There are no tours in July. The cost is NKr10 for adults, and children are free.

Stavanger
Outside of town are a ceramics factory and an outlet store: **Figgjo Ceramics** (Rte. E18, 4333 Figgjo, ☎ 51/67–00–00; 51/67–00–03 after 3:30) was started during World War II, when Norway was occupied by German forces. A museum traces the history of the factory; the seconds shop has discounts of about 50%. **Skjæveland Strikkevarefabrikk** (4330 Ålgård, ☎ 51/61–85–06) has a huge selection of men's and women's sweaters in both Norwegian patterns and other designs for about NKr200 less than prices found in the shops.

SPORTS AND OUTDOOR ACTIVITIES

Southern Norway is an outdoor paradise, with a mild summer climate and terrain varying from coastal flatland to inland mountains and forests. There's plenty of fish in the rivers and lakes, as well as along the coast. The region is particularly well suited to canoeing, kayaking, rafting, and hiking. Beavers, deer, foxes, and forest birds inhabit the area, so bring binoculars if you like to see them more closely.

Bicycling
Kristiansand has 70 kilometers (43 miles) of bike trails around the city. The tourist office can recommend routes and rentals.

From **Stavanger** you can take your bike onto the ferry that departs for Finnøy, one of the larger islands of the Ryfylke Archipelago. Spend the day or longer: Week-long cottage rentals are available from **Finnøy Fjordsenter** (4160, Judaberg, ☎ 51/71–26–46, FAX 51/54–17–62). For more information about cottages in the archipelago and maps, contact the Stavanger Tourist Board. The Ministry of the Environment can also provide information; call their **Bike Project** (Sandnes Turistinformasjon, Langgt. 8, 4300 Sandnes, ☎ 51/62–52–40).

Bird-Watching

The **Jærstrendene** in Jæren, from Randabergvika in the north to Ogna in the south, is a protected national park—and a good area for spotting puffins, cormorants, and black guillemots, as well as such waders as dunlins, little stints, and ringed plovers. Some areas of the park are closed to visitors, and it is forbidden to pick flowers, or for that matter, to disturb anything.

Fishing

Both Sørlandet, around Kristiansand, and Rogaland, around the Stavanger area, are famed for their fishing waters. For details on fishing holidays, contact the regional tourist boards.

KRISTIANSAND

Just north of Kristiansand there is excellent trout, perch, and eel fishing at Lillesand's **Vestre Grimevann** lake. You can get a permit at any sports store or at the tourist office (☎ 37/27–33–77). South of Kristiansand, in Mandal, sea trout run from mid-May to mid-September. The daily fishing fee is NKr50. For details, contact the tourist office (☎ 38/26–08–20).

STAVANGER

Three of the 10 best fishing rivers in Norway, the **Ognaelva, Håelva,** and **Figgjo,** are located in Jæren, just south of Stavanger. Fishing licenses, which are sold in grocery stores and gas stations, are required at all of them.

The longest salmon river in western Norway, the **Suldalslågen,** is also nearby, made popular 100 years ago by a Scottish aristocrat who built a fishing lodge there. **Lindum** still has cabins and camping facilities, as well as a dining room. Contact the **Lakseslottet Lindum** (N–4240 Suldalsosen, ☎ 52/79–91–61). The main salmon season is July through September (*see* also Water Sports, Stavanger, *below*).

Golf

At Randesund, southeast of **Kristiansand,** is a nine-hole golf course. Contact **Kristiansand Golfklubb**'s secretary (☎ 38/04–35–85) for details. The **Stavanger Golfklubb** (☎ 51/55–54–31) offers a lush, 18-hole, international-championship course and equipment rental.

Hiking

KRISTIANSAND

In addition to the gardens and steep hills of **Ravnedalen** (*see* Tour 2, *above*), the **Baneheia Forest,** just a 15-minute walk north from the city center, is full of evergreens, small lakes, and paths that are ideal for a lazy walk or a challenging run.

STAVANGER

Stavanger Turistforening (Postboks 239, 4001 Stavanger, ☎ 51/52–75–66, FAX 51/53–20–44) can plan a hike through the area, particularly in the rolling **Setesdalsheiene** and the thousands of islands and skerries of the **Ryfylke Archipelago.** The tourist board oversees 33 cabins for members (you can join on the spot) for overnighting along the way. Also in the Ryfylke area is a hike up to the **Kjerag,** a sheet of granite mountain that soars 3,555 feet, at the Lysefjord, near Forsand—ideal for thrill seekers.

Hunting

Throughout the Kristiansand and Stavanger areas, hunting laws are similar to those in the rest of Norway. For larger game, including elk, you must literally purchase a Norwegian's right, thereby ensuring that there is no overhunting. Beavers in the Kristiansand area and hare around Stavanger are numerous but still require the purchase of a permit. For information, contact **Info Sør** (Info South, Brokelandsheia, 4993 Sundrebru, ☎ 37/15–85–60).

Skiing

Skiing in Sirdal, two-and-a-half hours from Stavanger, is good from January to April. Special ski buses leave Stavanger on the weekends at 8:30 AM during the season. Especially recommended is Sinnes for its stunning views and non-hair-raising cross-country terrain. Downhill skiing is also available at Alsheia on the same bus route. Contact **SOT Reiser** (Treskeveien 5, 4040 Hafrsfjord, Stavanger, ☎ 51/55–60–66) for transportation information and the Kristiansand tourist office for more details.

Water Sports

KRISTIANSAND

Kuholmen Marina (Roligheden Camping, ☎ 38/09–67–22) arranges rentals of boats, water skis, and water scooters. **Anker Dykkersenter** (Randesundsg. 2, Kuholmen, ☎ 38/09–79–09) rents scuba equipment, and **Fun Sport** (Dronningensgt. 59, ☎ 38/02–24–45) rents Windsurfers and holds classes. **Kristiansand Diving Club** (Myrbakken 3, ☎ 38/01–03–32 between 6 PM and 9 PM) has information on local diving.

Combining history and sailing, the magnificent full-rig, square-sail school ship **Sørlandet** (Gravene 2, 4610 Kristiansand, ☎ 38/02–98–90, FAX 38/02–93–34), built in 1927, takes on passengers ranging from senior citizens to college students and younger for two weeks, usually stopping for several days in a northern European port. Prices range from NKr7,000 for adults to NKr6,000 for students.

STAVANGER

Diving is excellent all along the coast—although Norwegian law requires all foreigners to dive with a Norwegian as a way of ensuring that wrecks are left undisturbed. Contact **Dive In** (Madlaveien 5, Stavanger, ☎ 51/52–99–00), which rents equipment and offers a weekend rate.

On the island of **Kvitsøy,** in the archipelago just west of Stavanger, you can rent an apartment, complete with fish-smoking and -freezing facilities, and arrange to use a small sail- or motorboat. Contact **Kvitsøy Maritime Senter** (Box 35, 4090 Kvitsøy, ☎ 51/73–51–88, FAX 51/73–53–96).

DINING AND LODGING

Dining

Coastal Sørlandet is seafood country. Restaurants in this resort area are casual and unpretentious, and the cooking is simple. Better restaurants can usually be found in the hotels, especially in small towns.

Stavanger has many more good restaurants than other cities of comparable size, thanks to the influx of both foreigners and money to the city. More than 100 restaurants, bars, and cafés offer everything from Thai, Chinese, and Indian to Italian, French, and of course Norwegian cooking. Try the restored warehouse area in the harbor for some of the best restaurants.

Lodging

Hotels in the small towns along the coast are either modern and practical—suited for business guests—or quaint and old-fashioned. Prices are about the same regardless of style and are quite competitive during the summer months.

For price-category definitions, *see* How to Use this Book *in* On the Road with Fodor's.

Arendal

DINING

$$ Madam Reiersen. This authentic restaurant on the waterfront serves good food in an informal atmosphere. ✗ *Nedre Tyholmsvn. 3,* ☎ *37/02–19–00. No reservations. AE, DC, MC, V.*

LODGING

$$ Inter Nor Tyholmen. This maritime hotel, built in 1988, is at Tyholmen, with the sea at close quarters and a splendid view of the fjord. It also boasts an open-air restaurant. ☵ *Bryggekanten. Teaterpl. 2,* ☎ *37/02–68–00,* FAX *37/02–68–01. 60 rooms with bath. Restaurant, bar, sauna. AE, DC, MC, V.*

Bryne

DINING

$$ Time Station. It's a 40-minute train ride from Stavanger to Bryne, and the only place to eat in Bryne, this restaurant is next to the station. The specialty of the house is a seafood platter with salmon, monkfish, ocean catfish, mussels, and ocean crayfish in a beurre-blanc sauce. For dessert, try the *krumkake,* a cookie baked on an iron, wafer thin, shaped into a cone, and filled with blackberry cream. ✗ *Storgt. 346,* ☎ *51/48–22–56. Reservations required. AE, DC, MC, V. No weekday lunch. Closed Sun.*

Kristiansand

DINING

$$–$$$ Restaurant Bakgården. At this small and intimate restaurant the menu varies from day to day, but the seafood platter and lamb tenderloin are standard items. The staff is especially attentive to guests' wishes. ✗ *Tollbodgt. 5,* ☎ *38/02–79–55. AE, DC, MC, V. Dinner only.*

$$–$$$ Sjøhuset. Built in 1892 as a salt warehouse, this white-trimmed red building has since become a restaurant furnished with comfortable leather chairs and accented with maritime antiques. The specialty is seafood, appropriately, and the monkfish with Newburg sauce on green fettuccine is both colorful and delicious. ✗ *Østre Strandgt. 12,* ☎ *38/02–62–60. Reservations advised. AE, DC, MC, V.*

$ Mållaget Kafeteria. At this cafeteria everything is homemade (except for the gelatin dessert). That includes such dishes as meatballs, brisket of beef with onion sauce, and trout in sour-cream sauce. It's the best deal in town, but it closes right around the time most people think about eating dinner. ✗ *Gyldenløves Gt. 11,* ☎ *38/02–22–93. Reservations advised. No credit cards.*

LODGING

$$–$$$ Ernst Park. The rooms are decorated with chintz bedspreads and drapes and practical furniture. The corner rooms have a tower nook at one end. On Saturday the atrium restaurant is the local spot for a civilized tea and lovely cakes. ☵ *Rådhusgt. 2, 4611,* ☎ *38/02–14–00,* FAX *38/02–03–07. 112 rooms with bath or shower, 4 suites. Restaurant, 2 bars, nightclub, meeting rooms. AE, DC, MC, V.*

$$ **Hotel Norge.** This quiet, family hotel in the heart of town has an entrance more modern than that of the Ernst Park, but upstairs the difference is negligible. Here the rooms are furnished in bright colors and dark woods. Get up for breakfast to taste the homemade breads and rolls. ☎ *Dronningens Gt. 5, 4610,* ☎ *38/02–00–00,* FAX *38/02–35–30. 115 rooms with bath or shower. Restaurant, meeting rooms. AE, DC, MC, V.*

$$ **Rica Fregatten.** You're a stone's throw from the Town Hall and Cathedral in this medium-size hotel. The rooms are comfortable and well appointed, and there is a good restaurant, the Captain's Table. ☎ *Dronningens Gt. 66,* ☎ *38/02–15–00,* FAX *38/02–01–19. 47 rooms with bath. Restaurant, bar. AE, DC, MC, V.*

Larvik

DINING AND LODGING

$$ **Grand.** The rooms are spotless and the service attentive in this large hotel overlooking the fjord. There is a choice of good restaurants in which to sample the local fish soup and smoked-meat platters—especially good for lunch. ☎ *Storgt. 38–40,* ☎ *33/18–78–00,* FAX *33/18–70–45. 97 rooms with bath. Restaurant, bar, pub, dance club, nightclub. AE, DC, MC, V.*

Stavanger

DINING

$$$$ **Jans Mat & Vinhus.** The cellar setting is rustic, with old stone walls
★ and robust sideboards providing a nice counterpoint to the refined menu. As implied by the restaurant's name, there's an excellent selection of wines here as well. Saddle of Rogaland county lamb is boned and rolled around a thyme-flavored stuffing, and the fillet is topped with a crunchy mustard crust. For dessert, try the nougat parfait dusted with cocoa. ✗ *Breitorget,* ☎ *51/89–47–73. Reservations required. Jacket and tie. AE, DC, MC, V. Dinner only. Closed Sun.*

$$$ **Sjøhuset Skagen.** Just a few doors down from N.B. Sørensen's (*see below*), Sjøhuset Skagen is similar in decor, but with a greater variety of food. Try the crepes stuffed with roe of chapelin, onion, and sour cream, and the marinated salmon, Norwegian style, with potatoes in a dill-and-cream sauce. The brie served with cloudberries marinated in whiskey is excellent. ✗ *Skagen 16,* ☎ *51/89–51–80. Reservations recommended on weekends. AE, DC, MC, V.*

$$$ **Straen Fiskerestaurant.** Right on the quay with two old-fashioned dining rooms, this spot is considered by many the city's best fish restaurant. The three-course dinner of the day is always the best value. The house fish soup and the tournedos of monkfish with lobster sauce and a garnish of mussels and shrimp are excellent. A rock club, a rock café, and a pub are on the premises. ✗ *Nedre Strandgt. 15,* ☎ *51/52–62–30 or 51/52–61–00. Reservations advised. AE, DC, MC, V. Dinner only. Closed Sun.*

$$ **City Bistro.** This turn-of-the-century frame house with a tile roof is furnished with massive oak tables and benches. Choose from reindeer medallions with rowanberry jelly, deer fillet with lingonberries and pears, or halibut poached in cream with saffron, garnished with shrimp, crayfish, and mussels. The dish of the day is served from 5 to 6. ✗ *Madlavn. 18–20,* ☎ *51/53–95–70. Reservations required. AE, DC, MC, V. Dinner only.*

$$ **Harry Pepper.** This restaurant has two levels—the first has a trendy, popular bar that adjoins a Mexican restaurant. The color schemes are gaudy, as are the displays of tacky South American souvenirs. In contrast, the decor upstairs is subtle and modern, and the emphasis is on

meat dishes with an Italian touch. ✗ *Øvre Holmegt. 15,* ☎ *51/89–39–93. Reservations advised. AE, DC, V.*

$–$$ **N.B. Sørensen's Dampskibsexpedition.** In a restored warehouse right on
★ the quay, this bar and restaurant was once the offices of a shipping company. The decor is nautical and rustic, with ropes, gaslights, and barrels, and the food is Norwegian with a flair. Try the marinated shrimp appetizer and the baked monkfish. The dish of the day, as well as the red house wine, which is always waiting for customers in an N.B. Sørensen's bottle on each table, is one of the better deals in Stavanger. ✗ *Skagen 26,* ☎ *51/89–12–70. Reservations advised. AE, DC, MC, V.*

$ **Café Sting.** It's a restaurant–gallery–concert hall–meeting place day and night, located right at the foot of the Valbergtårnet. All food is made in-house and is better than most inexpensive fare in Norway. There's a skillet dish with crisp fried potatoes and bacon, flavored with leek, and topped with melted cheese and sour cream; and a meat loaf with mashed potatoes and sprinkled with cheese. The chocolate and almond cakes are good and they serve delicious hot chocolate that will satisfy winter sugar cravings. ✗ *Valberget. 3,* ☎ *51/53–24–40. AE, DC, V.*

LODGING

$$$–$$$$ **Reso Atlantic Hotel.** The largest hotel in Stavanger, the Atlantic is just off Breiavatnet in the heart of downtown. It is an international luxury hotel with several restaurants and the most popular nightclubs in town, but with little local flair. Rooms are immaculate and comfortable, with heavy quilts, thick carpets, and cozy stuffed chairs. ☎ *Olav V's Gt. 3, 4005 Stavanger,* ☎ *51/52–75–20,* FAX *51/53–48–69. 351 rooms with bath, 10 suites. Restaurant, bar, café, pub, dance club, nightclub, 12 meeting rooms. AE, DC, MC, V.*

$$–$$$ **Skagen Brygge.** This hotel incorporates three rehabilitated old sea houses. Almost all rooms are different, from modern to old-fashioned maritime, with exposed beams and brick and wood walls; many have harbor views. The hotel has an arrangement with 15 restaurants in the area—they make the reservations and the tab ends up on your hotel bill. ☎ *Skagenkaien 30, 4006,* ☎ *51/89–41–00,* FAX *51/89–58–83. 106 rooms with bath, 2 suites. Bar, indoor pool, health club, convention center. AE, DC, MC, V.*

$–$$$ **Victoria Hotel.** The oldest hotel in Stavanger, Victoria Hotel was built at the turn of the century and still retains a clubby, Victorian style, with leather couches, heavy curtains, and dark oil paintings. Rates are significantly lower with Scandinavian Bonuspass in summer and on weekends. Guests receive a 40% to 50% discount at the Trimoteket health club, just behind the hotel. ☎ *Skansegt. 1, 4006 Stavanger,* ☎ *51/89–60–00,* FAX *51/89–54–10. 107 rooms with bath, 3 suites. 2 restaurants, bar, breakfast room, meeting room. AE, DC, MC, V.*

$–$$ **Grand Hotel.** This hotel on the edge of the town center doesn't aim to be fancy; rooms are comfortable and bright, done in light pastels and white. In summer the rates drop significantly. ☎ *Klubbgt. 3, Boks 80, 4012,* ☎ *51/53–30–20,* FAX *51/56–19–42. 92 rooms with bath. Bar, breakfast room. AE, DC, MC, V.*

THE ARTS AND NIGHTLIFE

The Arts

STAVANGER

Stavanger Konserthus (Concert Hall, Bjergsted, ☎ 51/56–17–16) features local artists and hosts free summertime foyer concerts. Built on an island in the archipelago in the Middle Ages, today **Utstein Kloster**

is used for its superior acoustics and hosts classical and jazz concerts on some weekday afternoons from June to August.

Nightlife

KRISTIANSAND

As in most smaller cities, Kristiansand's nightlife centers around hotels.

STAVANGER

In summer people are out at all hours, and sidewalk restaurants stay open until the sun comes up. Walk along **Skagenkaien** and **Strandkaien** for a choice of pubs and nightclubs. Among media junkies the place for a beer and a bit of CNN is the **Newsman** (Skagen 14, ☎ 51/53–57–09). **Taket Nattklubb** (Nedre Strandgt.15, tel 51/52–61–00) and **Cobra** at the Atlantic Hotel (Olav V's Gt. 3, ☎ 51/52–75–20) are for the mid-twenties and above crowd, whereas **Checkpoint Charlie Hard Rock Cafe** (Lars Hertervigs Gt.5, ☎ 51/53–22–45) caters to a younger age group with an image to maintain.

SØRLANDET ESSENTIALS

Arriving and Departing

BY BOAT

Color Line (Strandkaien, Stavanger, ☎ 51/52–45–45) has four ships weekly on the Stavanger–Newcastle route. High-speed boats to Bergen are operated by **Flaggruten** (☎ 51/89–50–90). There is also a car ferry from Hirtshals, in northern Denmark, that takes about four hours to make the crossing. Another connects Larvik to Frederikshavn, on Denmark's west coast. In Denmark contact **DSB** (☎ 33/14–17–01); in Norway contact **Color Line** (☎ 51/52–45–45, 38/07–88–88 in Kristiansand). **DFDS Seaways** (☎ 22/41–90–90) sails the Kristiansand–Amsterdam route once a week June through September.

BY BUS

Aust-Agder Trafikkselskap (☎ 37/02–65–00), based in Arendal, has two departures daily in each direction for the 5½- to 6-hour journey between Oslo and Kristiansand.

Sørlandsruta (38/02–43–80), based in Mandal, has two departures in each direction for the 4½-hour trip from Kristiansand (Strandgt. 33) to Stavanger.

For information about both long-distance and local bus services in Stavanger, call 51/56–71–71; the bus terminal is outside the train station. In Kristiansand, call 38/02–43–80.

BY CAR

From Oslo, it is 329 kilometers (203 miles) to Kristiansand and 574 kilometers (352 miles) to Stavanger. Route E18 parallels the coastline but stays slightly inland on the eastern side of the country and farther inland in the western part. Although seldom wider than two lanes, it is easy driving because it is so flat.

BY PLANE

Kristiansand: Kjevik Airport, 16 kilometers (10 miles) outside town, is served by **Braathens SAFE** (☎ 38/02–14–10), with nonstop flights from Oslo, Bergen, and Stavanger, and **SAS** (☎ 38/06–30–33) with nonstop flights to Copenhagen. **MUK Air** serves Aalborg, Denmark, while **Agder Fly** serves Göteborg, Sweden, and Billund, Denmark. Tickets on the latter two can be booked with Braathen or SAS.

The airport bus (☎ 94/67–22–42) departs from the Braathens SAFE office, Vestre Strandgate, approximately one hour before every departure and proceeds, via downtown hotels, directly to Kjevik. Tickets cost NKr30 for adults, NKr15 for children.

Stavanger: Sola Airport is 14 kilometers (9 miles) from downtown. **Braathens SAFE** (☎ 51/51–10–00) has nonstop flights from Oslo, Sandefjord, Kristiansand, Haugesund, Bergen, Trondheim, and Newcastle. **SAS** (☎ 51/65–89–00) has nonstop flights from Bergen, Oslo, Copenhagen, Aberdeen, Göteborg, London, and Newcastle. **KLM** (☎ 51/65–10–22) and **British Airways** (☎ 51/65–15–33) have nonstop flights to Stavanger from Billund and London, respectively **Air UK** (☎ 51/65–26–30) flies nonstop from London.

The **Flybussen** to town goes every 15 minutes and takes 15 minutes. It stops at hotels and outside the railroad station. Tickets cost NKr30.

BY TRAIN

The **Sørlandsbanen** leaves Oslo S Station four times daily for the approximately 5-hour journey to Kristiansand and three times daily for the 8½- to 9-hour journey to Stavanger. Two more trains travel the 3½-hour Kristiansand–Stavanger route. Kristiansand's train station is at Vestre Strandgata (☎ 38/02–27–00). For information on trains from Stavanger call 51/56–96–00 or 51/56–71–71.

Getting Around

BY BUS

Bus connections in Sørlandet are infrequent; the tourist office can provide a comprehensive schedule. Tickets on **Stavanger's** excellent bus network cost NKr14.

BY CAR

Sørlandet is flat, so it's easy driving throughout. The area around the Kulturhus in the **Stavanger** city center is closed to car traffic, and one-way traffic is the norm in the rest of the downtown area. Parking is available in numerous marked lots and is free with the **Stavanger Card.**

BY TAXI

All **Kristiansand** taxis are connected with a central dispatching office (☎ 38/03–27–00) as are **Stavanger** taxis (☎ 51/88–41–00). Journeys are charged by the taximeter within the city, otherwise by the kilometer. The initial charge is NKr24 (NKr34 at night), with NKr11 per kilometer during the day and NKr13 at night.

PASSES

Kristiansand: Kristiansandspasset, which costs NKr75 and is available June through August, gives free admission to many sights and a 20% discount on tickets to the zoo and the M/S *Maarten*. It can be purchased at the tourist office, the zoo, and at all hotels. If you stay at any hotel in the city for four nights, the pass is free.

Stavanger: The **Stavanger Card,** sold at hotels, post offices, and Stavanger Tourist Information, gives discounts of up to 50% on sightseeing tours, regional and long-distance, buses, car rentals, and other services and attractions. Parking, local buses, and museum admissions are free with the Stavanger Card, which costs NKr110, NKr190, or NKr240 for one, two, or three days, respectively. The **Stavanger Package** includes the Stavanger Card and steeply discounted lodging in some of the leading hotels.

Guided Tours

Kristiansand: Tours of Kristiansand run only in the summer. The **City Train** (Rådhusgt. 11, ☎ 38/03–05–24) runs a 15-minute tour of the

START PLANNING YOUR TRIP NOW. CALL 1·800·4EURAIL FOR PRICES AND INFORMATION ON SCANDINAVIAN RAIL TRAVEL

With Rail Europe's Scanrail Pass you get unlimited rail travel in Norway, Sweden, Finland and Denmark. Or enjoy the benefits of both rail and car with Scanrail 'n Drive.

DISCOUNTS
Scanrail pass holders get discounts on luxurious ferries, boats and buses throughout Scandinavia plus hotel discounts of 10-30% for selected hotels during June, July and August. Passengers under 26 and over 55 can enjoy additional discounts.

CAR RENTAL OPTIONS
Our Scanrail 'n Drive offers you the flexibility and convenience of both train and auto travel so you can take in the breath-taking sites of Scandinavia at any pace you choose. Call your travel agent or 1-800-4EURAIL today.

1-800-4EURAIL
www.raileurope.com

Reality check. Call home.

—— *AT&T USADirect® and World Connect®. The fast, easy way to call most anywhere.* ——

Take out AT&T Calling Card or your local calling card.** Lift phone. Dial AT&T Access Number for country you're calling from. Connect to English-speaking operator or voice prompt. Reach the States or over 200 countries. Talk. Say goodbye. Hang up. Resume vacation.

Austria[*†††]........................022-903-011	Luxembourg 0-800-0111	**Turkey**[*] 00-800-12277
Belgium[*] 0-800-100-10	**Netherlands**[*]..................06-022-9111	**United Kingdom**................0500-89-0011
Czech Republic[*]..............00-420-00101	Norway 800-190-11	
Denmark 8001-0010	Poland[†♦¹] ....0◊010-480-0111	
Finland 9800-100-10	**Portugal**[†] 05017-1-288	
France................................19-0011	**Romania**[*].......................01-800-4288	
Germany.............................0130-0010	**Russia**[*†] **(Moscow)** 155-5042	
Greece[*]..............................00-800-1311	**Slovak Rep.**[*]..................00-420-00101	
Hungary[*].....................00◊-800-01111	Spain[●]............................900-99-00-11	
Ireland 1-800-550-000	**Sweden** 020-795-611	
Italy[*]..............................172-1011	**Switzerland**[*] 155-00-11	

AT&T
Your True Choice

For a free wallet sized card of all AT&T Access Numbers, call: 1-800-241-5555.

center. The M/S *Maarten* (Pier 6 by Fiskebrygga, ☏ 38/02–60–65) offers two-hour tours of the eastern archipelago, and a three-hour tour of the western archipelago June 6–August 21.

Stavanger: A two-hour bus tour leaves from the Marina at **Vågen** daily at 1 between June and August. **Rødne Clipperkontoret** (Skagenkaien 18, ☏ 51/89–52–70) offers three different tours, including an eye-popping fjord tour of the Lysefjord and Pulpit Rock. **Rogaland Trafikkselskap** (☏ 51/56–71–71 or 51/52–26–00) does the same, in either high-speed boats or ferries.

Important Addresses and Numbers

DENTISTS

In Kristiansand, **Skoletannklinikken** (Festningsgt. 40, ☏ 38/02–19–71) is open 7–3. In Stavanger, the tourist office has a list of dentists available for emergencies.

DOCTORS

In Kristiansand, **Kvadraturen Legesenter** (Vestre Strandgt. 32, ☏ 38/02–66–11) is open 8–4.

EMERGENCIES

Police: ☏ 112. **Fire:** ☏ 111. **Ambulance:** ☏ 113. **Car Rescue:** in Kristiansand, ☏ 38/02–60–00, in Stavanger, ☏ 51/58–29–00.

HOSPITAL EMERGENCY ROOMS

In Kristiansand, **Røde Kors** (Red Cross) **Legevakt** (Egsvei, ☏ 38/02–52–20) is open weekdays 4 PM–8 AM *and* weekends 24 hours. In Stavanger, call **Rogaland Sentralsykehus** (☏ 51/51–80–00).

PHARMACIES

Elefantapoteket (Gyldenløvesgt. 13, Kristiansand, ☏ 38/02–20–12) is open Monday through Friday 8:30–8, Saturday 8:30–6, Sunday 3–6. **Løveapoteket** (Olav V's Gt. 11, Stavanger, ☏ 51/52–06–07) is open daily 8 AM–11 PM.

VISITOR INFORMATION

The tourist information office in **Kristiansand** is at Dronningensgt. 2, Box 592, 4601, ☏ 38/02–60–65, ᖴᗩᕽ 38/02–52–55; in **Stavanger** it's at Stavanger Kulturhus, Sølvberget, ☏ 51/89–66–00.

Other tourist offices in the region are in **Arendal** (SørlandsInfo, Arendal Næringsråd, Friholmsgt. 1, 4800, ☏ 37/02–21–93), **Flekkefjord** (Flekkefjord Turistinformasjon, 4400, ☏ 38/32–42–54), **Kragerø** (Kragerø Turistkontor, Jernbanetomta, 3770, ☏ 35/98–23–30), **Larvik** (Storgt. 48, 3250, ☏ 33/13–01–00), **Mandal** (Mandal og Lindesnes Turistkontor, Bryggegt., 4500, ☏ 38/26–08–20), and **Sundebru** (Info-Sør, Brokelandsheia, 4993, ☏ 37/15–85–60).

4 Bergen

PEOPLE FROM BERGEN LIKE TO SAY they do not come from Norway but from Bergen. Enfolded at the crook of seven mountains and fish-boned by seven fjords, Bergen does seem far from the rest of Norway.

Hanseatic merchants from northern Germany settled in Bergen during the 14th century and made it one of their four major overseas trading centers. The surviving Hanseatic buildings on Bryggen (the quay) are neatly topped with triangular cookie-cutter roofs and scrupulously painted red, blue, yellow, and green. A monument in themselves (they are on the UNESCO World Heritage List), they now house boutiques, restaurants, and museums. In the evening, when the harborside is illuminated, these modest buildings, together with the stocky Rosencrantz Tower and the yachts lining the pier, are reflected in the water—and provide one of the loveliest cityscapes in northern Europe.

During the Hanseatic period, this active port was Norway's capital and largest city. Boats from northern Norway brought dried fish to Bergen to be shipped abroad by the Dutch, English, Scottish, and German merchants who had settled here. By the time the Hansa lost power, the city had an ample supply of wealthy local merchants and shipowners to replace them. For years Bergen was the capital of shipping, and until well into the 19th century, it remained the country's major city.

Culturally Bergen has also had its luminaries, including dramatist Ludvig Holberg, Scandinavia's answer to Molière—whom the Danes claim as their own. Bergensers know better. Norway's musical geniuses Ole Bull and Edvard Grieg also came from the city of the seven hills. In fact, once you've visited Troldhaugen, Grieg's "Hill of Trolls," you'll understand his inspiration.

About 219,000 people live in the greater metropolitan area now, compared with nearly 500,000 in Oslo. Even though the balance of power has shifted to the capital, Bergen remains a strong commercial force, thanks to shipping and oil, and is a cultural center, with an international music and arts festival every spring. Although it's true that an umbrella and slicker are necessary in this town, the raindrops—actually 219 days per year of them—never obstruct the lovely views.

EXPLORING

Numbers in the margin correspond to points of interest on the Bergen map.

Many of Bergen's sights are concentrated in a small area, so walking tours are the best way to see the city.

Tour 1: Historic Bergen

★ ❶ Start at **Torget,** Bergen's marketplace, also called **Fisketorget** (Fish Market). At the turn of the century, views of this active and pungent square, with fishermen in Wellington boots and mackintoshes and women in long aprons, were popular postcard subjects. Times haven't changed, and it remains just as picturesque—bring your camera. ☺ *Mon.–Wed. and Fri., 7–4, Thurs. 7–7, and Sat. 7–3.*

★ ❷ Look over toward **Bryggen,** the row of 14th-century painted wooden buildings with gables facing the harbor, built by Hansa merchants. The buildings, which are on the UNESCO World Heritage List, are mostly reconstructions, with the oldest dating from 1702. Several fires, the latest in 1955, destroyed the original structures. Take time to walk the narrow passageways between buildings; shops and galleries are hidden among the wooden facades.

★ ❸ Follow the pier to the **Hanseatisk** (Hanseatic) **Museum** at Finnegården, which was office and home to an affluent German merchant. Apprentices lived upstairs, in boxed-in beds with windows cut into the wall, so the tiny cells could be made up from the hall. Although claustrophobic, they retained body heat, practical in these unheated buildings. *Bryggen,* ☎ *55/31–41–89.* ☛ *NKr35 adults, NKr20 children.* ☺ *June–Aug., daily 9–5; May and Sept., daily 11–2; Oct.–Apr., Sun., Mon., Wed., and Fri. 11–2. Tours in English at 11 and 1 daily.*

Past the historic buildings, at the end of the Holmen promontory, is ❹ **Bergenhus Festning** (Bergenhus Fort), dating from the mid-13th century. **Håkonshallen,** a royal ceremonial hall used as early as 1261, was badly damaged by the explosion of a Dutch ship in 1944 but was restored by 1961. *Bergenhus,* ☎ *55/31–60–67.* ☛ *NKr15 adults, NKr5 children.* ☺ *Mid-May–mid-Sept., daily 10–4; mid-Sept.–mid-May, daily noon–3, also Thurs. 3–6. Closed during Bergen International Music Festival.*

❺ The nearby **Rosenkrantztårnet** (Rosenkrantz Tower), damaged in the same explosion that rocked Håkonshallen, was built in the 1560s by the Danish governor of Bergenhus, Erik Rosenkrantz, as a fortified official residence. It is furnished in the same formal, austere style as the hall. *Bergenhus,* ☎ *55/31–43–80.* ☛ *NKr15 adults, NKr5 children.* ☺ *Early May–early Sept., daily 10–4; mid-Sept.–mid-May, Sun. noon–3.*

★ ❻ Retrace your steps to the SAS Royal Hotel. Nearby is **Bryggens Museum,** which houses artifacts found during excavations on Bryggen, including 12th-century buildings constructed on site from the original foundations. The collection provides a good picture of daily life before and during the heyday of the Hansa, down to a two-seater outhouse. *Bryggen,* ☎ *55/31–67–10.* ☛ *NKr15, children free.* ☺ *May–Aug., daily 10–5; Sept.–Apr., weekdays 11–3, Sat. noon–3, Sun. noon–4.*

❼ The 12th-century **Mariakirken** (St. Mary's Church) is just up the street. Bergen's oldest building began as a Romanesque church but has gained a Gothic choir, richly decorated portals, and a splendid Baroque pulpit, much of it added by the Hanseatic merchants who owned it during the 15th and 16th centuries. Organ recitals are held Tuesday and Thursday June 15 to August 26. *Dreggen,* ☎ *55/31–59–60.* ☛ *NKr10 in summer, children free.* ☺ *Mid-May –early Sept., weekdays 11–4; mid-Sept.–mid-May, Tues.–Fri. noon–1:30.*

From Øvregaten, the back boundary of Bryggen, you can look down toward the wharf along the narrow passages where the citizens of the ★ ❽ city lived. Walk about four blocks to the popular **Fløybanen,** the funicular (a cable car that runs on tracks on the ground) to **Fløyen,** a lookout point 1,050 feet above the sea. Several marked trails lead from Fløyen into the surrounding wooded area, or you can walk back to town on Fjellveien. ☛ *NKr28 adults, NKr14 children; one-way tickets are half-price. Rides every half-hour 8 am–11 pm.*

Bergen

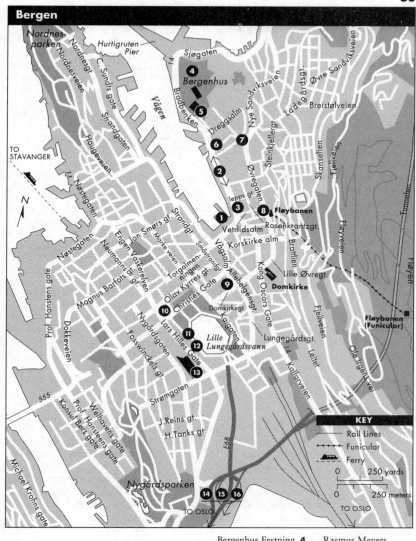

Bergenhus Festning, **4**
Bryggen, **2**
Bryggens Museum, **6**
Fantoft Stavkirke, **15**
Fløybanen, **8**
Gamle Rådhuset, **9**
Grieghallen, **13**
Hanseatisk Museum, **3**
Lysøen, **16**
Mariakirken, **7**

Rasmus Meyers
Samlinger, **12**
Rosenkrantztårnet, **5**
Stenersens
Samling, **11**
Torget, **1**
Troldhaugen, **14**
Vestlandske
Kunstindustri-
museum, **10**

On Lille Øvregaten, and in the area of crooked streets and hodge-podge architecture nearby, you'll find most of Bergen's antiques shops. On your left at the intersection with King Oscars Gate is Bergen **Domkirke** (cathedral), another building constructed in a profusion of styles. The oldest parts, the choir and lower portion of the tower, date from the late 12th century. ☎ 55/31–04–70. ☉ *Weekdays 11–2 during the summer only.*

⑨ Walk down Domkirkegaten to Allehelgensgate, past the police station, and turn right. On the left is **Gamle Rådhuset** (Old City Hall), built in the 16th century as the residence of the governor. The city council still meets there.

Tour 2: For Art Lovers

⑩ From Torgalmenningen, walk to Nordahl Bruns Gate and turn left for the **Vestlandske Kunstindustrimuseum** (West Norway Museum of Decorative Arts). Seventeenth- and 18th-century Bergen silversmiths were renowned throughout Scandinavia for their heavy, elaborate Baroque designs. Tankards embossed with flower motifs or inlaid with coins form a rich display. *Permanenten, Nordahl Bruns Gt. 9,* ☎ *55/32–51–08. Admisssion: NKr 20 Adults, NKr 10 students, children free.* ☉ *Mid-May–mid-Sept., Tue.–Sun. 11–4, mid-Sept.–mid-May, Tue.–Sun. noon–3, Thurs. noon–7.*

⑪ Follow Christies Gate along the park and turn left on Rasmus Meyers Allé to reach **Stenersens Samling**, an art museum that concentrates on Norwegian art since the mid-18th century but also houses an impressive collection of modern art, including works by Max Ernst, Paul Klee, Vassily Kandinsky, Pablo Picasso, and Joan Miró, as well as Edvard Munch. *Rasmus Meyers Allé 3,* ☎ *55/97–80–00.* ☛ *NKr35 adults, children free.* ☉ *Mid-May–mid-Sept., Mon.–Sat. 11–4, Sun. noon–3; mid-Sept.–mid-May, Tues.–Sun. noon–3.*

⑫ Just beyond is **Rasmus Meyers Samlinger.** Meyer, a businessman who lived from 1858 to 1916, assembled a superb collection, with many names that are famous today but were unknown when he acquired them. You'll see the best Munchs outside Oslo, as well as major works by Scandinavian impressionists. The gallery also hosts summertime Grieg concerts. *Rasmus Meyers Allé 7,* ☎ *55/97–80–00.* ☛ *NKr35 adults, children free.* ☉ *Mid-May–mid-Sept., Mon.–Sat. 11–4, Sun. noon–3; mid-Sept.–mid-May, Tues.–Sun., noon–3.*

⑬ Next is **Grieghallen**, named for the city's famous son, composer Edvard Grieg (1843–1907). Built in 1978, this home of the Bergen Philharmonic Orchestra is a conspicuous slab of glass and concrete, but the acoustics are marvelous. It is the stage for the annual International Music Festival.

Tour 3: Troldhaugen and Fantoft

Follow Route 1 (Nesttun/Voss) out of town about 5 kilometers (3 miles). Composer Edvard Grieg began his musical career under the tutelage of his mother, then went on to study music in Leipzig and Denmark, where he met his future wife, Nina, a Danish soprano. Even in his early compositions, his own unusual chord progressions fused with elements of Norwegian folk music.

★ ⑭ Norway and its landscape were always an inspiration to him, and nowhere is this more in evidence than at his villa, **Troldhaugen** (Troll Hill) by Nordåsvannet, where he and Nina lived for 22 years beginning in about 1885. An enchanting white clapboard house with restrained green gingerbread trim, it served as a salon and gathering place for many Scandinavian artists and brims with paintings, prints, and memorabilia. On Grieg's desk you'll see a small red troll—which, it is said, he religiously bade good night before he went to sleep. The house also contains his Steinway piano, which is still used for special concerts. Behind the grounds, at the edge of the fjord, you'll find a sheer rock face that was blasted open to provide a burial place for the couple. In 1985 **Troldsalen** (Troll Hall), with seating for 200 people, was built for concerts. ☎ 55/91–17–91. ☛ *NKr40 adults, NKr25 children.* ☉ *May–Sept., daily 9:30–5:30.*

★ ⑮ On the return trip, visit **Fantoft Stavkirke** (Fantoft Stave Church),which is being rebuilt after a fire in 1992. It was originally built in the early 12th century in Sognefjord but was later moved to its present site. Stave churches are unique to Norway, representing a sort of first step, spiritually and architecturally, into Christianity, without complete relinquishment of pagan beliefs. They also parallel Viking ships, as they are built of strips of wood laid edge to edge rather than in log-cabin style. *Paradis.* ☉ *Mid-May–mid-Sept.*

Tour 4: Lysøen

Ole Bull, not as well known as some of Norway's other cultural luminaries, was a virtuoso violinist and patron of visionary dimension. In 1850, after failing to establish a "New Norwegian Theater" in America, he founded the National Theater in Norway. He then chose the young, unknown playwright Henrik Ibsen to write full-time for the theater and later encouraged and promoted another neophyte—15-year-old Edvard Grieg.

★ ⑯ Getting to his villa, **Lysøen,** is a 30-minute trek, but it's worth the effort. Take Route 1 or Route 586 to Fana, over Fanafjell to Sørestraumen. Follow signs to Buena Kai. The ferry, *Ole Bull,* leaves on the hour (Mon.–Sat. noon–3 and Sun. 11–4; last ferry leaves Lysøen Mon.–Sat. 4, Sun. 5; return fare is NKr30 adults, NKr15 children).

This Victorian dream castle, built in 1873, complete with an onion dome, gingerbread gables, curved staircase, and cutwork trim just about everywhere, has to be seen to be believed. Inside, the music room is a frenzy of filigree carving, fretwork, braided and twisted columns, and gables with intricate openwork in the supports, all done in knotty pine. Bull's descendants donated the house to the national preservation trust in 1973. ☎ 56/30–90–77. ☛ *NKr20 adults, NKr5 children.* ☉ *Mid-May–late Aug., Mon.–Sat. noon–4, Sun. 11–5; Sept., Sun. noon–4.*

What to See and Do with Children

Akvariet (the Aquarium) has 50 tanks with a wide variety of fish, but the main attractions are penguins—several kinds, one of which has a platinum feather "hairdo," strangely appropriate in this land of blonds. There are also several seals. It's on Nordnes Peninsula, a 15-minute walk from downtown, or take Bus 4. *Nordnesparken,* ☎ 55/23–85–53. ☛ *NKr35 adults, NKr15 children.* ☉ *May–Sept, daily 9–8; Oct.–April, daily 10–6. Feeding times: 11, 2, and 6.*

Off the Beaten Path

Drum and crossbow drill teams are unique to Bergen. **Buekorpsmuseet** (the Crossbow Drill Corps Museum) is at "Muren," built in 1562. The exhibits include medals, banners, drums, and pictures. *Wall Gt.* ☛ *Free. Consult the tourist office for opening times, which vary.*

Admire summer sunsets from the top of Ulriken mountain while enjoying free "Music on the Mountain" concerts Mondays and Fridays at 7 PM, May through September. Consult the tourist office or **Ulriksbanen** (Ulriken cable car, Ulriken 1, 5009 Bergen, ☎ 55/29–31–60) for transport up the mountain.

SHOPPING

Shopping Centers

Sundt City (Torgalmenningen 14, ☎ 56/38–80–20) is the closest you'll get to a traditional department store in Norway, with everything from fashion to interior furnishings. However, you will find better value for your kroner if you shop around for souvenirs and sweaters. **Kløverhuset** (Strandkaien 10, ☎ 55/32–17–20), between Strandgaten and the fish market, has forty shops under one roof. You'll find outlets for **Dale** knitwear, souvenirs, leathers and fur. **Galleriet,** on Torgalmenningen, is the best of the downtown shopping malls. Here you will find Christiana Glasmagasin and more exclusive small shops along with all the high street chains like **Hennes & Mauritz** and **Lindex. Bystasjonen,** by the bus terminal, is small but conveniently located for last-minute items. Shops specializing in Norwegian **crafts** are either near Torgalmenningen, on Bryggen or just behind it.

Specialty Stores

ANTIQUES

There are many **antiques** shops around the Fløybanen, especially on Øvregaten.

Cecilie Antikk (Kong Oscarsgt. 32, ☎ 55/96–17–53) deals primarily in antique Norwegian glass and ceramics and old and rare books.

GLASS, CERAMICS, PEWTER

Viking Design (Torgalmenning 1, ☎ 55/31–05–20) specializes in pewter—you'll find that some pieces can be picked up quite reasonably.

Tilbords, Bergens Glasmagasin a.s (Olav Kyrresgt.9, ☎ 55/31–69–67) boasts the town's largest selection of glass and china, both Scandinavian and European designs.

Prydkunst-Hjertholm (Olav Kyrresgt. 7, ☎ 55/31–70–27) is the ideal shop for gifts; most everything is of Scandinavian design. You'll find pottery and glassware of the highest quality—much of it from local artisans.

HANDICRAFTS

Husfliden (Vågsalmenning 3, ☎ 55/31–78–70) caters to all your handicrafts needs, including a department for Norwegian national costumes. Look for the handwoven textiles and hand-carved wood items.

Berle (Bryggen 5, ☎ 55/31–73–00) has a huge selection of traditional knitwear and other souvenir items—don't miss the troll cave. Downstairs is an interior-design shop with Scandinavian furniture. There's also an automatic foreign-money exchange machine.

Theodor Olsens Eftf (Ole Bulls Pl. 7, ☎ 55/23–18–85) stocks silver jewelry of distinctive Norwegian and Scandinavian design.

SPORTS AND FITNESS

Below is a sampling of activities for the Bergen area, but outdoors lovers should be aware that the city is within easy reach of the Hardangervidda, the country's great plateau, which offers limitless outdoor possibilities (*see* Sports and Outdoor Activities in Mountains and Valleys of the Interior, *below*).

Fishing

The **Bergen Angling Association** (Fosswinckelsgt. 37, ☎ 55/32–11–64, closed July) can provide tips and information on permits. Among the many charters in the area, the **Fiskestrilen** (☎ 56/33-75–00 or 56/33-87–40) offers evening fishing tours from Glesvaer on the island of Sotra, about an hour's drive from Bergen, where you can catch coal fish, cod, mackerel, or haddock. On the sail home, they'll cook part of the catch.

Golf

There is a nine-hole golf course at **Åstveit** (☎ 55/18–20–77), 15 minutes north of the city on Route 1. Or you can take the Åsane bus from the bus station.

Hiking

Take the funicular up **Fløyen,** and minutes later you'll be in the midst of a forest. For a simple map of the mountain, ask at the tourist information office for the cartoon **"Gledeskartet"** map, which outlines 1.5- to 5-kilometer (1- to 3-mile) hikes. **Mount Ulriken** is also popular with walkers and can be best reached near the Montana Youth Hostel (Bus 4); alternatively, take Ulriksbanen cable car (☎ 55/29–31–60) which operates May 15 to September 15, 9 AM to 9 PM. Maps of the many walking-tour opportunities around Bergen are available from bookstores and from **Bergens Turlag** (touring club; Tverrgata 2–4, 5017 Bergen, ☎ 55/32-22-30), which arranges hikes and maintains cabins for hikers.

In the archipelago west of Bergen, there are many hiking options, ranging from the simple path between Morland and Fjell to the more rugged mountain climb at Haganes. For details, contact the Sund Tourist Office (5382 Skogsvåg, ☎ 56/33–75–00).

Skiing

When there is snow on the ground you can take the funicular up to the mountains for nearby cross-country skiing. Otherwise, Bergen is close to the major skiing center of Voss (*see* Sports under Central Fjord Country, *below*).

Yachting

The **Bergen Yachting Club** (55/22–65–45) has its harbor at Hjellestad, about a half-hour bus ride from the city bus station. If you want to do more than ogle the boats, however, the 100-year-old Hardanger yacht, *Mathilde* (Stiftinga Hardangerjakt, 5600 Kaldestad, ☎ 56/55–22–77), with the world's largest authentic yacht rigging, does both one- and several-day trips, as well as coastal safaris.

DINING

Among the most characteristic of Bergen dishes is a fresh, perfectly poached, whole salmon, served with new potatoes and parsley-butter sauce. To try another typical Bergen repast, without the typical bill, stroll among the stalls at Fisketorvet (the fish market), where you can munch bagsful of pink shrimp, heart-shaped fish cakes, and round buns topped with salmon. Top it off with another local specialty, a *skillings-bolle,* a big cinnamon roll, sometimes with a custard center, but most authentic without.

For price-category definitions, *see* How to Use this Book *in* On the Road with Fodor's.

$$$$ **Lucullus.** Although the décor seems a bit out of kilter—modern art matched with lace doilies and boardroom chairs—the food in this restaurant is always good. Sautéed monkfish with lobster sauce and rack of reindeer with blueberry sauce are two of many superb dishes. ✕ *Hotel Neptun, Walckendorfsgt. 8,* ☎ *55/90–10–00. Reservations required. Jacket and tie. AE, DC, MC, V. Dinner only. Closed Sun.*

$$$–$$$$ **Finnegaardstuene.** This classic Norwegian restaurant near Bryggen has four small rooms that make for a snug, intimate atmosphere. Some of the timber interior dates from the 18th century. There's a seven-course gourmet menu. The emphasis here is on seafood, although the venison and reindeer are excellent. Traditional Norwegian desserts such as cloudberries and cream are irresistible. ✕ *Rosenkrantzgt. 5,* ☎ *55/31–36–20. Reservations advised. AE, DC, MC, V. Closed Sun.*

$$$ **Fiskekrogen.** It's right on Fisketorvet, and in good weather you can sit outside for lunch. The fish soup is a meal in itself; the appetizer plate is a sampling of specialties, from smoked shrimp to marinated moose; and the Fish Symphony features two or three kinds of fish with lobster sauce and a garnish of shellfish. Meat lovers should try the grilled moose or venison rib-eye steak with herb butter. ✕ *Zachariasbryggen, Fisketorvet,* ☎ *55/31–75–66. Reservations required. AE, DC, MC, V. Dinner only mid-Sept.–Apr.*

$$$ **To Kokker.** The name means "two cooks," and that's what there are. It's on Bryggen, in a 300-year-old building complete with crooked floors. Try the roasted reindeer or the marinated salmon. Desserts use local fruit. *Enhjørningsgården,* ☎ *55/32–28–16. Reservations required. AE, DC, MC, V. Dinner only. Closed Sun.*

$$ **Bryggestuen & Bryggeloftet.** It's always full, upstairs and down. The menu's the same in both places, but only the first floor is authentically old. Poached halibut served with boiled potatoes and cucumber salad, a traditional favorite, is the specialty, but there's also sautéed ocean catfish with mushrooms and shrimp, and grilled lamb fillet. ✕ *Bryggen 11,* ☎ *55/31–06–30. Reservations advised. AE, DC, MC, V.*

$$ **Munkestuen Café.** With its five tables and red-and-white-check tablecloths, this mom-and-pop place looks more Italian than Norwegian, but locals regard it as a hometown legend—make reservations as soon as you get into town, if not before. Try the monkfish with hollandaise sauce or the fillet of roe deer with morels. ✕ *Klostergt. 12,* ☎ *55/90–21–49. Reservations required. AE, DC, MC, V. Closed Sat. and 3 weeks in July. Dinner only.*

$ **Augustin Bistro** and **Augustus.** You can't beat these two cafeterias under the same management for lunch or for cake and coffee in the afternoon. Vegetarians will be impressed by the number of salads and quiches, in addition to pâté and open-faced sandwiches. ✕ *Augustin Bistro: C. Sundtsgt. 24,* ☎ *55/23–00–25. No reservations. Augustus: Galleriet,* ☎ *55/32–35–25. No reservations. No credit cards.*

$ **Banco Rotto.** The fanciest café in town used to be a bank, and appropriately for Norway—a country where a cocktail costs a fortune—the liquor is still kept in the safe. Depending upon the time of day, it changes its identity from café to restaurant to piano bar; it functions best at either end—as a lunch café in the afternoon and as an evening spot that attracts the young as well as the old. There is dancing and live music on Thursday, Friday, and Saturday nights. ✕ *Vågsalmenning 16,* ☎ *55/32–75–20. No reservations. AE, DC, MC, V.*

$ Børs Café. What began as a beer hall in 1894 is now more of a pub, with hearty homemade food at reasonable prices. The corned beef with potato dumplings is served only on Thursday and Friday, while meat cakes with stewed peas and fried flounder plus the usual open-faced sandwiches are always on the menu. *Børs* means stockmarket and the price of beer fluctuates according to demand. ✕ *Strandgt. 15,* ☎ *55/32–47–19. No reservations. No credit cards.*

$ Baker Brun. This Bergen institution, now in several locations, is great for a quick bite. Try *skillingsbolle,* a roll with cinnamon and sugar or *skolebrød,* a sweet roll with custard and coconut icing—both are scrumptious. For something less sweet, this bakery serves fresh-baked wheat rolls with Norwegian *hvit ost* (white cheese) and cucumber. ✕ *Zachariasbryggen,* ☎ *55/31–51–08; Søstergården, Bryggen* ☎ *55/31–65–12.*

LODGING

From June 20 through August 10, special summer double-room rates are available in 21 Bergen hotels; rooms can only be reserved 48 hours in advance. In the winter, weekend specials are often a fraction of the weekday rates, which are geared toward business travelers. All rates include breakfast. The tourist information office will assist in finding accommodations in hotels, guest houses, or private houses.

For price-category definitions, *see* How to Use this Book *in* On the Road with Fodor's.

$$–$$$ Hotel Admiral. This dockside warehouse from 1906, right on the water across Vågen from Bryggen, was converted into a hotel in 1987. The building is geometric Art Nouveau, and although the small rooms are ordinary, the larger rooms overlooking the harbor have some of the best nighttime views in town. The harborside restaurant, Emily, has a small but good buffet table. ☎ *C. Sundts Gt. 9–13, 5004,* ☎ *55/32–47–30, FAX 55/23–30–92. 107 rooms with bath or shower, 12 suites. Restaurant, bar. AE, DC, MC, V.*

$$–$$$ Hotel Norge. Other hotels come and go, but the Norge stays. It's an established luxury hotel in the center of town, right by the park. The architecture is standard modern, with large rooms that blend contemporary Scandinavian comfort with traditional warmth. ☎ *Ole Bulls Pl. 4, 5012,* ☎ *55/21–01–00, FAX 55/21–02–99. 348 rooms with bath, 12 suites. 4 restaurants, 2 bars, indoor pool, health club, nightclub, meeting rooms. AE, DC, MC, V.*

$$–$$$ SAS Royal Hotel Bryggen. This well-designed hotel is behind the famous buildings at Bryggen, one story taller, with the same width and roof pitch. Finished in 1982, the smallish guest rooms, with their subdued woven spreads and dark-wood beds, are beginning to look dated. More expensive rooms, on the top floor, have been refurbished. ☎ *Bryggen, 5003,* ☎ *55/54–30–00, FAX 55/32–48–08. 273 rooms with bath, 7 suites. 2 restaurants, 2 bars, indoor pool, sauna, health club, dance club, convention center. AE, DC, MC, V.*

$–$$ Augustin Hotel. This small, family-run hotel, one block from the harbor, is just off the main pedestrian shopping street. The rooms are small, but some overlook the harbor. The first-floor bistro offers simple meals, and the coffee shop, Augusta, serves wonderful cakes. ☎ *C. Sundts*

Gt. 22–24, 5004, ☎ *55/23–00–25,* ꘙ *55/23–31–30. 38 rooms with bath. 2 restaurants, meeting rooms. AE, DC, MC, V.*

$–$$ **Bryggen Orion.** Facing the harbor in the center of town, the Orion is within walking distance of many of Bergen's most famous sights, including Bryggen and Rosenkrantztårnet. The rooms are decorated in warm, sunny colors. The open fireplace at the bar is cozy in the winter. ☒ *Bradbenken 3,* ☎ *55/31–80–80,* ꘙ *55/32–94–14. 229 rooms with bath. Restaurant, bar, nightclub. AE, DC, MC, V.*

$–$$ **Hotel Park Pension.** Near the university, this small family-run hotel is in a well-kept Victorian building. Both the public rooms and the guest rooms are furnished with antiques. It's a 10-minute walk from downtown. A simple and delicious Norwegian breakfast—fresh bread, jams, cheeses, and cereal—is included in the price. ☒ *Harald Hårfagres Gt. 35, 5000,* ☎ *55/32–09–60,* ꘙ *55/31–03–34. 21 rooms with bath. Breakfast room, meeting rooms. AE, V.*

$ **Fantoft Sommerhotell.** This student dorm, 6 kilometers (3½ miles) from downtown, becomes a hotel from May 20 to August 20. Family rooms are available. Accommodation is simple but adequate. Take a bus No. 18, 19, or 20 to Fantoft. ☒ *5036 Fantoft,* ☎ *55/27–60–00,* ꘙ *55/27–60–30. 72 rooms with shower. Restaurant. AE, DC, MC, V.*

THE ARTS AND NIGHTLIFE

The Arts

Bergen is known for its **Festspillene** (International Music Festival), held each year during the last week of May and the beginning of June. It features famous names in classical music, jazz, ballet, the arts, and theater. Tickets are available from the Festival Office at **Grieghallen** (Lars Hillesgt. 3, 5015, ☎ 55/21–61–00).

During the summer, twice a week, the **Bjørgvin folk dance group** performs a one-hour program of traditional dances and music from rural Norway at Bryggens Museum. Tickets are sold at the tourist information center and at the door. *Bryggen,* ☎ *55/31–67–10. Cost: NKr70. Performances June 8–Aug. 26, Tues. and Thurs. 8:30.*

A more extensive program, **Fana Folklore** is an evening of folklore, with traditional wedding food, dances, and folk music, plus a concert, at the 800-year-old Fana Church. *A/S Kunst (Art Association) Torgalmenning 9,* ☎ *55/91–52–40, or Fana Folklore, 5047 Fana,* ☎ *55/91–52–40.* ☛ *NKr180 (includes dinner). June–Aug., Mon., Tues., Thurs., and Fri. at 7 pm.*

Concerts are held at **Troldhaugen,** home of composer Edvard Grieg (*see* Tour 3, *above*), all summer. Tickets are sold at the tourist information center or at the door. Performances are given June 26–August 29, Wednesday and Sunday at 7:30, Saturday at 2; and September–October, Sunday at 2.

Nightlife

Most nightlife centers around the harbor area. **Zachariasbryggen** is a restaurant and entertainment complex right on the water. **Kjøbmandsstuen** is a piano bar with a crowd on weekends. **Engelen** (the Angel) at the SAS Royal Hotel attracts a mixed weekend crowd when it blasts hip-hop, funk, and rock. The **Hotel Norge** piano bar and disco are more low-key, with an older crowd. **Dickens** (8–10 Ole Bulls Pl., ☎ 55/90–07–60), across from the Hotel Norge, is a relaxed meeting place for an afternoon or evening drink. Right next to Dickens is **Losjehavn** (☎ 55/90–08–20), an outdoor patio especially popular in summer. **Maxime** (☎ 55/90–22–23) is a packed week-end disco, not for the faint-hearted as it can get very boisterous. The complete opposite, **Wesselstuen,** also on Ole Bull Plads (☎ 55/90–08–20) is a cozy place where you'll find students and the local intelligentsia. **Holbergstuen** (Torgalm. 6, ☎ 55/31–80–15) is similar but often attracts a crowd of local sages who hold court. **Café Opera** (24 Engen, ☎ 55/23–03–15) is a sumptuous place to go for a drink or a coffee. It's very comfortable and great for people-watching and whiling away the time.

LIVE MUSIC

Bergensers love jazz, and **Bergen Jazz Festival** (Georgernes Verft 3, 5011 Bergen, ☎ 55/32–09–76) is held here during the third week of August. **Bergen Jazz Forum** (same address) is *the* place, both in winter and summer, when there are nightly jazz concerts. For rock, **Hulen** (the Cave; Olav Ryesvei 47, ☎ 55/32–32–87) has live music on weekends.

Bergen has an active gay community with clubs and planned events. **Homofil Bevegelse** (Gay Movement, Nygårdsgt. 2A, ☎ 55/31–21–39) is open Sunday 2–8 PM. **Café Finken** (same address, ☎ 55/31–21–39) is open daily until 1 AM.

BERGEN ESSENTIALS

Arriving and Departing

BY BOAT

Boats have always been Bergen's lifeline to the world. **Color Line** (Skute-viksboder 1–2, 5023, ☎ 55/54–86–60) ferries serve Newcastle. Others connect with the Shetland and Faroe islands, Denmark, Scotland, and Iceland. All dock at Skoltegrunnskaien.

Express boats between Bergen and Stavanger run three times daily on weekdays, twice daily on weekends, for the four-hour trip. All arrive and depart from Strandkai Terminalen (☎ 55/23–87–80).

The *Hurtigruten* (Coastal Express, Veiten 2B, 5012, ☎ 55/23–07–90) departs daily from Frielenes Quay, Dock H, for the 11-day round-trip to Kirkenes in the far north.

BY BUS

The summer-only bus from Oslo to Bergen, **Geiteryggekspressen** (literally, "Goat-Back Express," referring to the tunnel through Geit-eryggen Mountain, which looks like a goat's back, between Hol and Aurland) leaves the Nor-Way bus terminal (Galleri Oslo, ☎ 22/17–52–90) at 8 AM and arrives in Bergen 12½ hours later. Buses also connect Bergen with Trondheim and Ålesund. Western Norway is served by several bus companies, which use the station at Strømgaten 8 (☎ 55/32–67–80).

BY CAR

Bergen is 485 kilometers (300 miles) from Oslo. Route 7 is good almost as far as Eidfjord at the eastern edge of the Hardangerfjord, but then deteriorates considerably. The ferry along the way, crossing the Hardanger Fjord from Brimnes to Bruravik, runs continually 5 AM to midnight and takes 10 minutes. At Granvin, 12 kilometers (7 miles) farther north, Route 7 joins Route E68, which is an alternative route from Oslo, crossing the Sognefjorden from Refsnes to Gudvangen. From Granvin to Bergen, Route E68 hugs the fjord part of the way, making for spectacular scenery.

Driving from Stavanger to Bergen involves from two to four ferries and a long journey packed with breathtaking scenery. The Stavanger tourist information office can help plan the trip and reserve ferry space.

BY PLANE

Flesland Airport is 20 kilometers (12 miles) south of Bergen. **SAS** (☎ 55/99–76–10) and **Braathens SAFE** (☎ 55/23–55–23) are the main domestic carriers. **British Airways** (serviced by Braathens SAFE) and **Lufthansa** (☎ 55/99–82–30) also serve Flesland.

BETWEEN THE AIRPORT AND DOWNTOWN

By Bus: Flesland is a 30-minute ride from the center of Bergen at off-peak hours. The **Flybussen** (Airport Bus) departs three times per hour (less frequently on weekends) from the SAS Royal Hotel via Braathens SAFE's office at the Hotel Norge and from the bus station. Tickets cost NKr35.

By Taxi: A taxi rank is outside the Arrivals exit. The trip into the city costs about NKr200.

By Car: Driving from Flesland to Bergen is simple, and the road is well marked. Bergen has an electronic toll ring surrounding it, so any vehicle entering the city weekdays between 6 AM and 10 PM has to pay NKr5. There is no toll in the other direction.

BY TRAIN

The **Bergensbanen** has five departures daily plus an additional one on Sunday, in both directions on the Oslo–Bergen route; it is widely acknowledged as one of the most beautiful train rides in the world. Trains leave from Oslo S Station for the 7½- to 8½-hour journey. For information about trains out of Bergen, call 55/96–60–50.

Getting Around

The best way to see the small center of Bergen is on foot. Most sights are within walking distance of the marketplace.

BY BUS

Tourist tickets for 48 hours of unlimited travel within the town boundaries cost NKr70, payable on the yellow city buses. All buses serving the Bergen region depart from the central bus station at Strømgaten 8 (☎ 55/32–67–80). Buses between the main post office (Småstrandgt. and Olav Kyrres Gt.) and the railway station are free.

BY CAR

Downtown Bergen is enclosed by an inner ring road. The area within is divided into three zones, which are separated by ONE-WAY and DO-NOT-ENTER signs. To get from one zone to another, return to the ring road and drive to an entry point into the desired zone. It's best to leave your car at a parking garage (the Birkebeiner Senter is on Rosenkrantz Gata, and there is a lot near the train station) and walk. You pay an NKr5 toll every time you drive into the city—but driving out is free.

BY TAXI

Taxi ranks are located in strategic places downtown. All taxis are connected to the central dispatching office (☎ 55/99–77–00) and can be booked in advance (☎ 55/99–77–10).

PASSES

The 24-hour **Bergen Card,** which costs NKr110 for adults and NKr55 for children (NKr170 and NKr80, respectively, for 48 hours), gives free admission to most museums and attractions, and rebates of 25% to

50% off sightseeing, rental cars, and transportation to and from Bergen. It is available at the tourist office and in most hotels.

Guided Tours

Bergen is the guided-tour capital of Norway because it is the starting point for most fjord tours. Tickets for all tours are available from the tourist information office.

FJORD TOURS

Bergen is the much-acclaimed "Gateway to the Fjords," with dozens of fjord-tour possibilities. The following is only meant as a sampling; check with the tourist office (☎ 55/32–14–80) for additional recommendations. The ambitious all-day **"Norway-in-a-Nutshell"** bus/train/boat tour (you can book through the tourist office) goes through Voss, Flåm, Myrdal, and Gudvangen—truly a breathtaking trip—is the best way to see a lot in a short amount of time.

Traveling by boat is an advantage because the contrasts between the fjords and mountains are greatest at water level, and the boats are comfortable and stable (the water is practically still), so seasickness is rare. Stops are frequent, and all sights are explained. **Fjord Sightseeing** (☎ 55/31–43–20) offers a four-hour local fjord tour. **Fylkesbaatane** (County Boats) **i Sogn og Fjordane** (☎ 55/32–40–15) has several combination tours. Tickets are sold at the tourist information center (☎ 55/32–14–80) and at the quay. Students receive a 25% discount for most tours.

There are other combinations of tours through the Hardangerfjorden and Sognefjorden that include the surrounding countryside; some tours have options to fish or visit local villages or islands. Some of these tours are operated by **Winge of Scandinavia** (Karl Johans Gt. 35, Box 1705, Vika, 0121 Oslo, ☎ 22/42–76–50).

ORIENTATION

Bergen Guided Tours (☎ 55/28–13–30 or 55/96–55–00) offers four city tours departing from Hotel Norge, including one to Edvard Grieg's home and the Fantoft Stave Church. The excellent **Bryggen Guiding** (1½ hours, June–Aug., ☎ 55/31–67–10) offers a historic tour of the buildings at Bryggen, as well as entrance to Bryggens Museum, the Hanseatic Museum, and Schøtstuene after the tour, conducted by knowledgeable guides. **Bergens-Expressen** (☎ 55/18–10–19), a "train on tires," leaves from Torgalmenningen for a one-hour ride around the center of town.

Opening and Closing Times

Shops are open Monday–Wednesday and Friday 9–4:30. On Thursday, as well as Friday for some shops, the hours are 9–7. On Saturday shops are open 9–3. The shopping centers are open weekdays 9–8 and Saturday 9–4.

Important Addresses and Numbers

DENTISTS

The dental emergency center at Lars Hillesgate 30 (☎ 55/32–11–20) is open daily 10–11 AM and 7–9 PM.

EMERGENCIES

Police: ☎ 112. **Fire:** ☎ 111. **Ambulance:** ☎ 113.

EMERGENCY ROOMS

The outpatient center at Lars Hillesgate 30 (☎ 55/32–11–20), near Grieghallen, is open 24 hours.

PHARMACIES

Apoteket Nordstjernen (☎ 55/31–68–84), by the bus station, is open daily from 7:30 AM to midnight; Sundays from 8:30 AM.

VISITOR INFORMATION

The **Tourist Information Office** at Bryggen (☎ 55/32–14–80), by the wharf, has brochures and maps and can arrange for accommodations and sightseeing. There is also a currency exchange.

WHERE TO CHANGE MONEY

Outside normal banking hours, the Tourist Information Office on Bryggen can change money. Post offices exchange money and are open Monday through Wednesday and Friday 8 to 5, Thursday 8 to 6, and Saturday 9 to 2.

5 Mountains and Valleys of the Interior

THE CENTRAL PORTION OF NORWAY lies in the shadow of the famed fjords but doesn't lack majestic scenery. A land of wide-open vistas and deep forests, it's veined with swift-flowing streams and scattered with peaceful lakes— a natural setting so powerful and silent that a few generations ago, trolls were the only reasonable explanation for what lurked in, or for that matter plodded through, the shadows. These legendary creatures, serious Norwegians explain, boast several heads, a couple of noses (used to stir their porridge of course), and can grow to the size of a village. Fortunately for humans, however, they turn to stone in sunlight.

The tourist board aptly calls the triangle between Oppland and Hedmark counties, south to Lillehammer (and including Peer Gynt country, in Jotunheimen), Troll Park. The otherworldly quality of oblique northern light against wildflower-covered hills has inspired centuries of folk tales, and artists from Wagner to Ibsen, who was awarded a government grant to scour the land for these very stories. Even today, locals claim he applied for the grant just to have the opportunity to hike the hills.

The southern part of the interior, around Hardangervidda, is prime vacation land for wilderness sports lovers, with fishing, canoeing, rafting, hiking, and horseback riding over the plateau in the summer, and skiing, particularly on the slopes of Geilo, in winter. Northward, the land turns to rolling hills and leafy forests, and the principal town, Lillehammer, attracts skiers from around the world to its slopes and trails; in 1994 it hosted the Winter Olympics. At the northern end of the region is the copper-mining town of Røros—which is on UNESCO's World Heritage List—a bucolic little town that's changed little over the past 100 years.

EXPLORING

Numbers in the margin correspond to points of interest on the Mountains and Valleys of the Interior map.

Tour 1: Central Norway

The center of Norway is outdoor country for Norwegians and northern Europeans, who come to ski, hike, dogsled and, in recent years, river raft.

Route 7 from Drammen winds through the historic **Hallingdal Valley**, which is lined with small farming communities and ski resorts. Hallingdal is known for its many well-preserved wooden log buildings, including
❶ the late-12th-century stave church in **Torpo.** Its colorful painted ceiling is decorated with scenes from the life of St. Margaret. *3579 Torpo.* ☉ *June–Aug., daily 9:30–5:30.*

❷ **Geilo,** population 3,500, is 35 kilometers (21 miles) farther west, dead-center between Bergen and Oslo. The country's most popular winter resort, it often draws more than a million visitors a year from throughout northern Europe and Scandinavia to its alpine slopes and cross-country trails; many people ski directly from their hotels and cabins. Recently Geilo has become a popular summer destination, with fishing, boating, hiking, and riding—although, admittedly, it still looks like a winter resort minus the snow. Plan ahead if you want to visit at Easter, when Norwegians flock there for a final ski weekend.

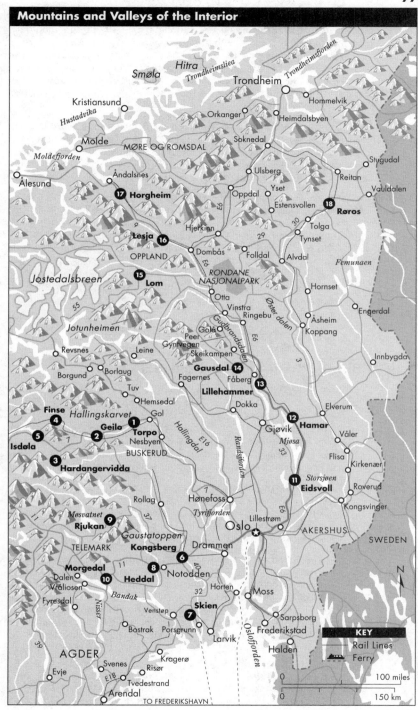

Smøla
Hitra
Trondheimsliea
Trondheim
Trondheimsfjorden

Kristiansund
Hustadvika
Orkanger
Hommelvik
Heimdalsbyen

Molde
MØRE OG ROMSDAL
Søknedal
Stugudal

Moldefjorden
Åndalsnes
Ulsberg
Reitan

Ålesund
Yset
Vauldalen

17 Horgheim
Oppdal
Estensvollen
18 Røros

Hjerkinn
Tolga
30

Lesja **16**
Dombås
Tynset
29

OPPLAND
Folldal
Alvdal
Femunaen

Jostedalsbreen
15 Lom
RONDANE NASJONALPARK
Hornset

Otta
Engerdal

Vinstra
Ringebu
Åsheim

Jotunheimen
Gola
Koppang

Revsnes
Leine
Peer
Gyntvegen
Skeikampen
3

Borglaug
Innbygda

Borgund
Gausdal **14**
Fagernes
Fåberg **13**

Tuv
Lillehammer

Finse
Hemsedal
Dokka
Elverum

4 Hallingskarvet
Gol
12 Hamar

5 Isdøla
2 Geilo
Torpo
Gjøvik
Våler

Nesbyen
Mjøsa
Flisa

3 Hardangervidda
BUSKERUD
Kirkenær

Randsfjorden
Roverud

Møsvatnet
9 Rjukan
Rollag
Hønefoss
Storsjøen
11 Eidsvoll
Kongsvinger

Gaustatoppen
Tyrifjorden
Lillestrøm

TELEMARK
Kongsberg
Drammen
Oslo
AKERSHUS
SWEDEN

Morgedal
11
6
8 Heddal
Notodden
Horten
Moss

Dalen
10
32

Vråliosen
Bandak
Skien
7
Venstøp
Sarpsborg

Fyresdal
Nisser
Bostrak
Porsgrunn
Larvik
Frederikstad

39
AGDER
Svenes
Kragerø
Halden

Evje
E18
Risør

Tvedestrand
100 miles

Arendal
TO FREDERIKSHAVN
150 km

KEY
Rail Lines
Ferry

★ ❸   Geilo is the gateway to **Hardangervidda,** Europe's largest mountain plateau and Norway's biggest national park—10,000 square kilometers of unique scenery, with the largest herd of wild reindeer in Europe, and home to many birds and animals on the endangered list. It also has rich and varied flora, about 450 different species. Touring the plateau, either on horseback or on foot, you can find a trail for any level of proficiency, and along the trails, the Norwegian Touring Association (DNT) has built cabins.

❹   The western settlement of **Finse** (on the Bergen railroad) is one of the most frigid places in southern Norway, with snow on the ground as late as August. Here polar explorers Nansen and Scott tested their equipment and the snow scenes in the *Star Wars* movies were filmed. It, too, is a good starting point for tours of Hardangervidda.

At the western end of the vidda, 72 kilometers (44 miles) beyond
❺   Geilo, is **Isdøla,** at the junction of the 1-kilometer (0.62 miles, but it seems like 10) road to Fossli and Vøringfossen (Vøring Falls), which has a 464-foot vertical drop. The road down to the valley of Måbødalen was blasted into the mountain early in the century; it has been improved steadily, and now most of the difficult parts are tunneled. Cyclists and hikers can go down the side of the mountain to the base of the falls on the original trail, with 124 swings and 1,300 steps—it takes about 30 minutes—but it's not for amateurs.

At the base is the innermost arm of the **Hardangerfjord.** Although it's not as dramatic as some of the other fjords, it is pastoral, with royal-blue water and lush apple orchards.

Tour 2: Historic Kongsberg and Telemark

Kongsberg, Norway's first industrial town, rose to prominence because of the discovery there of silver in its purest form. The town of Rjukan was the site of the country's entrance into modern technology, with hydroelectric power. Telemark was the birthplace of downhill skiing as we know it today, as well as the birthplace of many ancestors to Norwegian-Americans, for the poor farmers of the region were among the first to emigrate to the United States during the 19th century.

❻   **Kongsberg,** with 20,000 people, was Norway's silver town for more than 300 years. King Christian IV saw the town's natural potential when he noticed that a cow's horn had rubbed moss off a stone—to expose silver. Thereupon, the Danish builder king began construction of the town. The mines are now closed, but the Royal Mint is still going strong.

The **Norsk Bergverksmuseum** (Norwegian Mining Museum), in the old smelting works, documents the development of silver mining and exhibits the pure silver along with gold, emeralds, and rubies from other Norwegian mines. The Royal Mint Museum, in the same building, is a treasure trove for coin collectors, with a nearly complete assemblage of Norwegian coins. Children can pan for silver all summer. The **Kongsberg Ski Museum,** also part of the mining complex, houses exhibits of ancient skis and 23 Olympic and World Championship medals won by Kongsberg skiers. *Hyttegt. 3,* ☎ *32/73–32–60.* ☛ *NKr70 families, NKr30 adults, NKr10 children, NKr20 senior citizens.* ☼ *Mid-May–mid-Aug., weekdays 10–6, weekends 10–4; mid-late Aug., daily 10–4; Sept., daily noon–4; Oct.–mid-May, Sun. noon–4. Otherwise, by appointment.*

The **Sølvgruvene** (Silver Mines) in Saggrenda are 8 kilometers (5 miles) outside town, toward Notodden. Guided mine tours include a 2.3-kilometer (1.4-mile) ride on the mine train into Kongensgruve (the King's mine) and a ride on the first personnel elevator. The temperature in the mine is about 6°C (43°F) and the tour takes about one hour and 20 minutes, so dress accordingly. ☏ 32/73–32–60. ☛ NKr120 families, NKr50 adults, NKr20 children, NKr35 senior citizens. Tours mid-May–June, daily at 11, 12:30, 2; July–mid-Aug., daily at 11, 12:30, 2, 3:30; Sept.–mid-May, Sun. at 2.

Kongsberg Kirke (Kongsberg Church), finished in 1761, was built during the heyday of the silver mines, with an impressive gilded Baroque altar, organ, and pulpit all on one wall. It seats 3,000. The royal box and the galleries separated the gentry and mine owners from the workers. ☏ 32/73–19–02. ☛ NKr50 families, NKr20 adults, NKr10 children. ☉ Mid-May–Aug., guided tours lasting 45 min. on the hour, weekdays 10–noon, Sat. 10–1. Sun. services at 11 with tours afterward until 1:30. Organ concerts Wed. at 6 during the summer. Call to confirm times.

TIME OUT **Peckels Resept** (Peckels Gt. 12, ☏ 32/73–00–07), in the center of town, is a café with personality. It serves sandwiches and hot dishes, along with delicious cakes for lunch.

❼ South of Kongsberg on Routes 32 and 36 is **Skien,** the capital of the Telemark region. This town of 50,000 is best known as the birthplace of playwright Henrik Ibsen. The **Fylkesmuseet** (County Museum), a manor house from 1780, has a collection of Ibsen memorabilia, including his study and bedroom and the "blue salon" from his Oslo flat (other interiors are at the Norsk Folkemuseum in Oslo). The museum also has a display of Telemark-style folk art, including rosemaling and wood carving. Øvregt. 41, ☏ 35/52–35–94. ☛ NKr20 adults, NKr10 children. ☉ Garden, mid-May–Aug., daily 10–8; museum, mid-May–Aug., daily 10–6.

Venstøp, 5 kilometers (3 miles) northwest of the city, looks just as it did when the Ibsen family lived there from 1835 to 1843. The attic was the inspiration for The Wild Duck. The house is part of Skien's county museum. ☏ 35/52–57–49. ☛ NKr20 adults, NKr10 children. ☉ Mid-May–Aug., daily 10–6.

❽ **Heddal,** site of Norway's largest stave church, is 35 kilometers (20 miles) west of Kongsberg. The church dates from the middle of the 12th century and has exceptional stylized animal ornament, along with grotesque human heads, on the portals. ☏ 33/02–00–93. ☛ NKr15 adults, children free. ☉ Mid-May–late June, Mon.–Sat. 10–5; late June–late Aug., Mon.–Sat. 9–7; late Aug.–mid-Sept., Mon.–Sat. 10–5.. Sunday service at 12:30 (mid-May–mid-Sept).

Route 37 northwest from Kongsberg to Rjukan passes the 6,200-foot **Gaustatoppen,** a looming, snow-streaked table of rock popular with **❾** hikers. The town of **Rjukan** may not ring a bell, but mention "heavy water," and anyone who lived through World War II or saw the film The Heroes of Telemark knows about the sabotage of the "heavy water" factory there, which thwarted German efforts to develop an atomic bomb. Heavy water (used in nuclear reactors as a moderator) was produced as a by-product in the manufacture of fertilizer at **Vemork,** 6 kilometers (4 miles) west of town along Route 37, where a museum has been built. Exhibits document both the development of hydroelectric power and the World War II events. The first Saturday in July, the work of the saboteurs is commemorated, but their 8-kilometer (5-mile) path, starting at Rjukan Fjellstue (mountain lodge) and finishing at the museum, is marked and can be followed at any time. *Industriarbeidermuseet Vemork,* ☎ *35/09–51–53.* ☛ *NKr40 adults, NKr25 children.* ⊘ *Mid-June–mid-Aug., daily 10–6; May –mid-June, daily 10–4; mid-Aug.–Sept., weekdays 10–4, weekends 10–6; Oct. and Feb.–Apr. Sat., 10–4.*

Rjukan's history actually began in the decade between 1907 and 1916, when the population grew from a few hundred to 10,000 because of a different kind of water, hydroelectric power. Norsk Hydro, one of Norway's largest industries, which uses hydroelectric power to man-ufacture chemicals and fertilizer, was started here. It is also the site of northern Europe's first cable car, **Krossobanen,** built in 1928 by Hydro to transport people to the top of the mountain, where the sun shines year-round. ☛ *NKr20 adults, NKr10 children, NKr15 senior citizens.* ⊘ *Mid-Apr.–mid-Sept. Times vary. Call Rjukan tourist information for details,* ☎ *35/09–15–11.*

⑩ Farther into the heart of Telemark is **Morgedal,** the birthplace of mod-ern skiing, thanks to a persistent Sondre Nordheim, who in the 19th century perfected his skis and bindings and practiced jumping from his roof. His innovations included bindings that close behind the heel and skis that narrow in the middle to facilitate turning. In 1868, after re-vamping his skis and bindings, he took off for a 185-kilometer (115-mile) trek to Oslo just to prove it could be done. A hundred years ago, skiers used one long pole, held diagonally, much like high-wire artists. Eventually the use of two short poles became widespread, although purists feel that the one-pole version is the "authentic" way to ski. Nord-heim's traditional Telemark skiing is now the rage in Norway, though the revival was begun in the United States.

The **Bjåland Museum** in Morgedal is named for Olav Bjåland, who was chosen for Amundsen's expedition to Antarctica because he could ski in an absolutely straight line. The museum collections illustrate the de-velopment of Telemark skiing. Also on display are Bjåland's stream-lined polar sled and his photographs of the expedition. *Opposite Morgedal Turisthotell,* ☎ *35/05–42–50 or 35/05–41–56.* ☛ *NKr50 adults, NKr25 children, NKr 35 senior citizens and students.* ⊘ *Mid-June–mid-Aug., daily 9–7. mid-Aug.–mid-June, daily 11–5.*

Tour 3: Gudbrandsdal

The Gudbrandsdal (Gudbrand's Valley) is one of Norway's longest, extending from Lake Mjøsa, north of Oslo, diagonally across the country to Åndalsnes. At the base of the lake is **Eidsvoll,** where Nor-way's constitution was signed on May 17, 1814. Most visitors come to the region for the beautiful scenery and outdoor activities. Tourism in this area has increased substantially following the 1994 winter Olympics.

⑫ E6 follows the lake halfway to **Hamar.** During the Middle Ages, Hamar was the seat of a bishopric; four Romanesque arches, which are part of the cathedral wall, remain the symbol of the city today. The town got a new lease of life in 1994 when the Hamar Olympia Hall played host to the speed-skating and figure-skating events of the Lillehammer Winter Olympics.The hall, designed to look like an upside-down Viking Ship, was built to the highest environmental and construction standards. Contact Hamar Olympia Hall (Åkersvika, 2300 Hamar, ☎ 62/51–02–25) for details of tours and sports facilities.

Oslo University has sponsored digs around the cathedral precinct just outside town that have turned up thousands of artifacts, which are displayed nearby at **Hedmarkmuseet og Domkirkeodden** (the Hedmark Museum and Cathedral ruins). *Hedmarkmuseet and Domkirkeodden,* ☏ *62/53–11–66.* ☛ *NKr30 adults, NKr10 children.* ◷ *Mid-May–mid-June and mid-Aug.–Sept., daily 10–4; late June–mid-Aug., daily 10–6.*

⑬ The winter-sports center of **Lillehammer,** with 23,000 inhabitants, is next. In preparation for the 1994 Winter Olympics, this small town built a ski-jumping arena, an ice-hockey hall, a cross-country skiing stadium, and a bobsled and luge track, in addition to other venues and accommodations. However, far-sighted planning kept expansion surprisingly minimal, ensuring that the town was not left in a state of Olympic obsolescence. After the games, which proved hugely successful, many of the structures built to house the foreign media were turned over to the regional college, and one-third of the athletes' quarters were transported to Tromsø to be used as housing.

The **Lillehammer Olympic Information Center** ensures that the memories from the winter of 1994 will be kept alive and that those who weren't there can experience something of the atmosphere of the games. Understandably, considering their achievements (the enthusiastic Norwegians topped the medals count), much attention is given to Norwegian winter sports athletes. There's a boutique with Olympic clothing and souvenirs, and a cafeteria. *Lillehammer Olympiske Informasjonssenter. Elevgt. 19,* ☏ *61/26–07–00.* ☛ *NKr55 adults, NKr30 children, students, senior citizens.* ◷ *Mid-June–mid-Aug., Mon.–Sat. 10–8, Sun. noon–8. Otherwise Mon.–Sat. 10–5, Sun. 11–4.*

Kulturhuset Banken, a magnificent, century-old bank building, is the main venue for cultural events. It is decorated with both contemporary and turn-of-the-century art. Check out the murals on the ceiling of the ceremonial hall. *Kirkegt. 41,* ☏ *61/26–68–10. Tours by prior arrangement.* ☛ *NKr20. Café open daily 10–9.*

The new **Olympiaparken** (Olympic Park) includes the Lysgårdsbakkene ski jumping arena, where the Winter Olympics' opening and closing ceremonies were held. From the tower you can see the entire town. Also in the park are **Håkons Hall,** used for ice hockey, and the **Birkebeineren Stadion** (ski stadium), which holds cross-country and biathlon events.

The winter sports facilities provide amusement all year round in Lillehammer. You can try the **Downhill and Bobsled simulator** between Håkons Hall and Kristins Hall in the Olympic Park. It's a five-minute ride that replicates the sensations of being on a bobsleigh. ☛ *NKr35 adults, NKr20 children.* ◷ *Jan.–late June, daily 11–4; late June–mid-Aug., daily 10–7; late Aug., daily 11–4.*

Those over the age of 12 can try the **Bobsleigh on wheels**—it's the real thing with wheels instead of blades—at the **Lillehammer Bobsleigh and Luge Stadion.** Speeds of 100 kilometers per hour are reached, so you'll get a distinct impression of what the sport is all about. ☏ *61/27–75–50.* ☛ *Arena, NKr 15.* ◷ *Daily 8 am–8 pm.* ☛ *Wheeled bobsleigh, NKr120.* ◷ *Mid-June–late Aug., noon–8.*

A highlight of Lillehammer's ski year is the Birkebeineren cross-country ski race, which commemorates the trek of two warriors whose legs were wrapped in birchbark (hence *birkebeiner*—birch legs), which was customary for people who couldn't afford wool or leather leggings. They raced across the mountains from Lillehammer to Østerdalen in 1205, carrying the 18-month-old prince Håkon Håkonsson away from his enemies. The race attracts 6,000 entrants annually. Cartoon figures of Viking children representing Håkon on skis and his aunt Kristin (on ice skates) were the official mascots for the Olympic games.

Lillehammer claims fame as a cultural center as well. Sigrid Undset, who won the Nobel Prize in literature in 1928, lived in the town for 30 years. It is also the site of **Maihaugen,** Norway's oldest (and, according to some, Scandinavia's largest) open-air museum, founded in 1887. The massive collection was begun by Anders Sandvik, an itinerant dentist who accepted folksy odds and ends—and eventually entire buildings—from the people of Gudbransdalen in exchange for repairing their teeth. Eventually Sandvik turned the collection over to the city of Lillehammer, which provided land for the museum. In addition to more than 130 structures and 50,000 objects from all over Norway, it has a main building with reconstructed artisans' workshops. *Maihaugvn 1,* ☎ *61/28–89–00.* ☞ *NKr60 adults, NKr25 children, NKr50 senior citizens.* ☼ *June–Aug., daily 9–7; May and Sept., daily 10–5. Ticket includes guided tour.*

Lillehammer is also home to the **Norsk Vegmuseum** (Norwegian Museum of Transport History), a collection of vehicles ranging from the infancy of the horseless carriage to the present. *Hunder, 2638 Fåberg,* ☎ *61/25-61–65.* ☞ *Free.* ☼ *May–Aug., daily 10–7.*

One of the most important art collections in Norway is housed at the **Lillehammer Bys Malerisamling** (Lillehammer Art Museum). In addition to Munch pieces, the gallery has one of the largest collections of works from the national romantic period. *Kirkegt. 71, Stortorget,* ☎ *61/26–94–44.* ☞ *NKr30 adults, NKr20 children and senior citizens.* ☼ *Fri.–Wed. 11–5, Thu. 11–8. Tours daily at 1 pm.*

⑭ At **Gausdal,** just north of Lillehammer, you can turn onto the scenic, well-marked **Peer Gynt Vegen** (Peer Gynt Road), named for the real-life person behind Ibsen's character. A feisty fellow, given to tall tales, he is said to have spun yarns about his communing with trolls and riding reindeer backward. Traveling along the rolling hills sprinkled with old farmhouses and rich with views of the mountains of Rondane, Dovrefjell, and Jotunheimen, the road is only slightly narrower and just 3 kilometers (2 miles) longer than the main route. It passes two major resorts, **Skeikampen/Gausdal** and **Golå/Wadahl,** before rejoining E6 at Vinstra. Between Vinstra and Harpefoss, at the Sødorp Church, you can visit Peer Gynt's stone grave and what is said to be his old farm. Although you can walk the grounds, the 15th-century farm is privately owned.

From Vinstra, E6 continues along the great valley of the River Mjøsa, birthplace of Gudbrandsdalsost, a sweet brown goat cheese. The route offers lovely, rolling views of red farmhouses and lush green fields stretching from the valley to the mountainsides.

⑮ At Otta, Route 15 turns off for the 62-kilometer (38-mile) ride to **Lom,** in the middle of **Jotunheimen** national park. It is a picturesque, rustic town, with log cabin architecture, a stave church from 1170, and plenty of decorative rosemaling.

Lom Stavkirke (Lom Stave Church), a mixture of old and new construction, is on the main road. The interior, including the pulpit, a large collection of paintings, pews, windows, and the gallery, is Baroque. ☼ *June–Aug., Mon.–Sat. 10–5, Sun. noon–5.* ☞ *NKr20 adults, NKr15 children, students, senior citizens.*

⑯ Upper Gudbrandsdal has breathtaking scenery. The area around **Lesja** is trout-fishing country; Lesjaskogvatnet, the lake, has a mouth at either end, so the current changes in the middle. The landscape becomes more dramatic with every mile, as jagged rocks loom up from the river, leaving the tiny settlement of **Marstein** without sun for five months of the year.

🄗 **Horgheim** used to have a gingerbread hotel for elegant tourists—often European royalty—to view **Trollveggen,** the highest overhanging vertical rock face in Europe. However, the hotel has been a private home for the past 50 years, and the tourists have been replaced by expert rock climbers and daredevil sky divers from around the world. Åndalsnes, the end station on the railroad, is the perfect departure point for tours of Central Fjord Country (*see below*).

Tour 4: Røros

🄘 At the northern end of the Østerdal, the long valley to the east of Gudbrandsdalen, lies **Røros,** for more than 300 years a one-company town: Practically everyone who lived there was connected with the copper mines. The last mine in the region closed in 1986, but the town has survived thanks to other industries, including tourism, especially after it was placed on UNESCO's World Heritage List.

The main attraction is the **Old Town,** with its 250-year-old workers' cottages, slag dumps, and managers' houses, one of which is now City Hall. Descendants of the man who discovered the first copper ore in Røros still live in the oldest of the nearly 100 protected buildings. The tourist office has 75-minute guided tours of this part of town, starting at the information office and ending at the church. ☛ *NKr25 adults, NKr20 senior citizens and students, NKr15 children. Tours: June and late Aug.–mid-Sept., Mon.–Sat. at 11; late June–mid-Aug., Mon.–Sat. at noon and 3, Sun. at 3. Oct.–May, Sat. at 11.*

The **Røroskirke** (Røros Church), which towers above all the other buildings in the town, is an eight-sided stone structure from 1784, with the mines' symbol on the tower. It can seat 1,600, quite surprising in a town with a population of only 5,000 today. The pulpit looms above the center of the altar, and seats encircle the top perimeter. Two hundred years ago wealthy locals paid for the privilege of sitting there. ☎ *72/41–15–55.* ☛ *NKr15 adults, NKr12 senior citizens and students, NKr10 children.* ⊙ *Early June and late Aug.–mid-Sept., weekdays 2–4, Sat. 11–1; late June–mid-Aug., Mon.–Sat. 10–5. Oct.–May, Sat. 11–1.*

Olavsgruva (Olaf's Mine), outside of town, is now a museum. The guided tour of Olavsgruva takes visitors into the depths of the mine, complete with sound-and-light effects. Remember to bring warm clothing and good shoes, as the temperature below ground is about 5°C (41°F) year-round. *Rte. 31,* ☎ *72/41–44–50.* ☛ *NKr35 adults, NKr25 senior citizens and students, NKr20 children. Guided tours early June–and late Aug.–Sept., Mon.–Sat. at 1 and 3, Sun. at noon; late June–mid-Aug., daily at 10:30, noon, 1:30, 3, 4:30, 6. Oct.–May, Sat. at 3.*

Back in town, in the old smelting plant, is the **Rørosmuseet** (Røros Museum), which documents the history of the mines, with working models in one-tenth scale demonstrating the methods used in mining. ☎ *72/41–05–00.* ☛ *NKr30 adults, NKr25 senior citizens and students, NKr20 children.* ⊙ *Weekdays 11–3:30, weekends 11–2; Easter holiday 4–6.*

What to See and Do with Children

Hamar

The **Jernbanemuseet** (Railway Museum) documents the development of rail transportation in Norway, with locomotives and rolling stock on both normal and small-gauge track. *Tertittoget*, NSB's last steam locomotive, gives rides from mid-May to mid-August. *Strandvn. 132,* 🕾 *62/51–31–60.* 🖝 *NKr25 adults, NKr15 children and senior citizens.* ۞ *June and Aug., daily 10–4; July, daily 10–6.*

Lillehammer

Hunderfossen Park, 13 kilometers (8 miles) north of Lillehammer, has rides and a petting zoo for small children, plus an energy center, with Epcot-influenced exhibits about oil and gas, and a five-screen theater. There's also the world's biggest troll. *2638 Fåberg,* 🕾 *61/27–72–22.* 🖝 *NKr125 adults, NKr100 children.* ۞ *Early June–mid-Aug., daily 10–5.*

Just beyond Hunderfossen is **Lilleputthammer,** a miniature version of Lillehammer as it looked at the turn of the century, complete with animated figures in period dress. *Øyer Gjestegård, 2636 Øyer,* 🕾 *61/27–73–35.* 🖝 *NKr40.* ۞ *Late June–late Aug., daily 10–7.*

Off the Beaten Path

Hamar

Take a ride on the world's oldest paddleboat, the 130-year-old **Skibladner,** also called the "white swan of the Mjøsa," which connects the towns along the lake. The schedule is complicated, with only three stops a week in Eidsvoll and Lillehammer but three stops daily three times a week in Gjøvik. Ask for a schedule from the tourist information or the *Skibladner* office. *Strandgt. 23, 2300 Hamar,* 🕾 *62/52–70–85.* ۞ *Late June–mid-Aug. The* Skibladner *is available for charter May 20–Sept. 20.*

Hell

West of Gudbrandsdalen you will find the lush Espedalen valley and some of Europe's biggest stone caldrons. The sight alone is worth a look, and barbecues are held on Sunday throughout the summer, so you can shamelessly "fry in Hell." Visit in winter and you'll see Hell frozen over.

Lillehammer

The composer of Norway's national anthem and the 1903 Nobel Prize winner in literature, Bjørnstjerne Bjørnson lived at **Aulestad,** in Gausdal, 18 kilometers (11 miles) northwest of Lillehammer, from 1875 until he died in 1910. After his wife, Karoline, died in 1934, their house was opened as a museum. *2620 Follebu,* 🕾 *61/22–03–26.* 🖝 *NKr30 adults, NKr15 children and senior citizens.* ۞ *Late May–Sept., daily 10–3:30.*

Skien

From Skien you can take boat tours on the **Telemark waterways,** a combination of canals and natural lakes between Skien and either **Dalen** or **Notodden.** (For trips to Dalen, contact Telemarkreiser, 🕾 *35/53–03–00;* Notodden is served by Telemarksbåtene, 3812 Akkerhaugen, 🕾 *35/95–82–11,* 🖷 *35/95–82–96.*) The trip to Dalen takes you through **Ulefoss,** where you can leave the boat and visit the neoclassical **Ulefoss Manor,** which dates from 1807. *Ulefoss,* 🕾 *35/94–56–10.* 🖝 *NKr20 adults, NKr10 children.* ۞ *Late May–Aug., weekdays 2–6, Sun. noon–3.*

SHOPPING

Geilo
Brusletto & Co., in central Geilo (☎ 32/09–02–00), is a purveyor of high-quality hunting knives with silver-inlaid handles made from burnished metal, walnut, and rosewood. Norwegian men wear these knives, used for hunting and hiking, on their belts—something akin to jewelry.

Lillehammer
In Lillehammer, most of the stores along Storgate sell souvenirs. Try **Fakkelmannen** (Elvegt. 17, ☎ 61/07–13–55) and **Pins'etten** (Storgt. 79, ☎ 61/25–96–50) for pins; **Ingeborg Svarstad's Vevstugu** (Reichweinsgt. 20, ☎ 61/25–12–42), **Marihøna** (Storgt. 79, ☎ 61/25–99–80), **Husfliden** (Sigrid Undsets Pl., ☎ 61/25–30–03), and **Reidun's Rosemaling og Brukskunst** (Storgt. 84A, ☎ 61/25–84–50) for traditional Norwegian sweaters and handicrafts; and **Toves Brukthandel** (Storgt. 81, ☎ 61/25–45–11) and **Loftet Bruktklær** (Storgt. 81) for good bargains in the secondhand market.

SPORTS AND OUTDOOR ACTIVITIES

Although skiing, especially cross-country, is the most popular sport in the area, striking scenery and fresh air make outdoor possibilities endless—summer or winter. The following is only a sampling of what is available. For additional information on outdoor activities, contact the regional tourist boards or **Telemarkreiser** (☎ 35/53–03–00). Some of the organized activities operate only in summer. If you can't reach them, call the local tourist board.

Bicycling
You can rent a bike and get local maps through any local tourist board.

Dogsledding
In **Jotunheimen,** Magnar Aasheim and Kari Steinaug (Sjoa Rafting, ☎ 61/23–87–50, FAX 61/23–87–51) have one of the biggest kennels in Norway, with more than 80 dogs. You can travel as a sled-bound observer or control your own team of four to six dogs, most of which are ridiculously friendly Siberian and Alaskan huskies.

Fishing
Fishing throughout the region is excellent, and lakes and rivers are well stocked with trout, grayling, and char. Among the highlights is the Hardanger area, with the Eidfjord, Granvin, and Jondal good choices for salmon and trout. In Kvam, salmon run in the Strandadalselva, Moelven, and Øysteselva rivers, and trout are plentiful in the mountain lakes. Within the Troll Park, the Gudbrandsdalåen is touted as one of the best-stocked rivers in the country, and the size of Mjøsa trout (locals claim 25 pounds) is legendary. For seasons, permits (you'll need both a national and a local license), and tips, call local tourist boards.

Hiking
You can pick up maps and the information-packed **"Peer Gynt"** pamphlet at the tourism office in Vinstra; then hike anywhere along the 50-kilometer (31-mile) circular route, passing Peer's farm, cottages, and monument. Overnighting in cabins or hotels is particularly popular on the Peer Gynt Trail, where you can walk to each of the **Peer Gynt Hotels** (Box 115, N–2647 Hundorp, ☎ 61/29–66–66, FAX 61/29–66–88).

The national parks are also a good hiking choice (*see also* National Parks, *below*). Elsewhere in the area, hiking possibilities are limitless—particularly around Hardanger and Troll Park. Check with the local tourist board for maps and tips.

In summer you can hike single-file (for safety purposes, in case of calving or cracks) on the ice and explore ice caves on the **Galdhøpiggen** glacier. Call Lom Fjellføring (☎ 61/21–17–87) or the tourist board (☎ 61/21–12–86).

Horseback Riding

For day- or week-long trips to the Hardangervidda, on horses or husky Norwegian ponies, contact **Eivindsplass Fjellgård** (☎ 32/09–48–45) or **Geilo Hestesenter** (☎ 32/09–01–81). There are several stables in the Peer Gynt area, including **Sulseter Riding School** (☎ 61/29–01–53) and the **Peer Gynt Sommerarena** (☎ 61/29–85–28), both of which offer mountain trips.

Hunting

Just south of Lillehammer you can hunt for beavers, and the Østerdalen offers good elk and reindeer hunting. As elsewhere in Norway, you'll need local and national licenses, and in some regions you are permitted to hunt only with a Norwegian. For information, call **Troll Park** (Lillehammer, ☎ 61/28–99–00).

Mountain Climbing and Touring

Near **Hardangerjøkulen** (Hardanger Glacier), about an hour's drive north of Geilo, you can take a guided hike to the archaeological digs of 8,000-year-old Stone Age settlements. Contact the Geilo Tourist Office (☎ 32/09–13–00).

From 1932 to 1953, **musk ox** were transported from Greenland to the Dovrefjell, where about 60 still roam—bring binoculars to see them. For information on safaris, call the **Dombås Tourist Office** (☎ 61/24–14–44). **Elk safaris** leave Ringebu Tourist Office (☎ 61/28–05–33) every Tuesday and Thursday in the summer. **Elk safaris** in the Bjødnhovd (not far from Fagernes), and **bear safaris,** in southern Valdres, are also organized. Call the **Valdres Tourist Office** (☎ 61/36–04–00).

National Parks

The interior is a land of superlatives, home to several varied national parks. The **Hardangervidda**, Europe's largest plateau and Norway's biggest park, is flat in the east and at its center and more mountainous in the west. Europe's largest herd of reindeer roams the plateau, and trout and char abound in the lakes and streams. About 150 kilometers (94 miles) north are **Ormtjernkampen,** a virgin spruce forest, and **Jotunheimen,** a rougher area spiked with glaciers, as well as Norway's highest peak, the Galdhøpiggen. Farther north are the scrubby, flat, and wide **Rondane** and the **Dovrefjell,** peaked to the west with some of the country's steepest mountains and home to wild musk ox, reindeer, and birds.

Rafting and Canoeing

In Geilo they've combined rafting and canoeing with skiing, outfitting rubber rafts with a wood rudder and taking off down the slopes for a bracing, if peculiar, swoosh. Contact the tourist board for details. For rafting in **Dagali** or **Voss,** contact **Dagali-Voss Rafting** (Dagali Hotel, ☎ 32/09–37–00) for information on organized trips.

The **Sjoa River,** closer to Lillehammer, offers some of the most challenging rapids in the country. Contact **Heidal Rafting** (☎ 61/23–60–

37). **Flaate Opplevelser** (☎ 61/23–50–00) and **Norwegian Wildlife and Rafting** (☎ 61/23–87–27) also have trips in the **Sjoa** and **Dagali** areas.

Skiing

Telemark is famous as the cradle of skiing, and the region is a center for ski touring. Just to the north, between Bergen and Oslo, is **Geilo Skiheiser** (24 kilometers/15 miles of alpine slopes, 130 kilometers/81 miles of cross-country trails; 18 lifts; also a ski-board tunnel, tel 32/09–03–33). Among the area's other four ski centers, **Vestlia** (☎ 32/09–01–88), west of the Ustedalsfjord, is a good choice for families, as children can play under the guidance of the Troll Klub while their parents ski; **Halstensgård** (☎ 32/09–10–20) and **Slaatta** (☎ 32/09–17–10) have a range of alpine and cross-country trails; and **Havsdalsenteret** (☎ 32/09–17–77) attracts a young crowd to its long alpine slopes. One ski pass (NKr185 for adults, NKr135 for children, ☎ 32/09–03–33) gives access to all lifts in all five centers. Vestlia is connected to the eastern ski centers by ski taxis (NKr13, ☎ 32/09–10–00).

North of Geilo is **Hemsedal** (34 kilometers/21 miles of alpine slopes, 175 kilometers/108 miles of cross-country trails; 17 ski lifts), which together with several nearby areas offers hundreds of miles of alpine and cross-country trails along with comfortable, modern facilities. Norwegian World Cup skiers often practice in the top local ski center, Hemsedal Skisenter (☎ 32/06–22–08).

The Vinterlandkortet ski pass is accepted at all 71 ski slopes in Geilo, Hemsedal, Uvdal, and Ål, and is available at ski centers or tourist offices.

North of Oslo, **Lillehammer,** the 1994 Winter Olympics town, is another major skiing center (20 kilometers/12 miles of alpine, 400 kilometers/248 miles of cross-country trails; 7 ski lifts). Within the Lillehammer area, there are five ski centers: **Hafjell** (☎ 61/27–70–78), 10 kilometers (6.3 miles) north, is an Olympic venue with moderately steep alpine slopes; **Kvitfjell** (☎ 61/28–21–05), 50 kilometers (31 miles) north, another Olympic site, has some of the most difficult slopes in the world; **Skei** (☎ 61/22–85–55), near Gausdal, 30 kilometers (19 miles) north, has both cross-country and alpine trails; **Galdhøpiggen Sommerskisenter** (☎ 61/21–21–42 or 61/21–17–50), 135 kilometers (84 miles) northwest of Lillehammer, sits on a glacier, which makes it great for summer skiing; **Peer Gynt** (☎ 61/29–85–28), 80 kilometers (50 miles) northwest, has respectable downhill but is stronger as a cross-country venue. One ski-lift ticket, called a **Troll Pass** (NKr175 for adults, NKr135 for children), is good for admission to all the lifts at all five sites.

To the east of the Gudbrandsdalen is the **Troll-løype** (Troll Trail), 250 kilometers (156 miles) of country trails that vein across a vast plateau that's bumped with mountains, including the Dovrefjells to the north. Ski as much or as little of the tracks as you want, and you can also choose accommodations en route. For information, contact the **Otta Tourist Office** (2670 Otta, ☎ 61/23–02–44).

Beitostølen (9 kilometers/5 miles of downhill slopes, 150 kilometers/93 miles of cross-country trails; 7 ski lifts), on the southern slopes of the Jotunheim range, has everything from torchlit night skiing to paragliding. At the northern end of the region is **Oppdal** (45 kilometers/27 miles of alpine pistes, 186 kilometers/115 miles of cross-country trails; 10 ski lifts), a World Cup venue. Like most other areas, it has lighted trails and snow-making equipment.

DINING AND LODGING

For price-category definitions, see How to Use this Book *in* On the Road with Fodor's.

Dalen

DINING AND LODGING

$$$ **Hotel Dalen.** At the end of the Telemark Canals, Hotel Dalen was restored in 1992 to its original Victorian, "Swiss-style" opulence, complete with dragon carvings, stained-glass windows, and a balcony overlooking the stunning entrance hall. Rooms are relatively small and furnished with plain Norwegian antiques. All meals are provided on request; if you're not a guest, call a day in advance to reserve. You'll be served traditional Norwegian fare and Telemark specialties: porridge, dried mutton, flatbread, and lefse, the venerable Norwegian staple. ⌕ *3880 Dalen,* ☎ *35/07–70–00,* FAX *35/07–70–11. 38 rooms with bath. Breakfast room, lobby lounges, meeting rooms. AE, V. In winter, make advance reservations at Telemarkreiser,* ☎ *35/53–03–00,* FAX *35/52– 70–07.*

Elveseter

LODGING

$ **Elveseter Hotell.** About 136 kilometers (85 miles) north of Lillehammer in Bøverdalen, this family-owned hotel is like a museum. Imagine a swimming pool in a barn dating from 1579. Every room has a history, and doors and some walls have been painted by local artists. In the public rooms are museum-quality paintings and antiques. There's no place like it. ⌕ *2687 Bøverdalen,* ☎ *61/21–20–00,* FAX *61/21–21– 01. 100 rooms with bath or shower. 2 restaurants, bar, indoor swimming pool, meeting rooms. No credit cards. Closed mid-Sept.–mid-May. In winter, make advance reservations at* ☎ */fax 61/25–48–74.*

Geilo

DINING AND LODGING

$$$ **Dr. Holms Hotell.** Renovated in 1989 to include two new wings and a new kitchen, Dr. Holms is among Norway's top resort hotels. Chef Jim Weiss has made the gourmet restaurant (not to be confused with the dining room) worth a special trip. Don't miss the game sausages, which are full of flavor, and the butterscotch pudding with crunchy topping is sensational. An après-ski stop at Dr. Holms is a must. ⌕ *3580 Geilo,* ☎ *32/09–06–22,* FAX *32/09–16–20. 124 rooms with bath or shower. 2 restaurants, 3 bars, exercise room, indoor pool, meeting rooms. AE, DC, MC, V.*

Golå

DINING AND LODGING

$$$ **Golå Høyfjellshotell og Hytter.** Tucked away in Peer Gynt territory, this
★ peaceful hotel is furnished in Norwegian country, with all the extras. The restaurant has a down-to-earth menu of fresh local fish and game, prepared simply and elegantly. ⌕ *2646 Golå,* ☎ *61/29–81–09,* FAX *61/29–85–40. 42 rooms with shower. Restaurant, downhill skiing, outdoor swimming pool, meeting rooms, children's Troll Klub. AE, DC, MC, V.*

Kongsberg

DINING

$$ **Gamle Kongsberg Kro.** Beside the waterfall at Nybrofossen, with a minigolf course nearby, this newly restored café offers hearty Norwegian dishes at moderate prices. ✕ *Thornesvn. 4,* ☎ *32/73–16–33. No reservations. AE, DC, MC, V.*

LODGING

$-$$ **Grand.** A statue of Kongsberg's favorite son, Olympic ski-jumper Birger Ruud, stands in the park in front of this modern, centrally located hotel. ⊞ *Kristian Augustsgt. 2, 3600,* ☎ *32/73–20–29,* FAX *32/73–41–29. 95 rooms with bath or shower, 2 suites. 2 restaurants, 2 bars, exercise room, indoor swimming pool, nightclub, meeting rooms. AE, DC, MC, V.*

Lillehammer

DINING

$$–$$$ **Nikkers Spisested.** Right on Storgata you'll find this café and restaurant. The interior is light and airy, the cuisine traditional, and the staff service-minded. The fare is classic Norwegian with cakes, sandwiches, and hot dishes. The restaurant serves lunch specials and à la carte evening meals. ✕ *Elvegt. 18,* ☎ *61/27–05–56. AE, DC, MC, V. Closed Sun.*

$$–$$$ **Lundegården Brasserie & Bar.** A piece of the Continent in the middle of Storgata, this restaurant is a haven where guests can enjoy a light snack in the bar area or a full meal. The varied menu offers such dishes as baked salmon with pepper-cream sauce and seasonal vegetables. No detail is overlooked, whether it's the rattan furnishings in the bar or the starched white tablecloths in the dining room. ✕ *Storgt. 108A,* ☎ *61/26–90–22. Reservations required. AE, DC, MC, V. Dinner only.*

$ **Shanghai Chopstick.** This is a nice, clean café serving typical Chinese food. ✕ *Storgt 83,* ☎ *61/25–98–68.*

$ **Zeki Grill og Gatekjøkken.** When your purse is empty, everything else is closed, or homesickness overcomes you, come here. A Chicago hot dog costs NKr25. ✕ *Storgt 83,* ☎ *61/25–85–81.*

LODGING

$$$ **Lillehammer Hotel.** A five-minute walk from Maihaugen, the hotel is next door to Olympic Park, a housing development made from the buildings that were the hub of the games. The rooms are big but anonymous. ⊞ *Turisthotellvn. 27B, 2600,* ☎ *61/28–60–00,* FAX *61/25–73–33. 248 rooms with bath or shower. 2 restaurants, bar, exercise room, indoor swimming pool, nightclub. AE, DC, MC, V.*

$$–$$$ **Hammer Hotel.** A member of the Home Hotel chain, this hotel on Storgata opened in August 1991, but it's named for the old Hammer farm, which first opened its doors to guests in 1665. The rooms are decorated in shades of green with oak furniture, both modern and rustic. Waffles, an evening meal, and light beer are included in the price. ⊞ *Storgt. 108, 2600,* ☎ *61/26–35–00,* FAX *61/26–37–30. 71 rooms with shower. Lobby lounge, sauna, exercise room, meeting rooms. AE, DC, MC, V.*

$$–$$$ **Mølla Hotell.** This converted mill houses one of Lillehammer's newer hotels. The intimate reception area on the ground floor gives the feeling of a private home. The bar, Toppen, on the top floor, has a good view of Mjøsa, the town, and the ski jump arena. Egon, the restaurant, is on three levels linked by stairs that wind down into the basement. Some of the old mill equipment has been kept for atmosphere among seating nooks. Try the fried fillet of catfish with shrimp and capers. ⊞ *Elvegt. 12,* ☎ *61/26–92–94,* FAX *61/26–92–95. 58 rooms with bath. Bar, sauna. AE, DC, MC, V.*

$$ **Gjestehuset Ersgaard.** Dating from the 1500s, originally called "Eiriksgård" (Eirik's Farm), today this white manor house has all modern facilities but retains its homey atmosphere. The surroundings are beautiful, including views of Lillehammer and Lake Mjøsa, which can be enjoyed from the large terrace. ⊞ *Nordsetervn. 201 (at the Olympic Park),* ☎

61/25–06–84, FAX *61/25–06–84. 30 rooms, 20 with bath. Playground. DC, MC, V.*

$–$$ Dølaheimen Breiseth Hotell. This friendly hotel is right beside the railroad station and within walking distance of shops and businesses. The Dølaheimen Kafe serves hearty Norwegian meals. ☎ *Jernbanegt. 1– 5,* ☎ *61/26–95–00,* FAX *61/26–95–05. 89 rooms. Bar, brasserie, sauna. AE,DC, MC, V.*

$–$$ Birkebeineren Motell & Apartments. In these central accommodations the rooms are functional, and breakfast is included in the price. ☎ *Olympiaparken,* ☎ *61/26–47–00,* FAX *61/26–47–50. 52 hotel rooms, 35 motel rooms, 40 chalets. Dining room, sauna. AE, DC, MC, V.*

Lom

DINING AND LODGING

$–$$ Fossheim Turisthotell. Arne Brimi's cooking has made this hotel famous. He's a self-taught champion of the local cuisine and now a household name in Norway; his dishes are based on nature's kitchen, with liberal use of game, wild mushrooms, and berries. Anything with reindeer is a treat in his hands, and his thin, crisp wafers with cloudberry parfait make a lovely dessert. ☎ *2686,* ☎ *61/21–10–05,* FAX *61/21– 15–10. 54 rooms with bath or shower. Restaurant, bar. AE, DC, MC, V.* ·

Oppdal

LODGING

$–$$ Oppdal Hotell. A rather severe, modern, concrete-and-glass, slopefront addition obscures this fine brick building, but inside the mood is lighter. The public rooms are overdecorated, but the small bedrooms are understated and tastefully furnished, with light wood and pale woven textiles. It's basically a resort with sports—skiing, kayaking, canoeing, hiking, and rock climbing—year-round. ☎ *O. Skasliens vei, 7340,* ☎ *72/42–11–11,* FAX *72/42–08–24. 72 rooms with bath or shower. 2 restaurants, bar, health club, nightclub, convention center. AE, DC, MC, V.*

Øyer

DINING AND LODGING

$$–$$$ Hafjell Hotell. The largest hotel between Oslo and Trondheim, near the Olympic alpine facilities, opened in the spring of 1992. It is built in a modern yet rustic Norwegian style. Stig Søvik, one of Norway's finest chefs, prepares updated versions of Norwegian classics at the restaurant. ☎ *2636,* ☎ *61/27–77–77,* FAX *61/27–77–80. 210 rooms with bath, 6 suites. Restaurant, bar, indoor pool, sauna, dance club, meeting rooms. AE, DC, MC, V.*

Rjukan

DINING AND LODGING

$$ Park Hotell. This small hotel with a traditional, family atmosphere is in the center of town. The rooms are tastefully decorated in light colors. The restaurant, with the curious name Ammonia, offers a wide selection of dishes. *Sam Eydes Gt. 67, 3660,* ☎ *35/09–02–88,* FAX *35/09– 05–25. 39 rooms with bath or shower. Restaurant, bar, pub, nightclub. AE, DC, MC, V.*

LODGING

$$ Gaustablikk Høyfjellshotell. Built at the foot of Gaustatoppen near Rjukan, this modern timber hotel is a popular ski resort, with nine downhill slopes and 80 kilometers (50 miles) of cross-country trails. In summer, these marked trails are perfect for walks and hikes. ☎ *3660,* ☎ *35/09–14–22,* FAX *35/09–19–75. 91 rooms with bath or shower, 14* *suites. Restaurant, bar, indoor pool, sauna, exercise room, children's playroom. AE, DC, MC, V.*

Røros

DINING AND LODGING

$$–$$$ **Bergstadens Hotel.** The lobby is big, but when there's a fire in the stone fireplace it is quite cozy. Most of the rooms are decorated in shades of light blue, rose, and gray. The main draw here is the dining room: Chef Agnar Risvik sticks to local traditions and products—fish from mountain streams and berries from the nearby forest. ⌘ *Oslovn. 2, 7460,* ☎ *72/41–11–11,* FAX *72/41–01–55. 73 rooms with bath or shower, 2 suites. 2 restaurants, 2 bars, sauna, nightclub, pool, meeting rooms. AE, DC, MC, V.*

Skien

DINING

$$ **Boden Spiseri.** Boden serves an excellent pepper steak, but it also has Norwegian-style food, such as medallions of reindeer. For dessert, "Gjoegler Boden"—ice cream with rum, raisins, and a touch of ginger—is a delight. ✕ *Landbrygga 5,* ☎ *35/52–61–70. AE, DC, MC, V. Dinner only.*

LODGING

$–$$ **Høyers Hotell.** The old-fashioned quality of the exterior, all cornices and pedimented windows, is reflected in the Høyers's lobby, which is an incongruous mixture of old and new. The rooms are modern and light, thanks to the big windows. ⌘ *Kongensgt. 6, 3700,* ☎ *35/52–05–40,* FAX *35/52–26–08. 69 rooms with bath, 1 suite. Restaurant, bar, meeting rooms. AE, DC, MC, V.*

THE ARTS

Bø i Telemark

From June 29 to July 2, Bø holds its annual **Telemarksfestival** for international folk music and dancing, with musicians and dancers from distant lands as well as Norwegian and Sami artists. Nearly every weekend during the summer there's entertainment at **Telemark Sommarland** in Bø—everything from gospel singers to jazz. For more details call 35/95–18–80.

Geilo

On the first Saturday in August, the **Holsdagen** festival presents folk music and a traditional wedding ceremony in the **Hol Stave Church** and **Hol Folkemuseum** (Hol Kommune, Kulturkontoret, 3576 Hol, ☎ 32/08–81–40).

Kongsberg

Every June jazz fans descend on Kongsberg for its annual **jazz festival.** Contact the tourist office for information.

Skien

Henrik Ibsen's home town celebrates its favorite son every August with the **Ibsen-Kultur-festival** (Skien Tourist Office, Box 192, 3701 Skien, ☎ 35/53–49–80), which includes concerts as well as drama.

Vinstra

Henrik Ibsen's *Peer Gynt* is performed (in Norwegian) on the first two weekends in August at a small outdoor theater on the shores of Lake Golaa. Contact the Vinstra Tourist Board (Nedregt. 5A, 2640 Vinstra, ☎ 61/29–01–66) for additional information.

INTERIOR ESSENTIALS

Arriving and Departing

BY BUS

The many bus lines that serve the region are coordinated through Nor-Way Bussekspress in Oslo (Bussterminalen, Galleri Oslo, ☎ 22/17–52–90, FAX 22/17–59–22).

BY CAR

On Route E18 from Oslo, the drive southwest to Kongsberg (84 kilometers/52 miles) takes a little more than an hour. The wide, two-lane Route E6 north from Oslo passes through Hamar and Lillehammer. Route 3 follows Østerdalen (the eastern valley) from Oslo. Route 30 at Tynset leads to Røros and E6 on to Trondheim, 156 kilometers (97 miles) farther north.

BY TRAIN

The train from Oslo S Station to Kongsberg takes 1 hour and 25 minutes. There are good train connections between Oslo and the major interior towns to the north.

Getting Around

BY BUS

Buses in the region rarely run more than twice a day, so get a comprehensive schedule from the tourist office or Nor-Way Bussekspress and plan ahead.

BY CAR

Roads in the southern part of the interior region are open and flat, while those to the north become increasingly hilly and twisty as the terrain roughens into the central mountains. E18 and Routes 11 and 7 are the chief routes of the south; the northern end of the region is threaded by E16, E6, and Routes 51 and 3. Don't speed: High-tech markers at the roadside, particularly prevalent in the area of Vinstra and Otta, are actually cameras. Exceed the speed limit and you'll receive a ticket in the mail.

BY TRAIN

The only train service in the southern part of the region is the Oslo–Stavanger line (via Kristiansand). The mid-region is served by the Oslo–Bergen line, which is as much an attraction as a means of transportation. The northern part is served by the Oslo–Trondheim line and two other lines.

Visitor Information

The main tourist offices of the region are in **Geilo** (☎ 32/09–13–00); **Golå** (Fjell og Fjord Ferie, DBC–Senteret, ☎ 32/07–45–44); **Hamar** (Vikingskipet, Olympia Hall, ☎ 62/51–02–17 or 62/51–02–25); **Kongsberg** (Storgt. 35, ☎ 32/73–50–00); **Lillehammer** (Lilletorget, ☎ 61/25–92–99); **Lom** (☎ 61/21–12–86); **Notodden** (☎ 35/01–20–22); **Øyer** (☎ 61/27–79–50); **Rjukan** (Torget 2, ☎ 35/09–15–11); **Røros** (Peder Hiortsgt. 2, ☎ 72/41–00–00); and **Skien** (Reiselivets Hus, N. Hjellegt. 18, ☎ 35/53–49–80).

6 Central Fjord Country

THIS FJORD-RIDDLED COAST, from south of Bergen to Kristiansund, is stippled with islands and grooved with deep barren valleys, with most of the fertile land edging the water. The farther north one travels, the more rugged and wild the landscape. The motionless Sognefjord is the longest inlet, snaking 190 kilometers (110 miles) inland. It is 4,000 feet deep—a depth that often makes it appear black. Some of its sections are so narrow, with rock walls looming on either side, that they look as if they've been sliced from the mountains.

At the top of Sogn og Fjordane county is a succession of fjords referred to as Nordfjord, with Jostedalsbreen, mainland Europe's largest glacier, to the south. Sunnfjord is the coastal area between Nordfjord and Sognefjord, with Florø, the county seat, on an island close to Norway's westernmost point.

The mountains of Møre og Romsdal county are treeless moonscapes of gray rock, stone cliffs that hang out over the water far below. Geirangerfjord is the most spectacular fjord, with a road zigzagging all the way down from the mountaintops to the water beside a famous waterfall.

There is more to the central region than fidgety coasts and peaks. In fact, tourists have been visiting central fjord country ever since the English "discovered" the area some 150 years ago in their search for the ultimate salmon. One of these tourists was Germany's Kaiser Wilhelm, who spent every summer except one, from 1890 to 1913, in Molde and helped rebuild Ålesund into one of the most fantastic fits of architectural invention in Scandinavia.

EXPLORING

The best way to see the fjord country is to make an almost circular tour—from Oslo to Åndalsnes, out to the coastal towns of Ålesund, Molde, and Kristiansund, then over Trollstigveien to Geiranger, by ferry to Hellesylt, down to Stryn, around Loen and Olden and through the subglacial tunnel to Fjærland, by ferry to Balestrand, connecting with another ferry down to Flåm, where the railroad connects with Myrdal on the Bergen line (*see* Excursions from Bergen, *above*). Then the trip can either continue on to Bergen or back to Oslo.

Numbers in the margin correspond to points of interest on the Central Fjord Country map.

Tour 1: Åndalsnes and the Coast

★ ❶ **Åndalsnes,** an industrial town of 3,000 people, has at least three things going for it: As the last stop on the railroad, it is a gateway to fjord country; **Trollstigveien** (Trolls' Path), one of Europe's most fantastic zigzag roads, starts here; and **Trollveggen** (the Trolls' Wall), the highest sheer rock wall in Europe (3,300 feet), which attracts climbers from around the world, is just outside of town.

★ ❷ West 240 kilometers (150 miles), on three islands and between two bright blue fjords, is **Ålesund,** home to 36,000 inhabitants and one of Norway's largest harbors for exporting dried and fresh fish. Nearly 800 buildings in the center of town were destroyed by fire in 1904, which is said to have been started by a tipped oil lamp. In the rush to shelter the 10,000 homeless victims, Kaiser William II led a mercurial re-

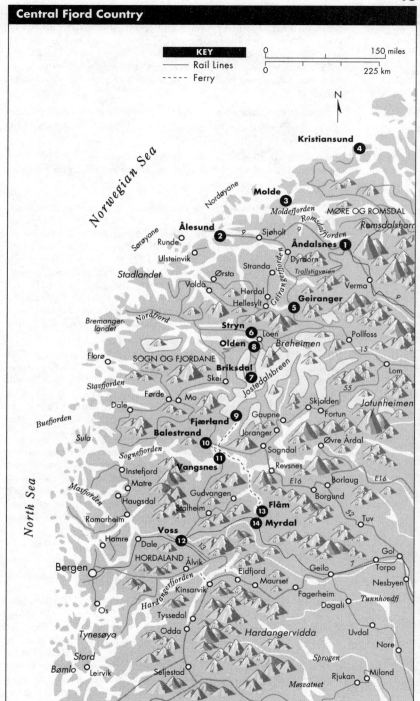

KEY
— Rail Lines
----- Ferry

0 _____ 150 miles
0 _____ 225 km

N

Norwegian Sea

Kristiansund **4**

Nordøyane

Molde **3**
Moldefjorden

Romsdalsfjorden

MØRE OG ROMSDAL

Romsdalshorn

Ålesund **2**
Sjøholt
Åndalsnes **1**

Sørøyane
Runde
Dyrdorn
Verma

Ulsteinvik
Stranda
Trollstigveien

Stadlandet
Ørsta
Herdal
Geiranger **5**

Volda
Hellesylt
Geirangerfjorden

Nordfjord
Stryn **6**
Loen
Breheimen

Bremanger-
landet
Olden **8**
Pollfoss

Florø
SOGN OG FJORDANE
Briksdal **7**
Jostedalsbreen
15

Stavfjorden
Skei
Lom

Førde
Mo
Skjolden
55
Jotunheimen

Dale
Fjærland **9**
Gaupne
Fortun

Buefjorden
Balestrand **10**
Joranger
Øvre Årdal

Sula
11
Sogndal

Sognefjorden
Revsnes
E16

Instefjord
Vangsnes
E16
Borlaug

Matre
Gudvangen
Borgund

Masfjorden
Haugsdal
Stalheim
Flåm **13**
52
Tuv

Romarheim
Myrdal **14**

Hamre
Voss **12**
Gol

North Sea
Dale
Torpo

HORDALAND
Ålvik
Geilo
7

Bergen
Hardangerfjorden
Eidfjord
Nesbyen

Os
Kinsarvik
Maurset
Tunnhovdfj

Fagerheim

Tynesøya
Tyssedal
Dagali

Odda
Hardangervidda
Uvdal

Stord
Seljestad
Nore

Bømlo
Leirvik
Sprogen

Rjukan
Miland

Møsvatnet

building that married the German Art Nouveau with Viking roots—much of it carried out by an army of young, foreign architects who threw in their own rabid flourishes. Delightfully, nothing has changed. Winding streets are crammed with warehouses topped with turrets, spires, gables, dragonheads, and curlicues, all in a delirious spirit that's best seen while wandering behind the local dock to Kongensgate, the walking street.

You can drive or take a bus (☎ 70/12–41–70) up nearby Aksla Mountain to a vantage point, **Kniven** (the knife), for a splendid view of the city—which absolutely glitters at night.

TIME OUT   Fjellstua (☎ 70/12–65–82), a modern lodge at the very top of the mountain, has a terrace with a cafeteria, where the view is especially good.

Near Ålesund is **Runde,** Norway's southernmost major bird rock, one of the largest in Europe, and a breeding ground for some 130 species, including puffins, gannets, and shags. The island is otherwise known for the "Runde Hoard," 1,300 kg of silver and gold coins, which were retrieved from a Dutch ship that sank in 1725. A catamaran leaves from Skateflua quay for the 25-minute trip to Hareid, where it connects with a bus for the 50-kilometer (31-mile) trip to Runde. A path leads from the bus stop to the nature reserve. It is also possible to sail around the rock on the yacht *Charming Ruth,* which leaves from Ulsteinvik at 11 on Wednesday and Sunday. Call the Runde tourist office (☎ 70/08–59–96) for more information.

❸ North of Ålesund on Route 668 is **Molde.** During World War II the German air force suspected that King Haakon VII was staying in a red house here and bombed every red house in town. These days, Molde is a modern town, after being almost entirely rebuilt, and is known for its yearly jazz festival at the end of July, when big names from around the world gather for a huge jam session. Tickets can be purchased at all post offices in Norway.

❹ **Kristiansund,** north of Molde on Route 64, was spared the destruction of its historic harbor, Vågen. Many buildings in the town—which celebrated its 250th birthday in 1992—are well preserved, including **Woldbrygga,** (Dalevn. 17, ☎ 71/67–15–78) a cooper's (barrel maker's) workshop from 1875 to 1965, with its original equipment still operational. ☛ *NKr25 adults, NKr10 children.* ⊘ *Tue.–Fri., 10–2, Sun. noon–3.*

Tour 2: Geirangerfjord to Sognefjord

Geiranger is the ultimate fjord, Norway at its most dramatic, with the finest sightseeing in the wildest nature compressed into a relatively small area. The mountains lining the Geiranger Fjord tower 6,600 feet above sea level. The most scenic route to Geiranger is the two-hour drive along Route 63 over **Trollstigveien** (Trolls' Path) from Åndalsnes. This road took 100 men 20 summers (from 1916 to 1936) to build, in a constant fight against rock and water. Trollstigveien and Ørneveien (at the Geiranger end) zigzag over the mountains separating two fjords. They're open only during the summer, but there's enough snow for skiing well into July. Trollstigveien has 11 giant hairpin turns, each one blasted from solid rock. Halfway up, the spray from **Stigfoss** (Path Falls) blows across the bridge.

TIME OUT   Trollstigen Fjellstue (☎ 71/22–14–65), near the top of Trollstigveien, is cozy and rustic. The *medisterkaker* with *surkål* (mild sausage cakes with caraway-flavored sauerkraut) is a good, hearty meal—be sure to pick up a little tub of *tyttebær* (lingonberries).

★ ❺ The Ørneveien (Eagles' Road), down to **Geiranger,** completed in 1952, with 11 hairpin turns, leads directly to the fjord. The 16-kilometer (10-mile) -long, 960-foot-deep Geirangerfjord's best-known attractions are its waterfalls—the Seven Sisters, the Bridal Veil, and the Suitor—and the abandoned farms at **Skageflå** and **Knivsflå,** which are visible (and accessible) only by boat (*see* Guided Tours, *below*). Perhaps the inhabitants left because provisions had to be carried from the boats straight up to Skageflå—a backbreaking 800 feet.

If you continue on to Stryn, take the ferry across the Geiranger Fjord to Hellesylt, a 75-minute ride. It's about 50 kilometers (30 miles) from Hellesylt to Stryn on Route 60. Stryn, Loen, and Olden, at the eastern end of Nordfjord, were among the first tourist destinations in the re-
❻ gion more than 100 years ago. **Stryn** is famous for its salmon river and summer ski center, while Loen and Olden are starting points for expeditions to branches of Europe's largest glacier, **Jostedalsbreen.**

❼ **Briksdal** is the most accessible arm of the Jostedal glacier. Take a bus (from Stryn, Loen, or Olden) or drive to Briksdalsbreen Fjellstove. The glacier is a 45-minute walk from the end of the road, or you can ride there with pony and trap, as tourists did 100 years ago. Local guides lead tours (*see* Guided Tours, *below*) over the safe parts of the glacier. These perennial ice masses are more treacherous than they look, for there's always the danger of calving (breaking off), and deep crevasses are not always visible.

TIME OUT **Briksdalsbre Fjellstove** (☎ 57/87–38–11) celebrated its 100th anniversary in 1992. Stop at the gift shop or at the cafeteria for delicious homemade cakes, or spend the night at the modern lodge.

It is also possible to visit the **Kjenndal** arm of the glacier on the M/B *Kjendal* (Alexandra Hotel, Loen, ☎ 57/87–76–60), which departs from Sande, near Loen. It sails down the 14-kilometer (9-mile) arm of the lake under mountains covered by protruding glacier arms and past Ramnefjell (Ramne Mountain), scarred by rock slides, to **Kjenndalsbreen Fjellstove.** A bus runs between the lodge (which serves excellent trout) and the glacier.

❽ For many years **Olden** was the home of American landscape artist William H. Singer (d. 1943), scion of a Pittsburgh steel family. A philanthropist, he paid for the road and the regional hospital. You can visit his studio and see some 20 Singer paintings on display there. ☎ 57/87–33–21. ☛ *NKr20 adults, NKr10 children, students and senior citizens.* ☉ *June–Aug., daily 10-6.*

From Olden it's 62 kilometers (37 miles) of easy though not particularly inspiring terrain to **Skei,** at the base of Lake Jølster, where the road goes under the glacier for more than 6 kilometers (4 miles) of the
❾ journey to **Fjærland,** which, until 1986, was without road connections altogether. In 1991 the **Norsk Bremuseum** (Norwegian Glacier Museum) opened just north of Fjærland. It has a huge screen on which a film about glacier trekking plays and a fiberglass glacial maze, complete with special effects courtesy of the *Star Wars* movies' set designer. ☎ 57/69–32–88. ☛ *NKr60 adults, NKr30 children and senior citizens.* ☉ *June–Aug., daily 9–7; Apr., May, Sept., Oct., daily 10–4.*

By 1996 Fjærland should have road connections with Sogndal, but until
⑩ then, the only way to travel is by ferry, which stops at both **Balestrand,**
⑪ one of the famous destinations of old, and **Vangsnes** across from it on
the southern bank of **Sognefjord,** one of the longest and deepest fjords
in the world, snaking 200 kilometers (136 miles) into the heart of the
country. Along its wide banks are some of Norway's best fruit farms,
with fertile soil and lush vegetation (the fruit blossoms in May are spectacular). Ferries are the lifeline of the region.

⑫ From Vangsnes it is 80 kilometers (50 miles) south to **Voss,** birthplace
of American football hero Knut Rockne, and a good place to stay the
night, either in the town itself or 36 kilometers (23 miles) away at Stalheim. The road to Stalheim, an old resort, has 13 hairpin turns in one
1½-kilometer (1-mile) stretch of road that can be almost dizzying—it's
1,800 feet straight down—but well worth the trip because the view is
breathtaking. Voss is connected with Oslo and Bergen by train and by
roads (some sections are narrow and steep).

⑬ It is also possible to ride a ferry from Balestrand to **Flåm,** from which
⑭ you can make Norway's most exciting railway journey, to **Myrdal.** Only
20 kilometers (12 miles) long, it takes 40 minutes to travel 2,850 feet
up a steep mountain gorge, and 53 minutes to go down, with one stop
for photos each way. Don't worry about the brakes. The train has five
separate systems, any one of which is able to stop it. A masterpiece of
engineering, the line includes 20 tunnels. From Flåm it is also an easy
drive back to Oslo on E16 along the Lærdal River, one of Norway's
most famous salmon streams and King Harald's favorite.

Off the Beaten Path

Halfway across the southern shore of Lake Jølster (about a 10-minute
detour from the road to Fjærland) is **Astruptunet,** the farm of artist Nico-
lai Astrup (1880–1928). The best of his primitive, mystical paintings
sell in the $500,000 range, ranking him among the most popular Nor-
wegian artists. His home and studio are in a cluster of small turf-roofed
buildings on a steep hill overlooking the lake. ☎ *57/72–67–82 or 57/72–
81–05 ☛ NKr50 adults, NKr10 children, NKr 40 students and senior
citizens. ☉ July, daily 10–8; late May–June and Aug.–early Sept.,
Tue.–Sun. 10–5.*

SHOPPING

Skei in Jølster
Audhild Vikens Vevstove (Skei, ☎ 57/72–81–25) specializes in the handicrafts, particularly woven textiles, of the Jølster region as well as
handicrafts from neighboring areas, including brass, porcelain, and
leather goods.

Stryn
Strynefjell Draktverkstad (6890 Oppstryn, ☎ 57/87–72–20) is a
women's workshop, started in 1988, that specializes in stylish knick-
ers, trousers, and skirts made of heavy wool fabric. It's a 10-minute
drive east of Stryn on Route 15.

SPORTS AND OUTDOOR ACTIVITIES

Fishing
There are numerous lakes, rivers, and streams around Voss, with trout
everywhere; char, salmon, and sea trout reside in these waters. There's
also good salmon fishing in the Vosso River (June–mid-August), and

the Vangsvatnet and Lønavatnet lakes are good for ice fishing. You can also go sea fishing among the islands south of Bergen near Sund (call the tourist office, at ☎ 56/33–75–00), or fish for more trout and salmon in the Etne River in Sunnhordland. As always, a license is required.

Hiking

Walks and hikes are especially rewarding in this region, with spectacular mountain and water views everywhere. Be prepared for abrupt weather changes in spring and fall. Voss is a starting point for mountain hikes in Slølsheimen, Vikafjell, and the surrounding mountains. Contact the Voss Tourist Board (Uttraagata 9, ☎ 56/51–00–51) for tips. There's also good walking in Sunnhorldland, Osterfjorden, Sotra-Øygarden (among the islands), and the more rugged Nordhorland. The local tourist boards can help you plan hikes.

Skiing

Voss (40 kilometers/25 miles of alpine slopes; 1 cable car, 8 ski lifts; 8 illuminated and 2 marked cross-country trails) is an important alpine skiing center in Norway, although it doesn't have the attractions or traditions of some of its resort neighbors to the east. The area includes several schools and interconnecting lifts that will get you from run to run. Call the tourist information office (☎ 56/51–00–51) for details.

DINING AND LODGING

Outside of some roadside snack bars and simple cafeterias, restaurants are few in fjord country. The majority of visitors dine at the hotels, where food is generally abundant and simple. Most feature a cold table at either lunch or dinner.

For price-category definitions, *see* How to Use this Book *in* On the Road with Fodor's.

Ålesund

DINING

$$ Fjellstua. This mountaintop restaurant has tremendous views over the surrounding peaks, islands, and fjords. There are several different eating establishments here, but the main restaurant serves a variety of dishes and homemade desserts. ✗ *Fjellstua*, ☎ 70/12–65–82. *Reservations not necessary. AE, DC, MC, V. Closed Mar–Nov.*

$$ Gullix. The decor is a bit much, with stone walls, plants hanging from the ceiling, musical instruments, and even the odd old-fashioned record player, but you can't fault the food, which ranges from sautéed monkfish garnished with shrimp, mussels, and crayfish to grilled marinated filet mignon of lamb. ✗ *Rådstugt. 5B,* ☎ 70/12–05–48. *Reservations advised. AE, DC, MC, V.*

$$ Sjøbua. Within walking distance of the new hotels, this fish restaurant is typical Ålesund. Pick your own lobster from the large tank. The mixed fish and shellfish platter is the most popular dish on the menu. The lobster soup is excellent, too, but leave room for the raspberry ice cream with nougat sauce. ✗ *Brunholmgt. 1,* ☎ 70/12–71–00. *Reservations advised. AE, DC, MC, V. Closed Sun.*

$ Brosundet Cafe. Hotel Atlantica's coffee shop is one of the most popular restaurants in town. It has its own bakery, so there are always homemade bread and rolls. You can order anything from *bløtkake* (cream cake) or the ever-so-popular *nøttekake* (nut cake) to pepper steak. ✗ *R. Rønnebergsgt. 4,* ☎ 70/12–91–00. *No reservations. AE, DC, MC, V.*

$ Vesle Kari. This tiny maritime-themed café serves typical Norwegian fare—open-face sandwiches and such hot dishes as *kjøttkaker* (meat patties), which are predictable but tasty. ✗ *Apotekergt. 2*, ☎ *70/12–84–04. No reservations. No credit cards.*

LODGING

$$ Bryggen. Right on Brosundet, Bryggen, formerly a turn-of-the-century fish warehouse, was restored by the Home Hotel chain in early 1990. The decor in both lobby and guest rooms illustrates the importance of the fishing industry to Ålesund. A light evening buffet is included in the room price, and waffles and coffee are always available. Fishing equipment is available; although Bryggen is on the water, anglers are advised to go farther afield for a better catch. ⊡ *Apotekergt. 1–3, 6021*, ☎ *70/12–64–00*, FAX *70/12–11–80. 76 rooms, 3 junior suites. Sauna, steam room, exercise room, fishing, meeting rooms. AE, DC, MC, V.*

$$ Hotel Scandinavie. The impressive building with towers and arches dates from 1905, but the rooms are newly refurbished, with dark modern Scandinavian furniture, while some textiles pay a token tribute to Art Nouveau. ⊡ *Løvenvoldgt. 8, 6002*, ☎ *70/12–31–31*, FAX *70/13–23–70. 63 rooms with bath, 2 suites. Restaurant, bar, pizzeria, meeting rooms. AE, DC, MC, V.*

$$ Rica Parken. This modern business hotel near Aksla offers panoramic views from most of the rooms. They're small but well appointed, with rattan furniture and pastel colors. *Storgt. 16, 6002*, ☎ *70/12–50–50*, FAX *70/12–21–64. 138 rooms with bath, 6 suites. Restaurant, bar, health club, nightclub, meeting rooms. AE, DC, MC, V.*

$$ Scandic. This large, postmodern building complex stands next to the Exhibition Hall. Its interior design has a maritime theme. The rooms are both spacious and tastefully decorated. ⊡ *Molovn. 6, 6004*, ☎ *70/12–81–00*, FAX *70/12–92–10. 118 rooms with bath, 6 suites. Restaurant, bar, indoor pool, sauna, health club, nightclub. AE, DC, MC, V.*

Åndalsnes
LODGING

$$ Grand Hotel Bellevue. It looks like a white stucco apartment building from the 1950s. The rooms are spare but adequate, all with a view of either the mountains or the fjord. ⊡ *Åndalsgt. 5, 6300*, ☎ *71/22–10–11*, FAX *71/22–60–38. 45 rooms with bath or shower. 2 restaurants, bar, meeting rooms. AE, DC, MC, V.*

Balestrand
LODGING

$$ Kvikne's Hotel. This huge, wooden gingerbread house at the edge of
★ the Sognefjord has been a landmark since 1913. It is fjord country's most elaborate old hotel, with rows of open porches and balustrades. The rooms are comfortable—those in the old section have more personality, but the view is the best part. This spot also provides good swimming, canoeing, rowing, and fishing (fishing equipment can be rented). ⊡ *5850, Balholm*, ☎ *57/69–11–01*, FAX *57/69–15–02. 190 rooms with bath or shower. Restaurant, exercise room, fishing, nightclub. AE, DC, MC, V.*

Fjærland
DINING AND LODGING

$$–$$$ Hotel Mundal. This small, old-fashioned yellow-and-white gingerbread hotel opened in 1891. All rooms are individually and simply decorated. The dining room looks rather dreary, but the food is good. ⊡ *5855*, ☎ *57/69–31–01*, FAX *57/69–31–79. 35 rooms with bath. Restaurant, bar, meeting rooms. No credit cards.*

Flåm

DINING AND LODGING

$$ **Fretheim Hotell.** With the fjord in front and mountains in back, the setting is perfect. The hotel is anonymous, white, and functional. The inside has comfortable lounges, but the rooms won't win any decorating prizes. ☎ *5743,* ☎ *57/63–22–00,* FAX *57/63–23–03. 56 rooms with bath or shower, 28 without. 2 restaurants, bar, fishing. AE, MC, V.*

Geiranger

LODGING

$$$ **Union Turisthotel.** This family-owned hotel is more than 100 years old. The old building was torn down, but the present hotel is a tribute to the old style. It is modern and comfortable, with lots of windows facing the view, and light-colored furniture in the rooms, which are relatively large. ☎ *6216,* ☎ *70/26–30–00,* FAX *70/26–31–61. 155 rooms with bath or shower, 10 suites. Restaurant, bar, exercise room, indoor pool, pool, nightclub. AE, DC, MC, V.*

$ **Grande Fjord Hotell.** Idyllically situated at the edge of the fjord, this small hotel complex has more charm than the big hotels in the area. The rooms are simple but comfortable. Fishing equipment is available for rental, as are rowboats and motorboats. ☎ *6216,* ☎ *70/26–30– 90,* FAX *70/26–31–77. 19 rooms with bath, 10 with shower, 18 cabins with shower. Restaurant, sauna. No credit cards.*

Kristiansund

LODGING

$$–$$$ **Inter Nor Grand.** Practically every Norwegian town has a Grand Hotel. This one's primarily a conference hotel, but the rooms are nicer than most in the chain (certainly much nicer than the lobby), with brass beds and light-wood furniture. ☎ *Bernstorffstredet 1, 6500,* ☎ *71/67–30–11,* FAX *71/67–23–70. 130 rooms with bath/shower. Restaurant, bar, pub, sauna, exercise room, nightclub, convention center. AE, DC, MC, V.*

Loen

DINING AND LODGING

$$$ **Alexandra.** The building that houses Alexandra looks more like a
★ huge white hospital than a hotel. More than 100 years ago, English and German tourists stayed here. Even though the original dragon-style building exists only in pictures in the lobby, it is still the most luxurious hotel around. The facilities are first-rate, but the food, prepared by Chef Wenche Loen, is the best part. ☎ *6878,* ☎ *57/87–76–60,* FAX *57/87–77–70. 197 rooms with bath. 2 restaurants, bar, nightclub, indoor pool, exercise room, tennis courts, boating, convention center. AE, DC, MC, V.*

Molde

DINING AND LODGING

$$–$$$ **Inter Nor Alexandra Molde.** Spisestuen, the restaurant of this premier
★ hotel, is worth a special trip. Kåre Monsås prepares such dishes as pepper-marinated veal fillet. The ice-cream soufflé is an excellent dessert. The rooms, many of which overlook the water, are nondescript but comfortable, with dark-brown wood furniture and textiles in shades of blue. ☎ *Storgt. 1–7, 6400,* ☎ *71/25–11–33,* FAX *71/21–66–35. 150 rooms with bath/shower, 11 suites. 3 restaurants, bar, sauna, indoor pool, exercise room, meeting rooms. AE, DC, MC, V.*

Runde

LODGING

$ **Christineborg Turisthotel.** This modern hotel faces the sea and the bird rocks. It's surprisingly comfortable and civilized, a welcome setting for unwinding. ☎ 6096, ☏ 70/08–59–50, ⓕ𝐀𝐗 70/08–59–72. *31 rooms with shower. Restaurant, bar, fishing boat. MC, V.*

Stalheim
LODGING

$$$–$$$$ **Stalheim Hotel.** A large rectangular building, much like other Norwegian resort hotels, the Stalheim has been painted dark red and blends into the scenery better than most hotels. It has an extensive collection of Norwegian antiques and even its own open-air museum with 30 houses. ☎ 5715, ☏ 56/52–01–22, ⓕ𝐀𝐗 56/52–00–56. *127 rooms with bath or shower, 3 suites. Restaurant, bar, fishing. AE, DC, MC, V.*

Stryn
LODGING

$$$ **Kong Oscar's Hall.** Mike and Møyfrid Walston have brought back to life a derelict but magnificent hotel from the heyday of the dragon style, 1896, complete with a tower with dragon heads on the eaves. The Great Hall gives new meaning to the word *great* and the number of royal guests, both present and past, is impressive. ☎ 6880, ☏ *and* ⓕ𝐀𝐗, 57/87–19–53. *5 suites. Restaurant. No credit cards. Closed Sept.–Apr.*

Voss
LODGING

$$ **Fleischers Hotel.** The modern addition along the front detracts from the turreted and gabled charm of this old hotel. Inside, the old style has been well maintained, particularly in the restaurant. The rooms in the old section are comfortable and pleasantly old-fashioned; in the rebuilt section (1993) they are modern and inviting; there is also a children's playroom. The motel section has apartments as well. ☎ *Evangervegen 13, 5700,* ☏ *56/51–11–55,* ⓕ𝐀𝐗 *56/51–22–89. 90 rooms with bath or shower; 30 apartments. Restaurant, bar, nightclub, indoor pool, hot tub, sauna, exercise room, tennis courts. AE, DC, MC, V.*

CENTRAL FJORD COUNTRY ESSENTIALS

Arriving and Departing
BY BOAT
The *Hurtigruten* (the coastal steamer) stops at Skansekaia in **Ålesund,** northbound at noon, departing at 3, and stops southbound at midnight, departing at 1. A catamaran runs between Ålesund and Molde at least twice daily.

BY CAR
From Oslo, it is 450 kilometers (295 miles) on Route E6 to Dombås and then Route 9 through Åndalsnes to Ålesund. The well-maintained two-lane road is inland to Åndalsnes and then follows the coastline out to Ålesund.

The 380-kilometer (235-mile) drive from Bergen to Ålesund covers some of the most breathtaking scenery in the world. Roads are narrow two-lane ventures much of the time; passing is difficult, and in summer traffic can be heavy.

BY PLANE
Ålesund's **Vigra** Airport is 15 kilometers (9 miles) from the center of town. Braathens SAFE (☏ 70/12–58–00, Ålesund; 70/18–32–45, Vigra) has nonstop flights from Oslo, Bergen, Trondheim, and Bodø. It's a 25-minute ride from Vigra to town with Flybussen. Tickets cost NKr50. Buses are scheduled according to flights—they leave the air-

port about 10 minutes after all arrivals and leave town about 60 or 70 minutes before each flight.

BY TRAIN

The *Dovrebanen* and *Raumabanen* between Oslo S Station and **Åndalsnes** via Dombås run three times daily in each direction for the 6½-hour ride. At Åndalsnes, buses wait outside the station to pick up passengers for points not served by the train. The 124-kilometer (76-mile) trip to Ålesund takes close to two hours.

Getting Around

BY BOAT

In addition to regular ferries to nearby islands, boats connect Ålesund with other points along the coast. Excursions by boat are available through the tourist office.

BY BUS

Bus routes are extensive. The tourist office has information about do-it-yourself tours by bus to the outlying districts. Three local bus companies serve **Ålesund;** all buses depart from the terminal on Kaiser Wilhelms Gate.

BY CAR

Ferries are a way of life in western Norway, but they are seldom big enough or don't run often enough during the summer, causing built-in delays. Considerable hassle can be eliminated by reserving ahead, as cars with reservations board first.

Guided Tours

ORIENTATION

A 1½-hour guided stroll through **Ålesund,** concentrating mostly on the Art Nouveau buildings, departs from the tourist information center (Rådhuset) Saturday, Tuesday, and Thursday at 1 PM from June 13 to August 19. ☛ *NKr45 adults, children free.*

SPECIAL-INTEREST

Cruises: The **M/S *Geirangerfjord*** (☎ 70/26–30–07) offers 105-minute guided minicruises on the Geirangerfjord. *Tickets are sold at the dock in Geiranger.* ☉ *June–August. Tours are offered at 10, noon, 2, and 5; one extra tour is added June 25–Aug.15 at 3:30.*

Flying: Firdafly A/S (☎ 57/86–53–88), based in **Sandane,** has air tours over Jostedalsbreen. Hotel Alexandra in Loen (*see* Lodging, *above*) arranges group flights. Mørefly A/S (☎ 70/18–35–00) runs 20-minute fjord and mountain-sightseeing trips by helicopter from **Ålesund.**

Hiking: Aak Fjellsportsenter (mountain sport) **Center** (☎ 71/22–64–44) in **Åndalsnes** specializes in walking tours of the area, from rambling in the hills for beginners and hikers to full-fledged rock climbing, along with rafting on the Rauma River. These are the guys who hang out of helicopters to rescue injured climbers, so they know what they're doing.

From Easter through September, **Jostedalen Breførlag** (5828 Gjerde, ☎ 56/68–32–73) offers glacier tours, from an easy 1½-hour family trip on the Nigard branch (equipment is provided) to advanced glacier courses with rock and ice climbing.

Diving: Ålesund Dykkersenter (Brunholmgt. 2, ☎ 70/12–34–24) has equipment for hire. All certificates are accepted.

Important Addresses and Numbers

EMERGENCIES

Ålesund: Police: ☎ 112 or 70/12–13–21. **Fire:** ☎ 111. **Ambulance:** ☎ 113. **Hospital Emergency Rooms/**Doctors/Dentists: ☎ 70/12–33–48. **Car Rescue:** ☎ 70/14–18–33.

LATE-NIGHT PHARMACIES

Nordstjernen (Keiser Wilhelmsgt. 22, Ålesund, ☎ 70/12–59–45) is open Wednesday until 6 and Saturday and Sunday from 6 to 8.

VISITOR INFORMATION

Ålesund (Rådhuset, ☎ 70/12–12–02); **Åndalsnes** (corner Nesgt./Romsdalsvn., ☎ 71/22–16–22); **Balestrand** (dockside, ☎ 57/69–12–55); **Flåm** (railroad station, ☎ 57/63–21–06); **Geiranger** (dockside, ☎ 70/26–30–99); **Hellesylt** (dockside, ☎ 70/26–50–52); **Lærdal** (☎ 57/66–65–09); **Molde** (Storgt 1, ☎ 71/21–92–62); **Sogndal** (Sognefjorden Tourist Information, ☎ 57/67–30–83); **Stryn** (☎ 57/87–23–32); **Ulvik** (dockside, ☎ 56/52–63–60); **Voss** (Hestevangen 10, ☎ 56/51–00–51). **Fjord Norway** (Bergen, ☎ 55/31–93–00) is a clearinghouse for information on all of western Norway.

7 Trondheim and the North

THE COAST OF NORTHERN NORWAY fidgets up from Trondheim, scattering thousands of islands and skerries along the way, until it reaches the northernmost point of Europe. Then it continues even farther, straggling above Sweden and Finland to point a finger of land into Russia.

Long and thin, this area covers an astonishing variety of land- and cityscapes, from bustling Trondheim to elegant Tromsø to colorful Karasjok, capital of the Sami. Some areas, especially when seen from the deck of the mail boats, seem like endless miles of wilderness marked by an occasional dot—a lonely cabin or a herd of reindeer. Views are often exquisite: glaciers, fjords, rocky coasts, and celestial displays of the midnight sun in summer and northern lights (aurora borealis) in winter.

Nordkapp (North Cape) has a character that changes with the seasons. In summer it teems with visitors and tour buses, and in winter, under several feet of snow, it is bleak, subtle, and astonishingly beautiful. It is accessible then only by squealing snow cat: a bracing and thoroughly Norwegian adventure.

EXPLORING

Numbers in the margin correspond to points of interest on the Trondheim and the North map.

Tour 1: Trondheim

❶ **Trondheim**'s original name, Nidaros (still the name of the cathedral), is a composite word referring to the city's location at the mouth of the Nid River. After a savage fire in 1681, the wooden town was rebuilt according to the plan of General Cicignon, a military man from Luxembourg, who also designed Trondheim's fort. The wide streets of the city center are still lined with brightly painted wooden houses and picturesque warehouses.

Start at Torget, the town square, with the statue of St. Olav in the middle. South on Munkegate is one of the finest art collections in Scandinavia, the **Nordenfjeldske Kunstindustrimuseum** (Decorative Arts Museum). It has superb period rooms from the Renaissance to 1950s Scandinavian modern. The Tiffany windows are also magnificent. *Munkegt. 5,* ☎ *73/52–13–11.* ☛ *NKr25 adults, NKr10 children.* ☺ *Late June–late Aug., Mon.–Sat. 10–8, Sun. noon–5; late Aug.–late June, Mon.–Sat. 10–3, Thurs. 10–7, Sun. noon–4.*

Continue on Munkegate to **Nidaros Domkirke** (Nidaros Cathedral), built on the grave of St. Olav, who formulated a Christian religious code for Norway in 1024 while he was king. He was killed in battle against local chieftains at Stiklestad. After he was buried, water sprang from his grave and people began to believe that his nails and hair continued to grow beneath the ground. Following a series of other miracles, the town became a pilgrimage site for the Christians of northern Europe, and Olav was canonized in 1164.

Although construction was begun in 1070, the oldest existing parts of the cathedral date from around 1150. During the Catholic period (ca. 1000–1537) it attracted crowds of pilgrims, but after the Reformation its importance declined and fires destroyed much of it. The 1814 Constitution decreed that Norway's kings should be crowned at the

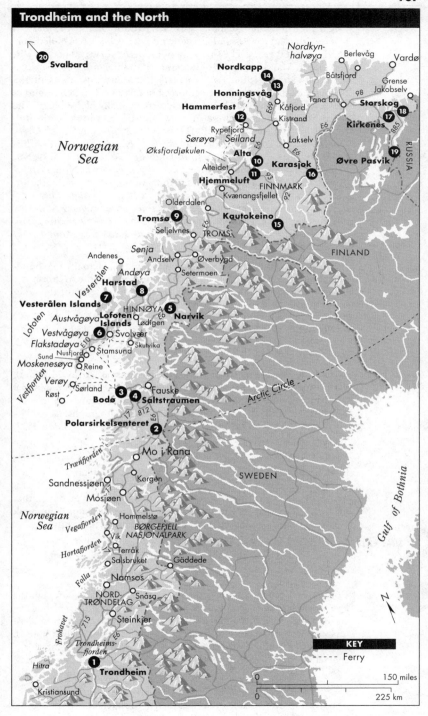

Nordkyn-
halvøya

Berlevåg

Vardø

Svalbard

Nordkapp 14

13

Båtsfjord

Grense
Jakobselv

Honningsvåg

Tana bru

98

Storskog

Hammerfest

Kåfjord

Kistrand

12

17 18

Rypefjord

E6

Kirkenes

*Norwegian
Sea*

Sørøya

Seiland

Lakselv

19

Øksfjordjøkulen

Alta

RUSSIA

Alteidet

10

Karasjok

Øvre Pasvik

11

16

Hjemmeluft

Kvænangsfjellet

FINNMARK

Olderdalen

Kautokeino

Tromsø 9

Seljelvnes

15

TROMS

Senja

FINLAND

Andenes

Andselv

Øverbygd

Andøya

Setermoen

Harstad

Vesterålen Islands 7

8

HINNØYA 5

Austvågøya

Narvik

**Lofoten
Islands**

Lødigen

6

Svolvær

Vestvågøya

Flakstadøya

Skutvika

Nusfjord

Stamsund

Sund

Moskenesøya

Reine

Vestfjorden

Verøy

Sørland

Røst

3 4

Bodø

Fauske

Saltstraumen

7 812

E6

Polarsirkelsenteret

2

Arctic Circle

Mo i Rana

Trænfjorden

SWEDEN

Sandnessjøen

Korgen

Mosjøen

*Norwegian
Sea*

Vegafjorden

Hommelstø

**BØRGEFJELL
NASJONALPARK**

Gulf of Bothnia

Vik

Hortafjorden

Terråk

Salsbruket

Gäddede

Folla

Namsos

**NORD-
TRØNDELAG**

Snåsa

715

Steinkjer

*Trondheims-
fjorden*

E6

Hitra

KEY

- - - - Ferry

Trondheim

Kristiansund

0 ——————— 150 miles
0 ——————— 225 km

cathedral. Restoration began around 1870 and the interior was completed in 1930. The facade is still being restored, and the western front, with twin towers and a rose window, has been reinstalled during the past 60 years. The first king of modern Norway, Haakon VII, and Queen Maud, daughter of Edward VII of England, were crowned in the cathedral in 1906. Two years later, the Constitution was altered to eliminate the coronation ceremony, but in 1957, King Olav, and in 1991, King Harald and Queen Sonja, were formally blessed here. The crown jewels, which visitors can view, are still kept in the cathedral. *Kongsgårdsgt. 2,* ☎ *73/52–52–33.* ☛ *NKr12 adults; NKr6 children, senior citizens, and students. Ticket also permits entry to Erkebispegården (see below).* ⊗ *Late June–late Aug., weekdays 9–5:30, Sat. 9–2, Sun. 1–4; May–mid-June and late Aug.–mid-Sept., Mon.–Sat. 9–3, Sat. 9–2, Sun. 1–4; Sept. 15–Apr., Mon.–Sat. noon–2:30, Sat. 11:30–2, Sun. 1–3.* ☛ *Tower, NKr5.* ⊗ *Late June–late Aug., daily every half-hour during regular opening hours. Crown jewels viewing Apr.–May and late Aug.–Oct., Fri. noon–2; June–late Aug., Mon.–Sat. 9:30–12:30, Sun. 1–4. Guided tours in English late June–late Aug., Mon.–Sat. at 11, 2, and 4.*

Next door is Scandinavia's oldest secular building (actually two buildings connected by a gatehouse), the **Erkebispegården** (the Archbishop's Palace). Dating from around 1160, it was the residence of the archbishop until the Reformation. After that, it was a Danish governor's palace, and later a military headquarters. ☎ *73/50–12–12.* ☛ *NKr12 adults, NKr6 children, senior citizens, and students. Ticket also permits entry to cathedral.* ⊗ *June–late Aug., weekdays 9–3, Sat. 9–2, Sun. noon–3.*

Within the Erkebispegården is the **Forsvarsmuseet** (Army Museum), with displays of uniforms, swords, and daggers. The **Hjemmefrontmuseet** (Resistance Museum), also there, documents the occupation of Norway during World War II through objects and photographs. ☎ *73/99–59–97.* ☛ *NKr5 adults, NKr2 children.* ⊗ *June–Aug., weekdays 9–3; year-round, weekends 11–3.*

On Bispegate turn right and follow the river. You'll pass the Gamle Bybro (Old Bridge) and reach Kjøpmannsgata, where you can turn left on Kongensgate. Behind the **Biblioteket** (Library, Peter Egges Pl. 1) are the remains of St. Olavskirke (St. Olav's Church). The crypt of another medieval church can be seen inside **Trondhjems og Strindens Sparebank** (a savings bank at Søndregate 2) during normal banking hours.

TIME OUT Two short blocks farther is Nordregate, a pedestrian mall. Pop into **Erichsens** restaurant/coffee shop (Nordregt. 10) for a quick lunch, cake and coffee, or a three-course meal.

Continue on Nordregate and turn left on Dronningens Gate. On the left is **Stiftsgården,** Scandinavia's largest wooden building, built in 1778 as a private home, the result of a competition between two sisters who were trying to outdo each other with the size of their houses. Today it is the king's official residence in Trondheim. The interior is sparsely furnished in threadbare Rococo, Empire, and Biedermeier. ☎ *73/52–13–11.* ☛ *NKr25 adults, NKr10 children.* ⊗ *June–late June, Tues.–Sun. 10-3 ; late June–late Aug., Tues.–Sun. 10–5.*

The street on the far side of Stiftsgården is Munkegate. To the right is **Ravnkloa Fiskehall** (fish market), by the water, where you can see an immense variety of seafood. Past the railroad station and the quay across the water, you'll come to a former prison that now houses the **Sjø-**

fartsmuseet (Maritime Museum). Inside are galleon figureheads, ship models, a harpoon cannon from a whaling boat, and a large collection of seafaring pictures. *Fjordgt. 6A,* ☎ *73/52–89–75.* ☛ *NKr10 adults, NKr5 children and senior citizens.* ۞ *Mon.–Sat. 9–3, Sun. noon–3; closed Sat. in winter.*

TIME OUT Down Kjøpmannsgata from the museum is a modern shopping mall, Olavskvartalet; in its center is **Torgcafeen,** run by the Grand Hotel Olav, which serves sandwiches, salads, and cakes.

Across the street is the Royal Garden Hotel, built in the same Hansa style as the buildings that line the wharf. Farther down are the oldest buildings on the river, dating from the 1700s.

For an unusual museum visit, you can take a half-hour ride to Fager-heim and the **Ringve Music Museum** at Ringve Gård, the childhood home of the naval hero Admiral Tordenskiold. Guides (music students) demonstrate the instruments on display and tell about their role in the history of music. Concerts are held regularly. *Lade Allé 60,* ☎ *73/92– 24–11.* ☛ *NKr50 adults, NKr30 senior citizens and students, NKr20 children. Guided tours in English late May–June, daily at noon, 2; July –mid-Aug., daily at 11, 12:30, 2:30, 4:30; mid-Aug.–late Aug., daily at 11, 12:30, 3; Sept., daily at noon; Oct.–mid-May, Sun. at 1:30. Tour lasts approximately 75 minutes.*

At the other end of town, **Trøndelag Folkemuseum** has a collection of rustic buildings from the turn of the century, including a dental office and a lace-and-ribbon-maker's workshop. The museum restaurant is from 1739 and serves traditional Norwegian food. *Sverresborg,* ☎ *73/ 53–14–90.* ☛ *NKr35 adults, NKr15 children and senior citizens.* ۞ *Late May–Aug., daily 11–6.*

Tour 2: Trondheim to Narvik

Nord Trøndelag, as the land above Trondheim is called, is largely agricultural. Taken on its own, it's beautiful, with farms, mountains, rock formations, and clear blue water, but compared with the rest of Norway, it is subtle, with only an undulating landscape—so many tourists just sleep through it on the night train, or fly over it on their way to the North.

The first town of any size is **Steinkjer,** a military base, boot camp for 3,000 Norwegian army recruits every year. North 350 kilometers (218 miles) is **Mo i Rana** (the poetic name means Mo on the Ranafjord), a center for iron and steel production using ore from nearby mines. Glacier fans can hike on the **Svartisen** (literally Black Ice), an ice cap 30 kilometers (19 miles) north of town.

② On a bleak stretch of treeless countryside 80 kilometers (50 miles) north of Mo i Rana is the Arctic Circle. The **Polarsirkelsenteret** (Arctic Circle Center), on E6, presents a multiscreen show about Norway. The post office has a special postmark, and you can get your Arctic Circle Certificate stamped. There's also a cafeteria and gift shop. *8242 Po-larsirkelen,* ☎ *75/16–60–66.* ☛ *NKr35.* ۞ *May–June, daily 10–8; July–Sept., daily 9 am–10 pm (Apr., Oct., cafeteria only).*

③ **Bodø,** a modern city of about 37,000 just above the Arctic Circle, is best known as the end station of the Nordlandsbanen railroad and the gateway to the Lofoten Islands and the North. At Bodø the midnight sun is visible from June 2 to July 10. Like many other coastal towns it began as a small fishing community, but today it is a commercial and administrative center.

Bodø is the best base for boat excursions to the coastal bird colonies on the Væren Islands. Bodø is also site of the **Nordland County Museum,** which depicts the life of the Sami and the regional history of the area, particularly its rich fishing heritage. *Prinsengt. 116,* ☎ *75/52–61–28.* ☛ *Free.* ⊙ *Weekdays 9–3, weekends noon–3.*

④ Saltstraumen, 33 kilometers (20 miles) southeast of Bodø on Route 80/17, is a 3-kilometer- (2-mile-) long and 500-foot-wide section of water between the outer fjord, which joins with the sea, and the inner fjord basin. During high tide, the volume of water rushing through the strait and into the basin is so great that whirlpools form. This is the legendary *malstrøm*—and the strongest one in the world. Sometimes as many as four separate whirlpools can be seen, and the noise made by these "cauldrons" can be both loud and eerie. All that rush of water brings enormous quantities of fish, making the malstrøm a popular fishing spot.

TIME OUT   **Saltstraumen Hotel** (☎ 75/58–76–85, ⅢⅩ 75/58–75–70) is practically on top of the malstrøm. The restaurant to the left of the entrance serves delicious steamed halibut in butter sauce.

⑤ Narvik, 336 kilometers (210 miles) north, is more easily reached by rail from Stockholm than from most places in Norway, as it is the end station on the Ofotbanen, the Norwegian railroad that connects with the Swedish railroad's northernmost line. It was originally established as the ice-free port for exporting Swedish iron ore mined around Kiruna.

On May 9, 1940, the German army invaded Norway through Narvik, and German occupying forces stayed for more than five years. After the war, Narvik, which had been leveled by the bombing, was rebuilt. The **Krigsminnemuseet** (War Memorial Museum) documents wartime events with artifacts, models, and pictures. *Torget,* ☎ *76/94–44–26.* ☛ *NKr20 adults, NKr10 children and senior citizens.* ⊙ *Mid-June–mid-Sept., Mon.–Sat. 10–10, Sun. 11–5; mid-Sept.–mid-June, Mon.–Sat. 11–2.*

Tour 3: The Lofoten Islands

⑥ Extending out into the ocean north of Bodø are the **Lofoten Islands,** a 190-kilometer (118-mile) chain of jagged peaks—mountaintops rising from the bottom of the sea like open jaws. The midnight sun is visible here from May 26 to July 17. In summer the idyll of farms, fjords, and fishing villages makes it a major tourist attraction, while in winter the coast facing the Arctic Ocean is one of Europe's stormiest.

Until about 40 years ago, fishing was the only source of income for the area. Cod and haddock were either dried or salted and sold on the Continent. Up to 6,000 boats with 30,000 fishermen would mobilize between January and March for the Lofotfisket, the world's largest cod-fishing event. During the season they fished in open boats and took shelter during stormy nights in *rorbuer,* simple cabins built right on the water. Today many rorbuer have been converted into lodgings, but Lofotfisket is still an annual tradition. In the summer, crisscrossing wooden racks are densely hung with drying cod while the midnight sun plays on the wooden boats in the harbor.

Svolvær, the main town, connected with the other islands by express boat and ferry, and by coastal steamer and air to Bodø, has a thriving summer art colony. A drive on E10, from Svolvær to the outer tip of Lofoten (130 kilometers/80 miles)—the town with the enigmatic name of Å—is an opportunity to see how the islanders really live. Scenic stops include **Nusfjord,** a 19th-century fishing village on the UNESCO list of historic monuments; **Sund,** with its smithy; and **Reine.**

TIME OUT **Gammelbua,** in Reine, serves excellent steamed halibut, homemade fish soufflé, and inspired desserts and cakes.

Off the tip of Moskenesøy, the last island with a bridge, is **Moskenesstraumen,** another malstrøm, not quite as dramatic as Saltstraumen, but inspiration to both Jules Verne, who wrote about it in *Journey Beneath the Sea,* and Edgar Allan Poe, who described it in his short story "A Descent into the Maelstrom."

❼ North of the Lofotens are the **Vesterålen Islands,** with more fishing villages and rorbuer, and diverse vegetation.

Tour 4: Harstad to the North Cape

❽ East of Vesterålen on Hinnøya, Norway's largest island, is **Harstad,** where the year-round population of 22,000 swells to 42,000 during the annual June cultural festival (the line-up includes concerts, theater, and dance) and its July deep-sea fishing festival.

❾ **Tromsø,** the most important city north of the Arctic Circle, and home to 50,000 people, is 318 kilometers (197 miles) northeast. At 2,558 square kilometers (987 square miles), it's Norway's largest city in terms of area, just about the same size as the country of Luxembourg. The midnight sun shines from May 21 to July 23, and the 13,000 students at the world's northernmost university are one reason the nightlife here is more lively than in many other northern cities.

Certainly the **Ishavskatedralen** (Arctic Cathedral) is the city's best-known structure. A looming peak of 11 descending triangles of concrete and glass, it is meant to evoke the shape of a Sami tent and the iciness of a glacier. Inside, an immense jewel-colored stained-glass window by Norwegian artist Viktor Sparre depicts the Second Coming. At the back of the church is a silver-and-copper organ, a modern adaptation of the omnipresent ships that hang in Scandinavian churches. ☎ 77/63–76–11. ☛ *NKr10 adults, children free.* ☉ *June–Aug., Mon.–Sat. 10–6, Sun. 1.30–6. Times may vary according to church services.*

The **Tromsø Museum,** part of Tromsø University, offers an extensive survey of local history, lifestyles, and nature, with dioramas on Sami culture, arctic hunting practices, and wildlife. *Universitetet, Lars Thøringsvei 10,* ☎ *77/64–50–00.* ☛ *NKr10 adults, NKr5 children.* ☉ *June–Aug., daily 9–9; Sept.–May, weekdays 8:30–3:30, Sat. noon–3, Sun. 11–4, Wed. evenings 7–10. At other times, call for hours.*

The **Polarmuseet** (Polar Museum), in an 1830s customs warehouse, documents the history of the polar region, with skis and equipment from Roald Amundsen's expedition to the South Pole and a reconstructed Svalbard hunting station from 1910. *Søndre Tollbugt. 11b,* ☎ *77/68–43–73.* ☛ *NKr25 adults, NKr5 children.* ☉ *Mid-May–mid-June, daily 11–6; mid-June–Aug., daily 11–8; Sept.–mid-May, daily 11–3.*

There are more museums in Tromsø, but to get a real sense of its northerly immensity and peace, take the **Fjellheisen** (cable car) from behind the cathedral up to the mountains, just a few minutes out of the city center. In the late afternoon and on weekends, summer and winter, this is where locals go to ski, picnic, walk their lucky dogs, and admire the view. ☎ *77/63–51–21.* ☛ *NKr 45 adults, NKr20 children.* ☉ *Late Apr.–late May, daily 10–5; late May–Sept., daily 10–1:30 am if it's sunny. At other times, call for hours.*

It's 409 kilometers (253 miles) to Alta on coastal road most of the way. Kautokeino Sami spend the summer in turf huts at **Kvænangsfjellet,** so you might see a few of their reindeer. **Øksfjordjøkelen,** the only glacier in Norway that calves into the sea, is 13 kilometers (8 miles) west of Alteidet.

⑩ **Alta** is a major transportation center into Finnmark, the far north of
⑪ Norway. Most people come just to spend the night before making the final ascent, but it's worth a trek to **Hjemmeluft,** southwest of the city, to see four groupings of 2,500- to 6,000-year-old **prehistoric rock carvings,** the largest in northern Europe. The pictographs, featuring ships, reindeer, and even a man with a bow and arrow, were discovered in 1973 and are included on the UNESCO World Heritage List. The rock carvings form part of the **Alta Museum,** which in 1993 won the "European Museum of the Year Award." The museum has displays delineating the history of the area from the Stone Age until today, including its destruction in World War II. ☎ *78/43–53–77 (Alta Museum).* ☛ *Summer, NKr40 adults; winter NKr30, children free.* ☉ *May, daily 9–6; June–mid-June and mid-Aug.–Sept., daily 8–8; mid-June–mid-Aug., daily 8 am–11 pm; Oct.–Apr., weekdays 9–3, weekends 11–4.*

On the way to the North Cape, 145 kilometers (90 miles) from Alta,
⑫ is the world's northernmost town, **Hammerfest,** an important fishing center. At these latitudes the "most northerlies" become numerous, but certainly the lifestyles here are a testament to determination, especially in winter, when night lasts for months. In 1891 Hammerfest decided to brighten the situation and purchased a generator from Thomas Edison. It was the first city in Europe to have electric street lamps. Hammerfest is also home to the **Royal and Ancient Polar Bear Society.** Don't visit the society if you don't like stuffed bears. *Town Hall Basement.* ☛ *Free.* ☉ *June–Aug., weekdays 8–8, weekends 10–5.*

The journey from Alta to the Cape is 217 kilometers (134 miles) and
⑬ includes a 45-minute ferry ride from Kåfjord to **Honningsvåg,** the last village before the Cape. Honningsvåg was completely destroyed at the end of World War II, when the Germans retreated and burned everything they left behind. Only a single wood church, which still survives, was not left in embers. The **Nordkappmuseet** (North Cape Museum), on the third floor of Nordkapphuset (North Cape House), documents the history of the fishing industry in the region as well as the history of tourism at the North Cape. *9750 Honningsvåg,* ☎ *78/47–28–33.* ☛ *NKr15 adults, NKr5 children.* ☉ *Mid-June–mid-Aug., Mon.–Sat. 9–8, Sun. 1–8; mid-Aug.–mid-June, weekdays 11–4.*

From Honningsvåg, it's 34 kilometers (21 miles) on treeless tundra,
⑭ with crumbling mountains and sparse dwarf plants, to **Nordkapp.** The contrast between this near-barren territory and the new **North Cape Hall** is striking. Blasted into the interior of the plateau, it includes a panorama restaurant. A tunnel leads past a small chapel to a grotto with a panoramic view of the Arctic Ocean and to the cliff wall itself, passing exhibits that trace the history of the Cape, from Richard Chancellor, an Englishman who drifted around it and named it in 1533, to Oscar II, king of Norway and Sweden, who climbed to the top of the plateau in 1873, and King Chulalongkorn of Siam (now Thailand), who visited the Cape in 1907. Out on the plateau itself, a hollow sculptured

globe is illuminated by the midnight sun, which shines from May 11 to August 31. *9764 Nordkapp,* ☎ *78/47–25–99.* ☛ *NKr150 adults, NKr70 children.*

Although this area is notoriously crowded in the summer, with endless lines of tour buses, it's completely different from fall through spring, when the snow is yards deep and the sea is frosty gray. Because the roads are closed in winter, the only access is from the tiny fishing village of Skarsvåg via Sno-Cat, a thump-and-bump ride that's as unforgettable as the beautifully bleak view. For winter information, contact **North Cape Travel** (☎ 78/47–25–99). Knivsjellodden, slightly west and less dramatic than the North Cape, is actually a hair farther north.

Tour 5: Samiland

Everyone has heard of Lapland, but few know its real name, Samiland. The Sami recognize no national boundaries, as their territory stretches from the Kola Peninsula in the Soviet Union through Finland, Sweden, and Norway. These indigenous reindeer herders are a distinct ethnic group, with a language related to Finnish. Although still considered nomadic, they no longer live in tents or huts, except for short periods during the summer, when their animals graze along the coast. They have had to conform to today's lifestyles, but their traditions survive through their language, music (called Joik), art, and handicrafts. Norwegian Samiland is synonymous with the communities of Kautokeino and Karasjok in Finnmark.

⑮ Kautokeino, 129 kilometers (80 miles) southeast of Alta, is the site of the Sami theater and the Nordic Sami Institute, dedicated to the study of Sami culture. It is a center for Sami handicrafts and education, complete with a school of reindeer herding.

Guovdageainnu (Kautokeino in the Sami language) **Gilisillju,** the local museum, documents the way of life of both the nomadic and the resident Sami of that area prior to World War II, with photographs and artifacts, including costumes, dwellings, and art. *9520 Kautokeino,* ☎ *78/45–62–03.* ☛ *NKr10 adults, children free.* ☺ *Mid-June–mid-Aug., weekdays 9–7, weekends noon–7; mid-Aug.–mid-June, weekdays 9–3.*

⑯ Karasjok, on the other side of the Finnmark Plateau, is the seat of the 39-member Sami Parliament and capital of Samiland. It has a typical inland climate, with the accompanying temperature extremes. The best time to come is at Easter, when the communities are celebrating the weddings and baptisms of the year and taking part in reindeer races and other colorful festivities. In summer, when many of the Sami go to the coast with their reindeer, the area is not nearly as interesting.

The **Samid Vuorka-Davvirat** (Sami Collections) are a comprehensive museum of Sami culture, with emphasis on the arts, reindeer herding, and the status of women in the Sami community. *Museumsgt. 17,* ☎ *78/46–63–05.* ☛ *NKr25 adults, NKr5 children, NKr15 students.* ☺ *Early June–late Aug., Mon.–Sat. 9–6, Sun. 10–6; late Aug.–Oct., weekdays 9–3, weekends 10–3; Nov.–Mar., weekdays 9–3, weekends noon–3; Apr.–early Jun., weekdays 9–3, weekends 10–3.*

From late fall to early spring you can go **reindeer sledding.** A Sami guide will take you out on a wooden sled tied to a couple of unwieldy reindeer, and you'll clop through the barren, snow-covered scenery of Finnmark. Wide and relatively flat, the colorless winter landscape is veined by inky alder branches and little else. You'll reach a *lavvu,* a traditional Sami tent, and be invited in to share a meal of boiled reindeer, bread, jam, and strong coffee next to an open alder fire. It's an extraordinary experience. *Karasjok Opplevelser,* ☎ 78/46–73–60.

Tour 6: The Finnish-Russian Connection

At its very top, Norway hooks over Finland and touches Russia for 122 kilometers (75 miles). The towns in east Finnmark have a more heterogeneous population than those in the rest of the country. A century ago, during hard times in Finland, many industrious Finns settled in this region, and their descendants keep the language alive there.

⓱ A good way to visit this part of Norway is to fly to **Kirkenes** and then explore the region by car. Only Malta was bombed more than Kirkenes during World War II—virtually everything you see in town has been built within the past 45 years.

From Kirkenes, it's about 60 kilometers (37 miles) to **Grense Jakobselv,** the Russian border. As a protest against constant Russian encroachment in the area, King Oscar II built a chapel right at the border
⓲ in 1869. Just east of Kirkenes is **Storskog,** for many years the only official land crossing of the border between Norway and Russia.

The southernmost part of Finnmark, a narrow tongue of land tucked
⓳ between Finland and Russia, is **Øvre Pasvik** national park. This subarctic evergreen forest is the western end of Siberia's *taiga* and supports many varieties of flora found only here. The area is surprisingly lush, and in good years all the cloudberries make the swamps shine orange.

Tour 7: Svalbard

⓴ About 640 kilometers (400 miles) north of the North Cape are the islands of **Svalbard,** the largest of which is Spitsbergen. Officially part of Norway only since 1920, they might have remained wilderness, with only the occasional visitor, if coal had not been discovered late in the 19th century. Today both a Norwegian and a Russian coal company have operations there, and there are two Russian coal miners' communities. The islands offer ample opportunities for ski, dogsled, and snowmobile exploring.

The best way to experience Svalbard is by organized tour, as accommodations and travel services on the islands themselves are sparse. The capital, **Longyearbyen,** is 90 minutes by air from Tromsø (there are no scheduled boats from the mainland to Tromsø). It was named for an American, John Monroe Longyear, who established a mining operation there in 1906. Only three species of land mammals besides humans—polar bears, reindeer, and Arctic foxes—and one species of bird—ptarmigan—have adapted to Svalbard winters, but during the summer months, more than 30 species of birds nest on the steep cliffs of the islands, and white whales, seals, and walruses also come for the season. Do heed warnings about polar bears: the bears can be a real hazard.

Because Svalbard is so far north, it has four months of continual daylight, from April 21 to August 21. Summers can be lush, with hundreds of varieties of wildflowers. The season is so compressed that buds, full-blown flowers, and seed appear simultaneously on the same plant.

What to See and Do with Children

Tromsø

Take Bus 28 to the mainland to ride Fjellheisen (*see* Tour 4, *above*) cable car to **Storsteinen** (the Big Rock), 1,386 feet above sea level, for a great view of the city.

Nordlysplanetariet (the Northern Lights Planetarium), at Breivika, is just outside town. Here, 112 projectors guarantee a 360-degree view of programs, which include a tour through the northern lights, the midnight sun, and geological history, as well as a film and multimedia show about the city. *Breivika,* ☎ *77/67–60–00.* ☛ *NKr50 adults, NKr25 children, NKr40 senior citizens.* ⊙ *June–Aug., shows in English daily at noon and 3; Sept.–May call for show times.*

At **Tromsø Museum** (*see* Tour 4, *above*) children can listen to animal sounds over earphones, match animals to tales about them, and play with a nearly life-size dinosaur. An open-air museum is on the same grounds.

Off the Beaten Path

In winter this entire region, blanketed by snow and cold, is off the beaten track. As the Norwegians say, there is no bad weather, only bad clothes—so bundle up and explore.

Kirkenes

From mid-June to mid-August, the **FFR** (Hammerfest, ☎ 78/41–10–00) operates visa-free day cruises to Murmansk, Russia, on a high-speed catamaran. Booking is required two weeks in advance.

St. Georgs Kapell, 45 kilometers (28 miles) west of Kirkenes, is the only Russian-Orthodox chapel in Norway, where the Orthodox Skolt-Sami had their summer encampment. It's a tiny building, and services are held outside, weather permitting.

Mo i Rana

Setergrotta and **Grønligrotta** are two of close to 200 caves 26 kilometers (16 miles) northwest of Mo i Rana. Setergrotta, with 7,920 feet of charted underground paths, many narrow passages, natural "chimneys," and an underground river, is for serious spelunkers. *Usually open from mid-June to mid-August, however, times vary with conditions. Check with the tourist office,* ☎ *75/15–04–21.* ☛ *NKr160 for a two-hour guided tour.*

Grønligrotta, Scandinavia's best-known show cave, even has electric lights. The 20-minute tour goes deep into the limestone cave to the underground river. ☛ *NKr40 adults, NKr20 children. Tours daily on the hour 10–7.* ⊙ *Mid-June–mid-Aug.*

Svartisen

Saltens Dampskibsselskap (☎ 75/72–10–20) offers seven-hour boat tours from Bodø to Svartisen, the second-largest glacier in Norway, near Mo i Rana, on Saturdays in summer. The easiest way to get to the glacier is from Mo, 32 kilometers (20 miles) by car to Svartisvatn lake. A boat crosses the lake every hour to within 2½ kilometers (1.5 miles) of the Østerdal arm of the glacier. If you plan to get to the glacier on your own, you should inquire at the tourist office about connecting with a guide. Glacier walking is extremely hazardous and should never be done without a professional guide—even though a glacier may appear fixed and static, it is always changing; there's always the danger of calving and hard-to-spot crevasses.

SHOPPING

Harstad
Trastadsenteret (Rik. Kaarbøsgt. 19, ☎ 77/06–29–08) sells pottery, weavings, and textile prints by local artists.

Kåfjord
Manndalen Husflidslag (☎ 77/71–62–73) at Løkvoll in Manndalen on E6 about 15 kilometers (9 miles) west of Alta is a center for Coastal Sami weaving on vertical looms. Local weavers sell their rugs and wall hangings along with other regional crafts.

Karasjok
The specialties of the region are Sami crafts, particularly handmade knives. In **Samelandssenter** (☎ 78/46–73–60) is a large collection of shops featuring northern specialties, including **Knivsmed Strømeng** (☎ 78/46–71–05).

Kautokeino
The Frank and Regina **Juhls** silver gallery (☎ 78/48–61–89) sells Sami crafts as well as its own modern jewelry.

Lofoten
Lofoten is a mecca for artists and craftspeople, who come for the spectacular scenery and the ever-changing subtle light; a list of galleries and crafts centers, with all locations marked on a map, is available from tourist offices.

Probably the best-known craftsperson in the region is Tor Vegard Mørkved, better known as **Smeden i Sund** (the blacksmith at Sund; ☎ 76/09–36–29). Watch him make wrought iron cormorants in many sizes, as well as candlesticks and other gift items.

Tromsø
The city has two major shopping centers: **Veita** (Storgt. 102, ☎ 77/68–07–87) and **Pyramiden** (Tromsdalen, ☎ 77/63–82–00).

Trondheim
Trondheim has an extraordinary number of high-quality art and handicraft stores. **Husfliden** (Olav Tryggvasonsgt. 18, ☎ 73/52–18–74) and **Yvonne Verkstedutsalg og Galleri** (Ørjaveita 6, ☎ 73/52–73–27) sell works of local artists. **Olavskvartalet,** across from the Royal Garden Hotel, is a shopping center with many specialty stores.

SPORTS AND OUTDOOR ACTIVITIES

Bird-Watching
From Moskenes, just north of Å (or from Bodø), you can take a ferry to the bird sanctuaries of **Værøy** and **Røst.** Hundreds of thousands of seabirds inhabit the cliffs of the islands, in particular the eider ducks, favorites of the local population, which build small shelters for their nests. Eventually the down collected from these nests ends up in *dyner* (feather comforters).

There are even more birds in Gjesvær on the east coast of the Honningsvåg. Contact Ola Thomassen (☎ 78/47–57–73) for organized outings.

Dogsledding
Canyon Huskies (☎ 78/43–33–06), in Alta, arranges all kinds of personalized tours, whether you want to stay in a tent or hotel, and

whether you want to drive your team or stay in the sled. Like most Norwegian sled dogs, these are very friendly.

Fishing

The Nidelven (Nid River) in **Trondheim** is one of Norway's best salmon and trout rivers. You can fish right in the city, but, as usual, you'll need a license. Ask at any sports store. In the waters of **Tromsø,** there are cod, coalfish, haddock, and the occasional catfish. In Finnmark, ice fishing is a passion, often with the entire family involved. (The Sami sometimes ice fish from tiny houses they pull onto the ice.) Check with the tourist board to find out if and where any competitions are scheduled. Bring at least your own ice drill.

Hiking

In **Tromsø** there's good hiking in the mountains above the city, reachable by funicular. Other regional possibilities begin anywhere outside the cities (usually only a few minutes away). In between the Alta and Karasjok areas, the **Finnmarksvidda** has marked trails with overnight possibilities in lodges. Contact the Norske Turistforening (Buks 1963 Vika, 0125 Oslo, ☎ 22/83–25–50, FAX 22/83–24–78) and the Finnmark Travel Association (☎ 78/43–54–44).

Hunting

Two licenses are needed to hunt, and for large game, especially moose, applicants must draw lots. Contact the Finnmark Travel Association (☎ 78/43–54–44).

Rafting

Deep-sea rafting is a relatively new sport in the area, but one that is as exhilarating as it is beautiful. Among the several tours is a three-hour trip to the North Cape. Call **Nordkapp Safari** (☎ 78/47–27–94).

Reindeer Sledding

Reindeer sledding is a wonderful Finnmark experience (*see* Tour 5, *above*).

Skiing

Bymarka and **Estenstadmarka,** the wooded areas on the periphery of Trondheim, are popular among cross-country skiers. At **Skistua** (ski lodge) in Bymarka, and at **Vassfjellet** south of the city, there are downhill runs. In Tromsø, the mountains, only eight minutes away by funicular, are not only a great place to ski, but also to hike (*see* Tour 4, *above*). Elsewhere, you'll have to ask specifics from the tourist board. Listen to the weather reports and heed warnings. Blizzards come in quickly over the water; the wind alone can knock a sizable person clear off his or her feet.

Beaches

In Trondheim the island of Munkholmen, easily reached by ferry from Ravnkloa, has a popular sandy beach. Elsewhere, most beaches are rocky, and the water is, as the Norwegians say, fresh. However, some of the beaches of Nordland are long and sandy, with temperatures reaching as high as 20°C (68°F).

DINING AND LODGING

Dining

Trondheim is known for several dishes, including *surlaks* (pickled salmon), marinated in a sweet-and-sour brine with onions and spices, and served with sour cream. A sweet specialty is *tekake* (tea cake), which looks like a thick-crust pizza topped with a lattice pattern of cinnamon and sugar.

If you visit northern Norway between May and August, try the specialty of *måsegg* and *Mack-øl*, more for curiosity value than for taste. *Måsegg* (seagulls' eggs) are always served hard-boiled and halved in their shells. They're larger than chicken eggs, and they look exotic, with greenish-gray speckled shells and bright orange yolks, but they taste like standard supermarket eggs. *Mack-øl* (similar to pils) is brewed in Tromsø at the world's northernmost brewery. Otherwise, as in the rest of provincial Norway, most better restaurants are in hotels.

Lodging

Most Trondheim hotels have summer rates, but for some, a hotel pass or special booking method is required. Unless otherwise noted, breakfast is included.

At times it seems as though the SAS and Rica hotel chains are the only ones in northern Norway, and often that is true. These are always top-rate, usually the most expensive hotels in town, with the best restaurant and the most extensive facilities. Rustic cabins and campsites are also available everywhere, as well as some independent hotels.

In the Lofoten and Vesterålen islands, *rorbuer*, fishing cottages that have been converted into lodgings or modern versions of these simple dwellings, are the most popular form of accommodation. These rustic quayside cabins, with minikitchens, bunk beds, living rooms, and showers, are reasonably priced, and they give a unique experience of the region. *Sjøhus* (sea houses) are larger, usually two- or three-storied buildings similar to rorbuer.

For price-category definitions, *see* How to Use this Book *in* On the Road with Fodor's.

Alta

LODGING

$$$ **SAS Alta Hotell.** This glass-and-white hotel does everything it can to make you forget that you are in a place where it is dark much of the time. Everything is light, from the reflectors on the ceiling of public rooms to the white furniture in the bedrooms. ✉ *Box 1093, 9501,* ☎ *78/43–50–00,* ℻ *78/43–58–25. 155 rooms with bath or shower. 2 restaurants, 2 bars, lobby lounge, sauna, exercise room, nightclub meeting rooms. AE, DC, MC, V.*

Bodø

DINING

$$–$$$ **Marlene Restaurant.** Set within the SAS Royal hotel (*see below*), the Marlene offers a superb seafood buffet throughout the summer. The salmon dishes, in particular, are excellent. ✕ *Storgt. 2,* ☎ *75/52–41–00. Reservations advised. AE, DC, MC, V.*

$$ **Turisthytta.** This mountaintop lodge is accessible only by car, but it is a fine place in which to have a meal while basking in the midnight sun. There is a good range of dishes, from snacks and open-faced sandwiches to fresh fish. ✕ *Turisthytta,* ☎ *75/58–33–00. Reservations advised. No credit cards.*

LODGING

$$ **Diplomat.** This hotel near the harbor is a short walk from the shopping district. The modern rooms are soberly decorated. The restaurant has live entertainment, but the food could be more imaginative. ✉ *Sjøgt. 23, 8000 Bodø,* ☎ *75/52–70–00,* ℻ *75/52–24–60. 104 rooms with* shower (no bathtubs). 2 restaurants, bar, exercise room, nightclub, convention center. AE, DC, MC, V.

$$ Norrøna. This bed-and-breakfast-style establishment is comfortable, with a location just as grand as that of the nearby Grand Royal but at a much more pleasant price. ☎ Storgt. 4B, ☎ 75/52–55–50, FAX 75/52–33–88. 105 rooms with bath or shower. AE, DC, MC, V.

$$ SAS Royal. This grandiose hotel pulses with life and has enough amenities to keep you entertained nearly around the clock. As with all SAS hotels, the rooms are spacious and well equipped, and the service is impeccable. ☎ Storgt. 2, ☎ 75/52–41–00, FAX 75/52–74–93. 194 rooms with bath. Restaurant, wine bar, sauna, health club, nightclub. AE, DC, MC, V.

Hammerfest

LODGING

$$$ Hammerfest Hotel. Right on the pleasant Rådhusplassen, this guest house has handsome, harborview rooms for tolerable prices in a town where hotels are expensive. ☎ Strandgt. 2–4, ☎ 78/41–16–22, FAX 78/41–21–27. 53 rooms with bath or shower. Restaurant, cafeteria, pub, sauna. AE, DC, MC, V.

$$–$$$ Rica Hotel Hammerfest. The rooms are functional and small, but the furniture is comfortable. There is also an informal pizza pub and a spacious bar. ☎ Sørøygt. 15, ☎ 78/41–13–33, FAX 78/41–13–11. 88 rooms with bath or shower. Restaurant, bar, pizzeria, sauna, health club, convention center. AE, DC, MC, V.

Harstad

DINING

$$$ Røkenes Gård. The farm was originally homesteaded in AD 400, and the large white wooden building with an intricately carved portal opened in 1750 as a commercial trading house and inn. The ninth generation of descendants restored it, and it is now a cozy restaurant serving regional specialties, such as reindeer gravlaks, and cloudberry parfait. Next door is the Gallery Harr, with the work of graphic artist Knut Erik Harr. ✗ 9400 Harstad, ☎ 77/01–74–65. Reservations required at least 24 hours in advance. AE, DC, MC, V. Closed Sun.

LODGING

$$–$$$ Grand Nordic. It's a neat, brick-red building in the Bauhaus style, with Norwegian 1970s-look leather furniture in the public rooms. Bedrooms, no bigger than necessary, have dark-wood furnishings. The restaurant and conference rooms are lighter and more modern. ☎ Strandgt. 9, 9400 Harstad, ☎ 77/06–21–70, FAX 77/06–77–30. 85 rooms with bath or shower, 3 suites. 2 restaurants, bar, nightclub, convention center. AE, DC, MC, V.

Honningsvåg

LODGING

$ Hotel Havly. This simple hotel is cozy and centrally located, with small, spic-and-span rooms, and an ample breakfast buffet. Because this is a seamen's hostel, no alcohol is served. ☎ 9751 Honningsvåg, ☎ 78/47–29–66, FAX 78/47–30–10. 35 rooms with shower. Restaurant, meeting rooms. AE, MC, V. Closed Dec. 24–Jan. 2.

Karasjok

DINING AND LODGING

$$$–$$$$ SAS Karasjok Hotell. This establishment feels more like a ski chalet than
★ a hotel, with bright rooms, done in warm blues and reds, that are cozy rather than industrial. The lobby is more staid, with a seating arrangement up front. The hotel's wonderful Sami restaurant, Storgam-

men, serves traditional fare, including reindeer cooked over open fires. ☎ *Box 38, 9731 Karasjok,* ☎ *78/46–74–00,* ⊞ *78/46–68–02. 56 rooms with shower. Restaurant, bar, saunas, meeting rooms. AE, DC, MC, V. Closed Dec. 24–Jan. 2.*

Kirkenes

$$–$$$$ **Rica Arctic Hotel.** Do not confuse this hotel with the Rica Hotel Kirkenes, an older establishment, which ends up costing the same during the summer. Rooms here are spacious and pretty, with white-painted furniture and light print textiles. ☎ *Kongensgt. 1–3, 9900 Kirkenes,* ☎ *78/99–29–29,* ⊞ *78/99–11–59. 80 rooms with bath. Restaurant, bar, indoor pool, beauty salon, sauna, exercise room, nightclub, convention center, shops. AE, DC, MC, V.*

Lofoten Islands

DINING

$$ **Fiskekrogen.** This quayside restaurant in the fishing village of Henningsvær will prepare your own catch. Chef-owner Otto Asheim's specialties include smoked *gravlaks* (smoking the dill-marinated salmon gives it extra depth of flavor) and sautéed ocean catfish garnished with mussels and shrimp. ✕ *8330 Henningsvær,* ☎ *76/07–46–52. Reservations required. DC, MC, V.*

LODGING

$$–$$$ **Nyvågar Rorbu og Aktivitetssenter.** This hotel and recreation complex is a 15-minute drive from the Svolvær airport. It looks old, but it was built in 1990. Activities are well organized, with fishing-boat tours, eagle safaris, and deep-sea rafting, as well as planned evening entertainment. ☎ *8310 Kabelvåg, Storvågan,* ☎ *76/07–89–00,* ⊞ *76/07–89–50. 30 rooms with shower (120 beds). 2 restaurants, meeting rooms. AE, DC, MC, V.*

$ **Henningsvær Rorbuer.** This small group of renovated turn-of-the-century rorbuer, all facing the sea, is just outside the center of Lofoten's most important fishing village. Breakfasts can be ordered from the cafeteria/reception, where there's a fireplace and a TV. Reservations are essential for July. ☎ *8330 Henningsvær,* ☎ *76/07–46–00,* ⊞ *76/07–49–10. 15 1- or 2-bedroom rorbuer with shower. Cafeteria, grill sauna, laundry service. MC, V.*

$ **Wulff-Nilsens Rorbuer.** A five-minute drive from Reine, which was named the country's prettiest village by Norwegian travel agents, this neat cluster of red-painted rorbuer is an excellent starting point for fishing excursions and mountain walks. Seagulls nest only yards from the cabins. The rorbuer are rustic but comfortably equipped; they have stoves and refrigerators. ✕ *Hamnøy, 8390 Reine,* ☎ *76/09–23–20,* ⊞ *76/09–21–54. 13 1-, 2-, or 3-bedroom rorbuer with shower, 2 without shower. No credit cards.*

Narvik

LODGING

$$–$$$ **Inter Nor Grand Royal.** It looks like an office building from the outside, but inside it is a comfortable top-class hotel, with big, rather formal rooms. The main restaurant is also quite formal. ☎ *Kongensgt. 64, 8500 Narvik,* ☎ *76/94–15–00,* ⊞ *76/94–55–31. 108 rooms with bath or shower. 2 restaurants, 2 bars, sauna, exercise room, nightclub, convention center. AE, DC, MC, V.*

Tromsø

DINING

$$–$$$ **Brankos.** Branko and Anne Brit Bartolj serve authentic Yugoslavian food—including *cevapcici* (small, spicy meatballs) and *raznici*—accompanied by their own imported Yugoslavian wines, in their art-filled dining room. ✕ *Storgt. 57,* ☎ *77/68–26–73. Reservations required. AE, DC, MC, V. No lunch.*

$$–$$$ **Compagniet.** An old wooden trading house from 1837 is now a stylish restaurant serving modern Norwegian food. Chef Anders Blomkvist prepares cream of lobster soup with a dash of brandy and escargot in garlic sauce for starters, while main dishes include grilled crayfish and marinated smoked reindeer. ✕ *Sjøgt. 12,* ☎ *77/65–57–21. Reservations required. AE, DC, MC, V. No lunch in winter.*

LODGING

$$–$$$ **Hotel With.** This recently constructed building on the waterfront in the dock area has spacious rooms decorated in shades of gray with the occasional colorful accent. The sauna/relaxation room on the top floor has the best view in town. As part the Home Hotel chain, Hotel With offers alcohol-free beer, a hot meal, and waffles and coffee at all times included in the room price. ▨ *Sjøgt. 35–37, 9000,* ☎ *77/68–70–00,* FAX *77/68–96–16. 76 rooms with shower. Exercise room, meeting rooms. AE, DC, MC, V.*

$$–$$$ **SAS Royal Hotel.** It's a new, modern hotel with splendid views over the Tromsø shoreline, but standard rooms are tiny, and even the costlier "Royal Club" rooms aren't big enough for real desks and tables, so modular ones have been attached to the walls. ▨ *Sjøgt. 7, 9000,* ☎ *77/60–00–00,* FAX *77/66–42–60. 193 rooms with bath, 6 suites. Restaurant, bar, nightclub, convention center. AE, DC, MC, V.*

$$ **Saga.** Central location on a pretty town square and a helpful staff make the Saga a good place to stay. Its restaurant has affordable, hearty meals, and the rooms—though somewhat basic—are quiet and comfortable. ▨ *Richard Withs Pl. 2,* ☎ *77/68–11–80,* FAX *77/68–23–80. 52 rooms with bath. Restaurant, cafeteria. AE, DC, MC, V.*

$–$$ **Polar Hotell.** This no-frills hotel gives good value for the money in winter, when none of the bigger hotels have special rates. Rooms are small, and the orange/brown color scheme is a bit dated, but it's a pleasant, unassuming place. ▨ *Grønnegt. 45, 9000,* ☎ *77/68–64–80,* FAX *77/68–91–36. 64 rooms with shower (no bathtubs). Restaurant, bar, meeting rooms. AE, DC, MC, V.*

Trondheim

DINING

$$$ **Bryggen.** The furnishings are in bleached wood, with dark-blue and
★ red accessories, and the atmosphere is intimate. The menu features a reindeer fillet salad with cranberry vinaigrette and an herb cream soup with both freshwater and ocean crayfish for appetizers. Meat dishes include breast of chicken with a red-wine sauce and lamb medley. ✕ *Øvre Bakklandet 66,* ☎ *73/52–02–30. Reservations required. AE, DC, MC, V. Closed Sun. Dinner only.*

$$–$$$ **Havfruen.** "The Mermaid" has a maritime dining room with an open kitchen at street level, while in the cellar, 200-year-old stone walls from the original building frame the setting. Fish soup is the most popular starter, while summer main dishes include poached halibut. Desserts are simple—the citrus parfait is especially good. ✕ *Kjøpmannsgt. 7,* ☎ *73/53–26–26. Reservations advised. AE, DC, MC, V. Closed Sun. Dinner only.*

$$ **Hos Magnus.** The price/value ratio is excellent at this old-fashioned, cozy restaurant in the new part of Bryggen. The menu ranges from old local specialty surlaks for appetizers to such modern dishes as rose of salmon cured and marinated with aquavit brandy. Lamb roulade stuffed with cheese and mushroom sauce is on the meat menu, and there

are ample fish and vegetarian choices, too. ✗ *Kjøpmannsgt. 63,* ☎ *73/ 52–41–10. Reservations advised. AE, DC, MC, V.*

$$ **Lian.** In the heights above the city, Lian offers beautiful scenery and Norwegian standards. The oldest part of the restaurant dates from 1700, but the round section, from the 1930s, commands the best view. The food is solid, honest, and hearty, with roast beef, reindeer, smoked pork loin, and the old standby, *kjøttkaker* (Norwegian meat cakes). ✗ *Lianvn.,* ☎ *72/55–90–77. No credit cards. Closed Mon.*

$$ **Tavern på Sverresborg.** This big, yellow, wooden former ferryman's
★   house at the Trøndelag Folkemuseum has been an inn since 1739. The food is authentic Norwegian, including meat and fish prepared with old methods—pickled, salted, and dried. Choices include a plate with four different kinds of herring, roast lamb ribs, trout, meat cakes, and rømmegrøt. Homemade oatmeal bread and rolls accompany all dishes. ✗ *Sverresborg Allé,* ☎ *73/52–09–32. MC, V. Dinner only Sept. 2– May 19.*

$ **De 3 Stuer.** This small bistro chain serves everything homemade, and the daily special features such dishes as fish soufflé, fried fish with sour-cream sauce, split-pea soup with sausage, boiled beef, and lamb stew, all served with dessert and coffee. For lunch there's smørbrød, crescent rolls, salads, and cakes. ✗ *Trondheim Torg,* ☎ *73/52–92–20; Gågaten Leuthenhaven,* ☎ *73/52–43–42; Dronningens Gt. 11,* ☎ *73/52–63– 20. No reservations. No credit cards. Dronningens Gt. closed Sun.*

DINING AND LODGING

$$$ **Grand Hotel Olav.** Right in the center of town, this hotel boasts 27 different room models, all impeccably decorated. It is part of a complex that contains shops, conference rooms, and the Olavshallen Concert Hall (home of the Trondheim Philharmonic). ⌸ *Kjøpmannsgt. 48,* ☎ *73/53–53–10,* ℻ *73/53–57–20. 106 rooms, 5 no-smoking rooms. 3 restaurants, bar, pub, nightclub. AE, DC, MC, V.*

$$–$$$$ **Prinsen.** Rooms in this hotel in the center of the city are light, monochromatic to the point of being dull, and decorated with light pine furniture. Teatergrillen, named after a nearby theater, serves a good early dinner. ⌸ *Kongensgt. 30, 7002,* ☎ *73/53–06–50,* ℻ *73/53–06–44. 85 rooms with bath or shower, 1 suite. 3 restaurants, 3 bars, nightclub. AE, DC, MC, V.*

$$–$$$$ **Royal Garden.** The city's showcase hostelry, right on the river, was built in the same style as the old warehouse buildings that line the waterfront, but in glass and concrete instead of wood. It's a luxury hotel, with big rooms, light-wood furniture, and predominantly blue textiles. ⌸ *Kjøpmannsgata 73, 7010,* ☎ *73/52–11–00,* ℻ *73/53–17–66. 297 rooms with bath, 8 suites. 3 restaurants, bar, indoor pool, exercise room, shops. AE, DC, MC, V.*

$$ **Ambassadeur.** Take in the panoramic view from the roof terrace of this first-rate modern hotel, about 303 feet from the market square. The deep blue waters of the Trondheimsfjord reflect the dramatic and irregular coastline. Most rooms in the Ambassadeur have fireplaces, and some have balconies. ⌸ *Elvegt. 18,* ☎ *73/52–70–50,* ℻ *73/52–70– 52. 34 rooms with bath. Bar. AE, DC, MC, V.*

$–$$ **Bakeriet.** The hotel opened in March 1991 in a building built as a bak-
★   ery in 1863. Few of the rooms look alike, but all are large, with natural wood furniture and beige-and-red-stripe textiles, and stylish in their simplicity. Every room has a VCR and a window thermometer. There's no restaurant, but a hot evening meal is included in the room rate. You can borrow a track suit, and there's free light beer in the lounge by the sauna. ⌸ *Brattørgt. 2, 7011, Trondheim,* ☎ *73/52–*

52–00, ℻ 73/50–23–30. *98 rooms with bath or shower, 1 suite. Sauna. AE, DC, MC, V.*

$–$$ **Trondheim.** If you've always wanted to try mead, the fermented honey drink of the Vikings, do it here—it's produced on the premises. The building is old on the outside, with a curved corner and wrought-iron balconies, but inside it's completely remodeled. The rooms are big and light, with what is now considered to be classic Scandinavian bentwood furniture. ⊡ *Kongensgt. 15, 7013,* ☎ *73/50–50–50,* ℻ *73/51–60–58. 131 rooms with shower or bath. Restaurant, bar, meeting room. AE, DC, MC, V.*

THE ARTS AND NIGHTLIFE

The Arts
TRONDHEIM
Olavshallen (Kjøpmannsgt. 44, ☎ 73/53–40–50 or toll-free 800/33–133), a concert and cultural center built in 1989, is the home of Trondheim's symphony and the nearly 3,000 music students in the city. The auditorium seats 1,300. The concert and entertainment season is from September through May.

During the last week in July, the *St. Olav Play* is performed at the outdoor amphitheater in **Stiklestad,** 98 kilometers (60 miles) from Trondheim. The play, with a cast of 300, commemorates the life of King Olav Haraldsson, who united the country and brought Christianity to Norway. Tickets are available from any post office, Stiklestad Nasjonale Kulturhus (☎ 74/07–12–00), or Olavsfestdagene (☎ 73/50–97–97).

TROMSØ
Every year in January the city celebrates **Nordlysfestivalen** (the Northern Lights Festival) with a series of concerts by distinguished visiting artists at the Kulturhuset (Culture House; Grønnegata 87, ☎ 77/68–20–64). For concert information and reservations, contact the festival (☎ 77/68–08–63, ℻ 77/68–01–09).

THE NORTH
Nature takes precedence over the arts in northern Norway, but Harstad hosts the yearly **Northern Norway Festival** in June.

During Easter, Kautokeino holds its annual **Easter Festival,** including theater, joik (a haunting, ancient form of solo, a cappella song, often in praise of nature), concerts, weddings, and exhibits of traditional crafts. Contact Finnmark Opplevelser, 9500 Alta, ☎ 78/43–54–44.

From June 15 to August 15, **Beaivváš Sami Theater** (9250 Kautokeino, ☎ 78/48–68–11) offers summer programs of traditional Sami folk songs and modern works.

Nightlife
TRONDHEIM
Olavskvartalet (*see* Shopping, *above*) is the center of much of the city's nightlife, with a disco, a jazz and blues club, and a bar and beer hall in the cellar. **Hotell Prinsen** (*see* Lodging, *above*) has a summer restaurant, **Sommer'n,** open from mid-May to the end of August, with live music and dancing. **Monte Cristo** (Prinsensgt. 38–40, ☎ 73/52–18–80) has a restaurant, bar, and disco under the same roof and is popular with the mid-twenties and upwards age group. Students and younger people in search of cheap drinks, music, and dancing tend to gravitate towards **Strossa** (Elgeseter Gt. 1, ☎ 73/89–95–10), which is run by

students. **Cafe Remis** (Kjoepmannsgt. 12, ☎ 73/52–05–52) is the center for gay nightlife in Trondheim.

TROMSØ

Tromsø brags that it has 10 nightclubs, not bad for a city of 50,000 at the top of the world. **Compagniet** (*see* Dining, *above*) has the classiest nightclub; **Charly's** at the SAS Royal Hotel is also popular. **Boccaccio** (☎ 77/68–49–06) is a good place to go for live bands and attracts a younger crowd. **Dampen** is more alternative than any other venue in Tromsø in terms of live music and clientele. It also has a disco (Kai Gt.1).

TRONDHEIM AND THE NORTH ESSENTIALS

Arriving and Departing

BY BOAT

Hurtigruten (the coastal express boat, which calls at 35 ports from Bergen to Kirkenes) stops at Trondheim, southbound at St. Olav's Pier, Quay 16, northbound at Pier 1, Quay 7. Call 73/52–55–40 for information on Hurtigruten and local ferries.

BY BUS

Buses run only from Oslo to Otta, where they connect with the train to Trondheim. Buses connect Bergen, Molde, Ålesund, and Røros with Trondheim. **Nor-Way Bussekspress** (☎ 22/17–52–90) can help you to put together a bus journey to the North. The Express 2000 travels three times a week between Oslo, Kautokeino, Alta, and Hammerfest. The journey, via Sweden, takes 24, 26, and 29 hours, respectively.

BY CAR

Trondheim is about 500 kilometers (310 miles) from Oslo: seven to eight hours of driving. Speed limits are 80 kmh (50 mph) much of the way. There are two alternatives, E6 through Gudbrandsdalen or Route 3 through Østerdalen. Roads are decent for the most part but can become thick with campers during midsummer, sometimes making the going slow. It's 727 kilometers (450 miles) from Trondheim to Bodø on Route E6, which goes all the way to Kirkenes. There's a 20NKr toll on E6 just south of Trondheim for travelers in both directions. Cars entering the downtown area must pay a 10NKr toll (6 AM–10 PM).

BY PLANE

Trondheim's **Værnes** Airport is 35 kilometers (22 miles) northeast of the city. **SAS** (☎ 74/82–49–22), **Braathens SAFE** (☎ 74/82–32–00), and **Widerøe** (☎ 74/82–49–22) are the main domestic carriers. SAS also has one flight between Trondheim and Copenhagen daily, except Sunday, and daily flights to Stockholm.

With the exception of Harstad, all cities in northern Norway are served by airports less than 5 kilometers (3 miles) from the center of town. Tromsø is a crossroads for air traffic between northern and southern Norway and is served by Braathens SAFE, SAS, and Widerøe. SAS flies to eight destinations in northern Norway, including Bodø, Tromsø, Alta, and Kirkenes. Braathens SAFE flies to five destinations, including Bodø and Tromsø. Widerøe specializes in northern Norway and flies to 19 destinations in the region, including Honningsvåg, the airport closest to the North Cape.

The **Dovrebanen** has five departures daily, four on Saturday, in both directions on the Oslo–Trondheim route. Trains leave from Oslo S Station for the seven- to eight-hour journey. Trondheim is the gateway to the North, and two trains run daily in both directions on the 11-hour Trondheim–Bodø route. For information about trains out of Trondheim, call 73/53–00–10. The **Nordlandsbanen** has two departures daily in each direction on the Bodø–Trondheim route, an 11-hour journey. The **Ofotbanen** has one departure daily in each direction on the Stockholm–Narvik route, a 21-hour journey.

Getting Around
BY BOAT
Boat is the ideal transportation in Nordland. The *Hurtigruten* stops twice daily (north and southbound) at 20 ports in northern Norway. It is possible to buy tickets between any harbors right on the boats. **Saltens Dampskibsselskab** (Bodø, ☎ 75/52–10–20) has express boats between Bodø and Hamarøy and Svolvær, while **OVDS** (Narvik, ☎ 76/92–37–00) ferries and express boats serve many towns in the region. **TFDS, Troms Fylkes Dampskibsselskap** (Tromsø, ☎ 77/68–60–88) operates various boat services in the region around Tromsø.

BY BUS
Trondheim: Most local buses in **Trondheim** stop at the Munkegata/Dronningens Gate intersection. Some routes end at the bus terminal (Skakkes Gt. 40, ☎ 73/52–44–74). Tickets cost NKr12 and allow free transfer between buses (☎ 73/54–71–00) and streetcars (**Gråkallbanen,** ☎ 72/55–23–55).

The North: North of **Bodø** and **Narvik** (a five-hour bus ride from Bodø), beyond the reach of the railroad, buses go virtually everywhere, but they don't go often. Get a comprehensive bus schedule from a tourist office or travel agent before making plans. Local bus companies include **Saltens Bilruter** (Bodø, ☎ 75/52–50–25), **Ofotens Bilruter** (Narvik, ☎ 76/92–35–00), **Tromsbuss** (Tromsø, ☎ 77/67–02–33), **Tromsøexpressen** (Tromsø, ☎ 77/67–27–87), and **Finnmark Fylkesrederi og Ruteselskap** (FFR, Alta, ☎ 78/43–52–11, Hammerfest, ☎ 78/41–10–00).

BY CAR
The roads aren't a problem in northern Norway—most are quite good, although there are always narrow and winding stretches, especially along fjords. Distances are formidable. Route 17—the *Kystriksvegen* (Coastal Highway) from Namsos to Bodø—is an excellent alternative to E6. Getting to Tromsø and the North Cape involves additional driving on narrower roads off E6. In the northern winter, near-blizzard conditions and icy roads sometimes make it necessary to drive in a convoy. You'll know it when you see it: Towns are cut off from traffic at access roads, and vehicles wait until their numbers are large enough to make the crossing safely.

You can also fly the extensive distances and then rent a car for sightseeing within the area, but book a rental car as far in advance as possible. There's no better way to see the Lofoten and Vesterålen islands than by car. Nordkapp (take the plane to Honningsvåg) is another excursion best made by car.

BY PLANE
Northern Norway has excellent air connections through SAS, Braathens SAFE, and Widerøe. (*See* Arriving and Departing by Plane, *above.*)

BY TAXI

Taxi ranks are located in strategic places in downtown **Trondheim.** All taxis are connected to the central dispatching office (☎ 73/50–50– 73). Taxi numbers in other towns are: **Harstad,** ☎ 77/06–20–50; **Narvik,** ☎ 76/94–65–00; and **Tromsø,** ☎ 77/68–80–20.

Guided Tours

SAMILAND

Contact Sami Travel A/S (Kautokeino, ☎ 78/48–56–00) for adventure trips to Sami settlements.

SVALBARD

Svalbard Polar Travel (9170 Longyearbyen, ☎ 79/02–19–71) arranges combination air-sea visits, from three-day minicruises to 12-day trekking expeditions on the rim of the North Pole. **Spitsbergen Travel** (9170 Longyearbyen, ☎ 79/02–24–00) offers specialized "exploring" tours that focus on the plant and animal life of the region.

TROMSØ

The tourist information office sells tickets for **City Sightseeing** (Dampskipskaia) and **M/F Karlsøy,** an original Arctic vessel that runs a fishing tour in the waters around Tromsø Island.

TRONDHEIM

The Trondheim Tourist Association offers a number of tours. Tickets are sold at the tourist information office or at the start of the tour.

Important Addresses and Numbers

EMERGENCIES

Other Towns: Bodø, Harstad, Narvik, and **Tromsø:** ☎ 112.

Trondheim: Police: ☎ 112. **Fire:** ☎ 111. **Ambulance:** ☎ 113. **Car rescue:** ☎ 73/96–62–88. **Doctors:** ☎ 73/99–88–00. **Dentists:** ☎ 73/52– 25–00.

LATE-NIGHT PHARMACIES

Trondheim: St. Olav Vaktapotek (Kjøpmannsgt. 65, ☎ 73/52–66–66) is open Monday through Saturday 8:30 AM–midnight and Sunday 10 AM–midnight.

Tromsø: Svaneapoteket (Fr. Langes Gt. 9, ☎ 77/68–64–24) is open daily 8:30–4 and 6–9.

VISITOR INFORMATION

Trondheim (Munkegt. 19, 7000, ☎ 73/92–93–94). Other tourist offices in the region: **Alta** (Finnmark Opplevelser A/S, 9500, ☎ 78/43– 54–44); **Bodø** (Sjøgt. 21, 8006, ☎ 75/52–60–00); **Hammerfest** (9600, ☎ 78/41–21–85); **Harstad** (Torvet 8, 9400, ☎ 77/06–32–35); **Karasjok** (9730, ☎ 78/46–73–60); **Lofoten** (8300 Svolvær, ☎ 76/07–30–00); **Mo i Rana** (8600 Mo, ☎ 75/15–04–21); **Narvik** (Kongensgt. 66, 8500, ☎ 76/94–33–09); **Tromsø** (Storgt. 61, 9000, ☎ 77/61–00–00); **Vesterålen Reiselivslag** (8400 Sortland, ☎ 77/12–15–55); **Nordkapp,** (Nordkapphuset, Honningsvåg, ☎ 78/47–28–94); and **Svalbard** (9170 Longyearbyen, ☎ 79/02–23–03).

8 Portraits of Norway

NORWAY AT A GLANCE:
A CHRONOLOGY

c 1200 BC   The earliest human settlers reach Norway.

2,000 BC   Tribes from Southern Europe migrate toward Denmark. The majority of early settlers in Scandinavia were of Germanic origin.

c AD 770   The Viking Age begins. For the next 250 years, Scandinavians set sail on frequent expeditions stretching from the Baltic to the Irish seas and even to the Mediterranean as far as Sicily, employing superior ships and weapons and efficient military organization.

c 870   The first permanent settlers arrive in Iceland from western Norway.

c 900   Norwegians unite under Harald I Haarfager.

995   King Olaf I Tryggvasson introduces Christianity into Norway.

1000   Leif Eriksson visits America. Olaf I sends a mission to Christianize Iceland.

1016–1028   King Olaf II Haraldsson (St. Olaf) tries to complete conversion of Norway to Christianity. Killed at Stiklestad in battle with Danish king, he becomes patron saint of Norway.

1028–1035   Canute (Knud) the Great is king of England, Denmark (1018), and Norway (1028).

1045–1066   King Harald III (Hardraade) fights long war with Danes, then participates in and is killed during Norman invasion of England.

1217   Haakon IV becomes king of Norway, beginning its "Golden Age." His many reforms modernize the Norwegian administration; under him, the Norwegian empire reaches its greatest extent when Greenland and Iceland form unions with Norway in 1261. The Sagas are written during this time.

1319   Sweden and Norway form a union that lasts until 1335.

1349   The Black Death strikes Norway and kills two-thirds of the population.

1370   The Treaty of Stralsund gives the north German trading centers of the Hanseatic League free passage through Danish waters. German power increases throughout Scandinavia.

1397   The Kalmar Union is formed as a result of the dynastic ties between Sweden, Denmark, and Norway, the geographical position of the Scandinavian states, and the growing influence of Germans in the Baltic. Erik of Pomerania is crowned king of the Kalmar Union.

1520   Christian II, ruler of the Kalmar Union, executes 82 people who oppose the Scandinavian union, an event known as the "Stockholm blood bath." Sweden secedes from the Union three years later. Norway remains tied to Denmark and becomes a Danish province in 1536.

1536   The Reformation enters Scandinavia in the form of Lutheranism through the Hauseatic port of Bergen.

1559–1648   Norwegian trade flourishes.

1660   Peace of Copenhagen establishes modern boundaries of Denmark, Sweden, and Norway.

1814 Sweden, after Napoleon's defeat at the Battle of Leipzig, attacks Denmark and forces the Danish surrender of Norway. On 17 May, Norwegians adopt constitution at Eidsvoll. On 4 November, Norway is forced to accept Act of Union with Sweden.

1811 University of Oslo is established.

1884 A parliamentary system is established in Norway.

1903 Bjørnstjerne Bjørnson awarded Nobel Prize for literature.

1905 Norway's union with Sweden is dissolved.

1914 At the outbreak of World War I, Norway declares neutrality but is effectively blockaded.

1918 Norwegian women gain the right to vote.

1920 Norway joins the League of Nations. Novelist Knut Hansun receives Nobel Prize.

1928 Sigrid Undset receives Nobel Prize for literature.

1929–1937 Norway is ruled by a labor government.

1939 Norway declares neutrality in World War II.

1940 Germany occupies Norway.

1945 Norway joins the United Nations.

1946–1954 Norwegian statesman Trygve Lie presides as first Secretary-General of UN.

1949 Norway becomes a member of NATO.

1952 The Nordic Council, which promotes cooperation among the Nordic parliaments, is founded.

1968 Norway discovers oil in the North Sea.

1971 North Sea oil extraction begins, transforming the Norwegian economy.

1972 Norway declines membership in the EC.

1981 Gro Harlem Brundtland, a member of the Labor party, becomes Norway's first female prime minister.

1991 King Olav V dies. King Harald V ascends the throne. His wife, Queen Sonja, becomes first queen since the death of Maud in 1938.

1993 Norway's Minister of Foreign Affairs Thorvald Stoltenberg is appointed peace negotiator to Bosnia and Herzegovina.

1994 Norway hosts the XVII Olympic Winter Games at Lillehammer.

1995 In a national referendum, Norwegians again decline membership in the EC.

IN NORWAY AT CHRISTMAS

EVERY CULTURE REINVENTS the wheel. But every culture reinvents it slightly differently. In Norway, a traditional dining table may rest not on four legs, as tables usually do elsewhere, but on a cubic frame, like an imaginary cage that imprisons your feet while you eat.

I am a Chinese who has fallen in love with Norway. I was invited by my good friends Ole and Else to spend Christmas and New Year's with them in Oslo. It turned out to be the most marvelous Christmas of my fifty-two years.

It was one long feast, moving from household to household. On Christmas Eve we held hands and sang carols and danced ring-around-the-Christmas-tree. We skied at night on an illuminated track, whose lights switched off at ten, plunging us into obscurity on the downward slope. We played squash on the Norsk Hydro court and afterward relaxed in the sauna. We ushered in the New Year with fireworks on Oslo's frozen streets.

I am probably one of the few Chinese in two thousand years to have had such an intimate glimpse of Norwegian life. Of course, it is presumptuous of me to write about a people after an eight-day visit. Yet I have the feeling that Norwegians don't very much mind presumption (as long as it is straightforward and honest). Indeed, this exceptional tolerance of friendly rudeness bespeaks their generosity and is, to me, one of their most endearing qualities.

To begin with, to a Chinese who has seen something of the world, Norway is a most exotic country. Even ordinary, everday things are done exotically here. For example, I saw my Norwegian friends: drink aquavit at breakfast; eat breakfast in the afternoon; turn on an electric switch to heat the sidewalk in front of their house; get a thrill out of driving their car like a bobsled; leave the house lights on day and night, when they went out and when they slept; wash their dishes with soap without rinsing them.

Norwegians also love to give gifts and make philosophical speeches at festive dinners. They decorate their Christmas trees not with angels but with strings of Norwegian flags. They don't find it necessary to have curtains around their showers, because it's simpler to build a drain on the bathroom floor. Cold dishes are de rigueur in the winter. There is a national horror of hot, spicy foods, and a national pact to ignore vegetables.

The Norwegians and the Chinese share certain cultural traits. The most striking is their common fondness for rituals. Confucius insisted on the importance of rituals as a collective code of behavior that gives order to life. The Master said, "To suppress the self and submit to ritual is to engage in Humanity." This precept might just as well apply to the Norwegians as to the Chinese.

At Christmas, all the traditional rituals are performed, some older than Christianity in Norway. A great deal of effort goes into making sure that they are done right. After each one—the baking of the gingerbread houses, the decorating of the tree—the excitement palpably mounts.

Christmas begins on the eve, with the hostess welcoming the guests to the dinner table. She assigns to each a specific seat according to a careful arrangement. The seating plan is the one touch of originality that marks the occasion. It is, in some ways, the hostess's signature for the evening. (You find seating charts of past banquets faithfully recorded in a family book.) It's quite touching to see a young hostess assign a seat to her own mother, who has undoubtedly done the same many times herself. It signals the passing of the torch from one generation of women to another.

Once the guests are seated and the candles lit, the feast begins. It begins with the dessert: rice pudding (reminiscent of the rice gruel that Chinese eat for breakfast and when ill, albeit without milk and butter. Toasts are offered, followed by a chorus of *skaals*.

Then comes raw fish of every kind—salmon, eel, herring, enough to send a sashimi-loving Japanese into ecstasy. From the sea, the food parade marches onto land. A whole side of roast pork, skin done to a golden crisp, is served with meatballs and sausage, and buried under potatoes. Throughout there is much toasting with aquavit.

Finally, after two hours the meal is done. You get up from the table and stagger into the living room. There, in a role reminiscent of her mother's, the little daughter of the house hands out the gifts—there is a mound of them under the tree—to each recipient with charming solemnity.

Great care is taken by each household to do everything the same way, so that, as with the retelling of a familiar tale, all expectaions are happily satisfied. Once in a while, one may introduce an oddity, such as a Chinese guest from afar, to liven up the routine. But in general surprises tend to raise eyebrows.

If, for the Chinese, rituals recall the teachings of Confucius, for the Norwegians they go back to the pagans. In spite of the electric sidewalks, the past is very much alive in the modern Norwegian psyche. The feasting, the speech-making, the gift-giving, and especially the generous hospitality and the importance of friendship are all part of the Viking tradition. Yuletide was a pagan celebration of the winter solstice. The birth of Christ was a later liturgical imposition. In some families these days, it is celebrated almost as an afterthought.

The other thing that the Norwegians share with the Chinese is their strong attachment to the family. Like the Chinese, the Norwegians belong to extended families, practically clans. But what defines a family in Norway is not at all clear. The relations are so complex and intertwined that, rather than family trees, the Norwegians seem to have family bushes. To begin with, there is one's spouse and one's brothers and sisters and their spouses. And then there is one's former spouse and his or her present spouse. And then there is the former spouse of the present spouse of one's former spouse, who in some cases also happens to be one's present spouse. The children of the former spouse of one's spouse are somewhat like nephews and nieces. Beyond that, there are the living-together arrangements and the progeny thereof, which take on quasi-family status.

It's not unusual for people who are divorced to remain good friends. Their old pictures sometimes hang in each other's bedrooms, Christmastime finds them reunited with their old partners and all of their children, old and new. At first, this kind of marital pluralism is slightly unsettling. What, no bad blood? No bitterness or jealousy?

I ASKED A YOUNG NORWEGIAN if it upset him to be shuttling between his father's and mother's separate households. He looked at me with astonishment. "But that's normal," he said. "Every kid in my class is in the same situation."

His guileless reaction gave me food for thought. "And indeed what's wrong with that?" I asked myself. Why try to stay with an unhappy relationship when one feels the need to change? And once changed, why not try to reconcile the past with the present?

The Chinese family is a vertical structure. Like the society itself, it is hierarchical, ruled from the top down. Confucius said, "Let the prince be prince, the minister be minister, the father be father, the son be son." Patriarchy and gerontocracy are the order of things: old men will rule, and the young will obey. Repression is inevitable under such a hierarchy. The collective always takes precedence over the individual; order always takes precedence over freedom. This denial of the self is responsible for much of the envy, backbiting, and hypocrisy common in Chinese communities.

The Norwegian family, on the other hand—or perhaps I should say the *new* Norwegian family—is horizontal. Like a strawberry plant, it spreads in all directions. Wherever it touches soil, it sprouts a new shoot. An obvious sign of this strawberry-patch kinship is the diminished importance of the family name. These days people are known mostly by first names. Children, too, often address their parents by their first names. As more and more households are headed by women, the old nuclear family is giving way to a fluid tribalism.

One way to understand the difference between the vertical and the horizontal cultures is to compare thier concepts of space. To the Chinese, any space must have a center. The Chinese name for China, Zhongguo, means precisely Center Country. Every Chinese knows that the center of China is Beijing. Why? Because the vast expanse of China is not divided into time zones, and from the Pacific to Tibet every watch is set to Beijing time. Every Chinese also knows that the center of Beijing is the Forbidden City, the symbol of governmental power, and that inside the Forbidden City sits an old man whose word is law.

NO ONE WOULD DREAM of ordering Norway's space this way. Unlike elsewhere in Europe, you seldom see a square in a Norwegian town. People don't seem to feel the need to meet and sit in the sun and feed the pigeons. In some rural communities, the church stands not in the center of town but on a hill somewhere on the outskirts. The houses, in all forms and dispositions, are widely dispersed, disdaining to line up along a straight road. One gets the impression that zoning laws are not very strict in Norway.

The big question is, if the Norwegians are such confirmed individualists, how come they are so conformist? It's voluntary, true, they choose it, but it's conformity all the same. This is the question posed—but never answered—by Ibsen's plays.

For me, the key to understanding the Norwegians is to recognize that they are a nation of irreconciled opposites. They have taken on the contradiction of their seasons: the long happy summer days alternating with the gloomy nights of winter. They have inherited two pasts with totally different characters. For more than two hundred years, from the ninth to the eleventh centuries, they were the scourge of Europe. They raided Britain and discovered America; they ruled Kiev and besieged Paris; they served at the court of Byzantium, and—who knows?—maybe some of them even made it to China. Lusty, adventurous, destructive, and curious about the world, they were sea nomads, the maritime counter-

part of the horsemen of Genghis Khan, who conquered Russia and China. Then, as suddenly as they burst upon the world in their splendid ships, they retreated, went back to their home in the north. They were converted to Christianity and not heard from again.

Why the seafaring Vikings turned into God-fearing Christians is one of those mysteries that history doesn't explain very well. What made them turn their gaze inward? Why did they change from thinking big to thinking small? What, finally, made them give up violence for peaceful ways? There is no satisfactory answer.

In any case, as the final image of Ingmar Bergman's *Fanny and Alexander* so powerfully shows, there are two ghosts walking beside the Scandinavian soul: the ghost of the hard-drinking father and the ghost of the psalm-singing stepfather. They walk beside the boy, each with a hand on his shoulder, never exchanging a word.

So the Norwegian labors under a double identity. In one ear, the Viking ghost tells him to leave Norway, this cold, homogeneous, incurious community, and discover the world. Go! The center is elsewhere! There are wonderful places to see and fabulous riches to be had!

In his other ear, the Christian ghost tells him Stay! Go back to your roots! Embrace the tradition and preserve the social order.

This ambivalence is at the heart of Norway itself. You see it reflected on canvas in the National Gallery in Oslo. Among the painters of the late nineteenth century, one finds two divergent sensibilities: the naturalists, who took as their subject the Norwegian folk, and the cosmopolitans, who, having spent time in Paris or Rome, insisted that art was not sociology or geography but, simply and purely, a composition of color and light.

For eight centuries, Christian ethics held sway in Norway as in the rest of Europe. But since 1945 something important has changed. There is a gap between the values of the prewar and the postwar generations. Between the threat of nuclear destruction and the temptation of America, the influence of the church waned. More and more, people have stopped practicing their faith. As they do so, they are reverting their ancestral Viking instincts.

One clue to this reemergence of pagan consciousness is the marital pluralism that I observed. Another clue, probably closely related, is women's push for equality, a push that has been more forceful and more widely accepted in Scandinavia than anywhere else. A third indication of this new pagan way, I believe—and here I'm sticking my neck out—is the nation's collective decision, in the seventies, to turn Norway overnight into an oil economy.

There have been a lot of arguments about the reasoning behind this decision, but none of them address the Viking-versus-Christian dilemma. If Norway had listened to its Christian voice, it would have been content to remain a frugal, hard-working nation, tending the farm or the machine. Instead, after the oil crisis of 1973, Norway chose the Viking solution and went for broke. It decided to plunder the sea.

Agrarian people, like the Chinese, are naturally patient: it takes time to make things grow. The Vikings, on the other hand, never had patience. If they could survive by fishing and gathering berries, they would not care to cultivate. Whatever they could get by raiding, they would not care to make. It is still so today. Norwegians are willing to put all their ingenuity and technical skill into building gigantic derricks and drilling kilometers beneath the sea. They will do so in order to avoid making clothes and toys to compete with Hong Kong. This is the message I got from that magnificent Christmas feast: If it tastes good raw, *don't bother to cook it.* Take it raw. Don't transform. And nothing is rawer than oil.

In 1066, King Harald Hardraade left the shores of Norway to grab the big prize: the throne of England. At Stamford Bridge, he was offered by his enemy seven feet of English ground, "and more—if you are taller." Harald fought and lost. By nightfall, mortally wounded, he said, "I will accept that piece of kingdom that was offered me this morning."

I said to my friend Ole—who, as an oil engineer at Norsk Hydro, has staked his whole future on a challenge against the North Sea—"One day your oil will be depleted, and then where will you be?" He grinned and said, echoing King Harald's insouciance, "And then I will have nothing."

— *Chunglu Tsen*

Born in Shanghai, Chunglu Tsen grew up in Paris and received his education in England and the United States. Since 1974 he has worked as a translator for the United Nations in Geneva. This article appeared originally in the December 1990 issue of Wigwag.

NORWEGIAN VOCABULARY

English	Norwegian	Pronunciation

Basics

English	Norwegian	Pronunciation
Yes/no	Ja/nei	yah/nigh
Please	Vær så snill	**vehr** soh snihl
Thank you very much.	Tusen takk	**tews**-sehn tahk
You're welcome.	Vær så god	**vehr** soh goo
Excuse me.	Unnskyld	**ewn**-shewl
Hello	God dag	goo **dahg**
Goodbye	Adjø	ah-**dyur**
Today	i dag	ee **dahg**
Tomorrow	i morgen	ee **moh**-ern
Yesterday	i går	ee **gohr**
Morning	morgen	**moh**-ern
Afternoon	ettermiddag	**eh-terr**-mid-dahg
Night	natt	naht

Numbers

English	Norwegian	Pronunciation
One	en	ehn
Two	to	too
Three	tre	tray
Four	fire	**feer**-eh
Five	fem	fehm
Six	seks	sehks
Seven	syv, sju	shew
Eight	åtte	**oh**-teh
Nine	ni	nee
Ten	ti	tee

Days of the Week

English	Norwegian	Pronunciation
Monday	mandag	**mahn**-dahg
Tuesday	tirsdag	**teesh**-dahg
Wednesday	onsdag	**oonss**-dahg
Thursday	torsdag	**tohsh**-dahg
Friday	fredag	**fray**-dahg
Saturday	lørdag	**loor**-dahg
Sunday	Søndag	**suhn**-dahg

Useful Phrases

English	Norwegian	Pronunciation
Do you speak English?	Snakker De engelsk?	**snahk**-kerr dee **ehng**-ehlsk
I don't speak Norwegian.	Jeg snakker ikke norsk.	yay **snahk**-kerr **ik**-keh nohrshk

I don't understand.	Jeg forstår ikke.	yay fosh-**tawr** **ik**-keh
I don't know.	Jeg vet ikke.	yay veht **ik**-keh
I am American/ British.	Jeg er amerikansk/ engelsk.	yay ehr ah-mehr-ee-kahnsk/ehng-ehlsk
I am sick.	Jeg er dårlig.	yay ehr **dohr**-lee
Please call a doctor.	Vær så snill og ring etter en lege.	vehr soh snihl oh ring **eht**-ehr ehn **lay**-geh
Do you have a vacant room?	Jeg vil gjerne ha et rom.	yay vil **yehr**-neh hah eht room
How much does it cost?	Hva koster det?	vah **koss**-terr deh
It's too expensive.	Det er for dyrt.	deh ehr for **deert**
Beautiful	vakker	**vah**-kehr
Help!	Hjelp!	yehlp
Stop!	Stopp!	stop
How do I get to . . .	Hvor er	voor **ehr**
. . . the train station?	jernbanestasjonen	yehrn-bahn-eh-sta-**shoon**-ern
. . . the post office?	posthuset	**pohsst**-hewss
. . . the tourist office?	turistkontoret	tew-**reest**-koon-toor-er
. . . the hospital?	sykehuset	**see**-keh-hoo-seh
Does this bus go to . . . ?	Går denne bussen til . . . ?	gohr **den**-nah boos teel
Where is the W.C.?	Hvor er toalettene?	voor ehr too-ah-**leht**-ter-ner
On the left	Til venstre	teel **vehn**-streh
On the right	Til høyre	teel **hooy**-reh
Straight ahead	Rett fram	reht **frahm**

Dining Out

menu	meny	meh-**new**
fork	gaffel	**gahff**-erl
knife	kniv	kneev
spoon	skje	shay
napkin	serviett	ssehr-**vyeht**
bread	brød	brur
butter	smør	smurr
milk	melk	mehlk
pepper	pepper	**pehp**-per
salt	salt	sahlt

sugar	sukker	**sook**-kerr
water/bottled water	vann	vahn
The check, please.	Jeg vil gjerne betale.	yay vil **yehr**-neh beh-**tah**-leh

INDEX

NOTES

NOTES

NOTES

NOTES

NOTES

NOTES

NOTES

NOTES

Fodor's Travel Publications

Available at bookstores everywhere, or call 1–800–533–6478, 24 hours a day.

Gold Guides

U.S.

Alaska

Arizona

Boston

California

Cape Cod, Martha's Vineyard, Nantucket

The Carolinas & the Georgia Coast

Chicago

Colorado

Florida

Hawaii

Las Vegas, Reno, Tahoe

Los Angeles

Maine, Vermont, New Hampshire

Maui

Miami & the Keys

New England

New Orleans

New York City

Pacific North Coast

Philadelphia & the Pennsylvania Dutch Country

The Rockies

San Diego

San Francisco

Santa Fe, Taos, Albuquerque

Seattle & Vancouver

The South

U.S. & British Virgin Islands

USA

Virginia & Maryland

Waikiki

Washington, D.C.

Foreign

Australia & New Zealand

Austria

The Bahamas

Bermuda

Budapest

Canada

Cancún, Cozumel, Yucatán Peninsula

Caribbean

China

Costa Rica, Belize, Guatemala

Cuba

The Czech Republic & Slovakia

Eastern Europe

Egypt

Europe

Florence, Tuscany & Umbria

France

Germany

Great Britain

Greece

Hong Kong

India

Ireland

Israel

Italy

Japan

Kenya & Tanzania

Korea

London

Madrid & Barcelona

Mexico

Montréal & Québec City

Moscow, St. Petersburg, Kiev

The Netherlands, Belgium & Luxembourg

New Zealand

Norway

Nova Scotia, New Brunswick, Prince Edward Island

Paris

Portugal

Provence & the Riviera

Scandinavia

Scotland

Singapore

South Africa

South America

Southeast Asia

Spain

Sweden

Switzerland

Thailand

Tokyo

Toronto

Turkey

Vienna & the Danube

Fodor's Special-Interest Guides

Branson

Caribbean Ports of Call

The Complete Guide to America's National Parks

Condé Nast Traveler Caribbean Resort and Cruise Ship Finder

Cruises and Ports of Call

Fodor's London Companion

Gay USA

France by Train

Halliday's New England Food Explorer

Healthy Escapes

Italy by Train

Kodak Guide to Shooting Great Travel Pictures

Shadow Traffic's New York Shortcuts and Traffic Tips

Sunday in New York

Sunday in San Francisco

Walt Disney World, Universal Studios and Orlando

Walt Disney World for Adults

Where Should We Take the Kids? California

Where Should We Take the Kids? Family Adventures

Where Should We Take the Kids? Northeast

Special Series

Affordables
Caribbean
Europe
Florida
France
Germany
Great Britain
Italy
London
Paris

Fodor's Bed & Breakfasts and Country Inns
America's Best B&Bs
California's Best B&Bs
Canada's Great Country Inns
Cottages, B&Bs and Country Inns of England and Wales
The Mid-Atlantic's Best B&Bs
New England's Best B&Bs
The Pacific Northwest's Best B&Bs
The South's Best B&Bs
The Southwest's Best B&Bs
The Upper Great Lakes' Best B&Bs

The Berkeley Guides
California
Central America
Eastern Europe
Europe
France
Germany & Austria
Great Britain & Ireland
Italy
London
Mexico
Pacific Northwest & Alaska
Paris
San Francisco

Compass American Guides
Arizona
Chicago
Colorado
Hawaii
Idaho
Hollywood
Las Vegas
Maine
Manhattan
Montana
New Mexico
New Orleans
Oregon
San Francisco
Santa Fe
South Carolina
South Dakota
Southwest
Texas
Utah
Virginia
Washington
Wine Country
Wisconsin
Wyoming

Fodor's Citypacks
Atlanta
Hong Kong
London
New York City
Paris
Rome
San Francisco
Washington, D.C.

Fodor's Español
California
Caribe Occidental
Caribe Oriental
Gran Bretaña
Londres
Mexico

Nueva York
Paris

Fodor's Exploring Guides
Australia
Boston & New England
Britain
California
Caribbean
China
Egypt
Florence & Tuscany
Florida
France
Germany
Ireland
Israel
Italy
Japan
London
Mexico
Moscow & St. Petersburg
New York City
Paris
Prague
Provence
Rome
San Francisco
Scotland
Singapore & Malaysia
Spain
Thailand
Turkey
Venice

Fodor's Flashmaps
Boston
New York
San Francisco
Washington, D.C.

Fodor's Pocket Guides
Acapulco
Atlanta
Barbados

Jamaica
London
New York City
Paris
Prague
Puerto Rico
Rome
San Francisco
Washington, D.C.

Rivages Guides
Bed and Breakfasts of Character and Charm in France
Hotels and Country Inns of Character and Charm in France
Hotels and Country Inns of Character and Charm in Italy

Short Escapes
Country Getaways in Britain
Country Getaways in France
Country Getaways in New England
Country Getaways Near New York City

Fodor's Sports
Golf Digest's Best Places to Play
Skiing USA
USA Today The Complete Four Sport Stadium Guide

Fodor's Vacation Planners
Great American Learning Vacations
Great American Sports & Adventure Vacations
Great American Vacations
National Parks and Seashores of the East
National Parks of the West

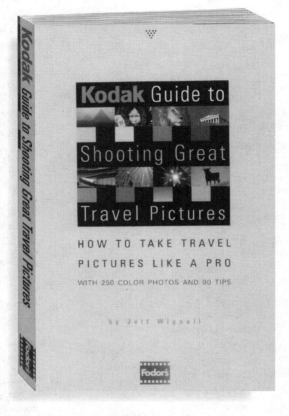